Rev Henry Davis 2⁰⁰

BIBLE
TRANSLATING

An Analysis of Principles and Procedures,
with Special Reference to
Aboriginal Languages

By EUGENE A. NIDA, Ph. D.

Secretary for Versions, American Bible Society

AMERICAN BIBLE SOCIETY

NEW YORK

TABLE OF CONTENTS

CONTENTS

PREFACE

THIS book has been prepared to assist missionaries in the task of finding the proper solutions to the many complex problems of Bible translating. The principles upon which this treatment is made are all ably stated in the *Guide for Translators, Revisers, and Editors* (see Appendix) published by the American Bible Society and conforming to the Guide published by the British and Foreign Bible Society. It has been found, however, that the bare statement of the principles has not always proven an adequate help for the translator. Some supplementary and illustrative material drawn from the experience of other translators has been continually requested. Accordingly, we are attempting to meet this need.

The source material for this volume is not as representative as the writer would desire, but it has seemed preferable to base the discussions upon data which could be personally investigated or adequately documented, rather than to undertake to discuss material which might prove unreliable. A considerable proportion of the illustrative data comes from languages in Latin America, where the writer has had most of his experience. It is hoped that in succeeding editions the illustrative base for this analysis of translation techniques may be considerably extended by investigations in other language areas. Supplementary information from missionary translators and linguists in all parts of the world will be greatly appreciated and should be of importance in making a future edition more representative and valuable.

Each of the problems and particular renderings of passages which are cited, as well as all anthropological data, may be fully validated. The sources of this material are: (1) the files of the American Bible Society covering problems which have been encountered in the process of checking manuscripts, (2) the experience of the writer on the field and in checking manuscripts for the Society, and (3) the experience of the writer's colleagues in the Summer Institute of Linguistics. When commendable renderings have been cited, the languages are named in most instances.

PREFACE

Where the renderings have not been good, the writer has purposely avoided indicating the language, in order that there may be no reflection upon the translator. There is nothing to be gained by stating the language and thus identifying the translator to many readers. The reader will have to trust the writer that the instances listed here are valid, but, were it necessary, much more flagrant errors could be cited than are commented upon in this book.

It will be noted that most of the problems which are listed come from the New Testament. This is because most translations which are published are the New Testament or parts of it. Nevertheless, the principles which are illustrated are equally applicable to the Old Testament, though in some instances the cultural setting is somewhat different.

The writer is dependent upon the rich and far more extensive experience of others. Dr. Eric M. North, General Secretary of the American Bible Society, has been responsible for the development of the extensive series of checks which are now employed by the Society and which are responsible for many very significant improvements in translation techniques. Dr. James Oscar Boyd, the writer's predecessor as Versions Secretary of the Society, has shown remarkable insight in the treatment of many technical problems. All this research has been made available and much of it has been incorporated into this book.

The writer is also deeply indebted to many missionary translators in various parts of the world, and also to students and colleagues of the Summer Institute of Linguistics, whose valuable suggestions and criticisms have been very important in the formulation and illustration of many principles of procedure.

New York, 1947   EUGENE A. NIDA

Chapter 1

MEN OF THE BOOK

"KALATE! KALATE!" ("The books! The books!") The shout resounded through the village. No man of Elat, here in the Camerouns, had to ask what books. These were *the* books—so long expected, so long delayed by war; some lost at sea, but some finally here—the translation of the Bible into their own Bulu tongue. To be sure, there were educated men among them who could speak French, the government language in this African mandate, and who could read the Bible in that language. But French did not speak to their hearts as did the Bulu. Parts of the Bible had been translated into Bulu before. But here it was, entire. "The books are here!" rang the shout.

Outside the infirmary, a great crowd gathered almost in a moment. Hundreds of hands were outstretched to receive a copy of the Bible. Lists had been made long ago of those who should receive them—the native evangelists, the Sunday-school teachers, the elders. But that was before all but 300 of the expected 2,000 copies had been lost in transit through war-disturbed waters. What to do now? One of the distributors gave up in despair, and tossed a copy out to the sea of hands. Two men caught it, and it was torn in two before they realized what they were doing. One evangelist held his copy tightly closed; he would not open it then. "No; first I must go and pray before I open and read it. How often I have prayed, 'I hope I will not die until the Bible comes.' My Father has answered my prayer. Now I must go to thank Him." Another took his book and went into the forest, away from the shouts and confusion. He must be alone to read the Word undisturbed. And so, one by one, the precious volumes found their way into the hands of a few of the 100,000 Bulu Christians of this West African community.

Drama was enacted in Elat that day; but behind the drama lay months and years of work. Sometimes the work was mere drudgery; sometimes it went swiftly to a peak of achievement. It is so

3

with every new venture into the field of Bible translation. There
are the weeks and months when the missionary translator is writing
down hundreds of words in his notebook or on small pieces of paper. All these strange words must be memorized. The missionary
may have asked for such a short word as 'bus,' to find the native give such a word as the Chichimeca gul'?us-we'doa-ko'pu?,
literally 'a house that walks on the land.' Or perhaps the missionary has not even had the advantage of an interpreter. He has
had to point at things, mimic all sorts of actions, and endanger his
reputation for sanity in order to elicit some of those very hard
words. A missionary among the Tarahumaras was trying to
obtain the word 'jump.' He acted it out by jumping around the
room. The natives responded with an expression; so he quickly
wrote it down, only to find out later that it meant 'What is wrong
with you?'

But it is not enough for the missionary to write down the words;
they have to be memorized and used. The only way to learn to
speak a language is to speak it, even though the mistakes may seem
tragic. For example, one missionary thought he was asking for
'help' but was actually inquiring for a 'wife.' That slip of the
tongue made him the welcome guest at any gathering of the natives, for they seemed never to cease laughing at this and similar
mistakes which he made. One can learn to play the piano by
practicing in seclusion, but no one ever learned to speak a language
well without an audience. Within a week all the stuffy self-con-
sciousness of the missionary must be lost or he will be a failure in
his work of learning the language.

After the initial failures and sometimes horrifying mistakes come
the long mosquito-filled evenings around the smoking camp fire,
listening to the palaver of the old men, the almost endless tales of
ancient wars, the gods and heroes who completely outclass Tarzan
and Buck Rogers with their amazing exploits.

The folktales are the word pictures of the aboriginal society,
the school of native wisdom. Here are the illustrations for ser-
mons which speak to the people as no foreign illustrations can
possibly do. What better illustration of temptation and the penalty for sin can the missionary find than in the San Blas story of
the little lobster who finally gets caught in the trap because he
will not heed the warning of his parents to avoid the temptation
of an easily procured meal! The translator may not be able to

translate our own figure of speech "jumping from the frying pan into the fire," but around the camp fires of West Africa he may hear the proverb about the man who was so afraid of the sword that he hid in the scabbard. To speak the language of the people, he must hear the people speak. In time he may conclude that in the knowledge of human nature his textbooks in college showed a contemptible ignorance when compared with the accumulative wisdom of centuries passed down from generation to generation around the smoldering camp fires in the jungle.

But languages are not mastered by listening, or even by practicing chance expressions picked up from natives. There is real 'boning' to be done. Hour after hour must be spent in compiling words into a dictionary, analyzing the grammatical structure of the language on the basis of the hundreds of pages of native stories which the translator has written down. His goal is to translate in the same form in which the people speak, in a style which seems so (1) natural to them that it speaks intimately and personally to their own hearts. If possible, he does not want this book to bear the marks of a foreign language, or even of his own imperfect knowledge of the native tongue. But to attain his goal requires months and years of concentrated effort.

When finally the translator has learned the language well enough that he can actually converse freely with the native speakers about the Bible and its contents, then come the weeks, and months, and even years of work with the native helpers: studying verse after verse of the text, carefully explaining the meaning, discussing the best manner of saying the same thing in the native language, writing it down, and finally going over it carefully to check for any errors.

The joy of sending off the final manuscript is usually swallowed up by the anxiety of not knowing whether the manuscript will arrive safely at the Bible Society offices. Then follow the final checks and the proofreading. Nothing can seem to be so hard as proofreading. But all this must go into the making of a new translation. It can be told so much more quickly than it can be done. However, to those who have had the privilege of completing the task, no joy has seemed quite so great as that experienced in giving to a new tribe of people the heritage of the Word of God in their own language.

By the time the translation is completed, the days of real pioneering have receded into the past. It may be hard for the translator to remember those times when he offended the people's sense of propriety by pointing at objects with his fingers in order to obtain the native words for all the things he saw. It was only after he had frightfully shocked his audience with his bad manners that he found out that he should have pointed with his lower lip. He tried never to offend again. Finally, pointing with the lip became so much a habit that he almost found himself doing it when he came home on furlough.

(2) Food habits also become changed as well as social and linguistic ones. One translator learned to relish fried ants, but he hardly wanted to admit to the folks at home that his daughter insisted that she preferred them to ice cream. After all, what would the folks at home say when they heard that a child had been brought up with such "heathenish" tastes? Yet he would not remonstrate with his daughter, for he was secretly inclined to agree with her.

However, it has generally been far easier to eat the strange food than to get accustomed to the beliefs of the people. How many times the missionary had unwittingly offended them! There was the time when he had picked up and carried to the hospital a little girl who had fallen out of a tree. When, however, she regained consciousness she insisted that someone be sent back immediately to the base of the tree in order to bring her spirit back to her. Of course, it would not help the girl to have someone go for her spirit, but should the poor girl die, the missionary knew that he would be blamed for her death. What was he to do? If he told them that their belief was false, how could they possibly believe him? He was just a foreigner. The death of this unfortunate girl would outweigh any arguments which he might bring. Perhaps some day there would be some of this girl's own people who would be able to explain to her that it was not necessary for someone to return to get her soul. Perhaps gradually the translator's considerate ministry to the people would convince them of the truth of the good news which he talked about. Certainly his life will give meaning to his words.

Some translators feel that they could have easily adjusted themselves to the life of the people if only it had not been for the terrifying problems of the language. For example, in the Kekchi language of Guatemala the only difference between 'our pig' and 'fire' is the kind of popping k sounds which occur in the last word and that do not occur in the first. It is exceedingly embarrassing to run down the street yelling, 'Our pig! Our pig!' instead of 'Fire! Fire!' Or perhaps the translator feels as did those working on the Mazatec language of Mexico, when much to their amazement they found that instead of saying, 'Our director has told us to come here' they had been saying, 'Our devil has told us to come here.' The only distinction between the word for 'director' or 'chief' and the word for 'devil' is a slight difference in the tone. Of course, to say that the devil had told them to carry out their work was only adding confirmation to what the local religious authorities had already said, namely, that these translators were out there under the auspices of Satan himself.

Long and short vowels and syllabic consonants are always a headache to missionaries. But few people have gotten into quite so much difficulty in one sentence as a missionary who was preaching in one of the Bantu languages of West Africa. Instead of saying that 'The children of Israel crossed the Red Sea and followed Moses' he declared that 'The children of Israel crossed the red mosquitoes and swallowed Moses.'

The eagerness with which some people receive the Word is usually matched by the fierce hatred with which others reject it. In 1943 a translator was approaching a village in a steaming tropical jungle of Latin America. A small band of men met him. One of them stepped out and grabbed him by the shoulder, brandished his razor-sharp machete, and drew it across the throat of the missionary. Then he warned him in no uncertain words that he would draw it across again and slit his throat if the missionary did not leave immediately. The people of this village were determined to keep out anyone who would bring them the book which they had been told was "the book of the Devil." This incident is not rare. The history of missions is full of the accounts of men and women who have been shot, beaten, and tortured because they dared to bring the Word of God to men who had not read and could not read it. No translator turns back in the task of giving the Word because it may cost him his life, not when other men have sacrificed so much before. Tyndale was driven from his own home, finally captured, strangled to death, and his body burned in the public square—all this by ecclesiastical authorities. He suffered such a fate because he was convinced that we as English-speaking people should have the Bible in our language. Tyndale knew the risks he was running. He knew that the ecclesiastical hierarchy had denounced Wyclif and had even exhumed his body, burned it, and cast the ashes into the river Swift in order that the body of such a man might not pollute the holy ground of England. But just as the physical remains of Wyclif were borne out to the open sea, so the influence of both the man and his translation has been carried from the narrow confines of England to the ends of the earth. Perils did not thwart the greatest of early missionaries, Paul. The modern translator cannot afford to falter, with need and example to spur him on.

But physical danger comes seldom. Great emergencies are not so wearing on the spirit as the endless details which fill the translator's life. Many a translator has dreamed of being undisturbed for the entire day in order that he might give himself completely to the task so close to his heart. But there are always innumerable things that must be done. Early in the morning the carriers come for their pay. A drunk staggers up to the house. He cannot be ordered away, for perhaps he is a good friend. Perhaps the missionary uses on him the technique which he has employed before, namely, plying him with so many questions about almost anything that the poor fellow becomes befuddled and goes off. Nevertheless he retains the conviction that certainly the missionary is interested in him or he would not have asked him so many questions. There is almost always some child who comes to have a splinter extracted. The translator is no doctor; he is probably not much of a nurse; but every missionary is somewhat of a doctor even if he knows only the most rudimentary things about first aid. A man may have gashed his leg and come many miles to be treated. He cannot be sent away. The translator does for him what he can, but giving him only one sulfa pill at a time, for if he were given ten pills he would take them all at once, reasoning that ten pills should be ten times more efficacious than one.

All these interruptions take time. They fill the day to the point where even the missionary's own friends and family may think that he is beside himself. But Jesus' family and friends thought the same of Him. Human suffering cannot go unattended. However, as the missionary ministers to needs of people in the name of Jesus, they will praise God for such a man, even as those of ancient times glorified God for Jesus.

In all the press of duties the translator must be a word-hunter. "How can one say 'glory' in this language?" he is perhaps saying to himself. These people do not know anything about the glory of God. Their own petty chieftains possess no glory. The translator may light upon the idea of using the term for 'radiance' for the basic underlying word, even as was done in the Mazatec language. But 'radiance' is not enough. This must be qualified. In the Mazatec one must first add a prefix to indicate that a quality is being spoken of. Then, by means of a final element one must indicate that this radiance has a personal and living significance. It is true that the Mazatec word is newly constructed by the translator, but it is made up exactly like many other Mazatec words. This word is recognizable by the people as 'the quality of living radiance.' When one is sure that the people do immediately understand it, another big stumbling-block has been removed from the road to final completion of the translation.

Words with broad, general meanings never seem to have parallels in the aboriginal language. The translators of the Mazatec struggled with "He must increase, but I must decrease," John 3:30, only to find that the expressions which they first chose meant 'to become 'tall and to become short'; 'fat' and 'skinny'; or 'huge' and 'puny.' There seemed to be no way of expressing the meaning of the Bible text, until one day the translators explained to the native helper that the verse did not imply becoming physically big and small but, rather, socially more important and less important. Immediately the native informant had the answer. The Mazatec way of saying this was, 'He must become more of a chief, and I must become more of a follower.' This translation meant something to a Mazatec Indian, for it came from his own culture. It was the way he would say it.

With all the careful attention to details, there are always items which escape attention. One may discover as one translator did that one vowel on the end of a word had been omitted, with the result that the manuscript declared that Jesus was asleep 'behind the boat' rather than asleep 'in the back part of the boat.'

Wherever the translator goes, he becomes identified as the man of the Book. It may be along the hot jungle trail where he is seated to rest and the men ask him to take out his book to read to them. It may be in the evening twilight around the flickering light of the fire or the rapidly melting candle that he reads the story of life. But always he is the man of the Book.

In a village in Mexico the local authorities denounced the man who was translating the Bible into their language. After all, he was a foreigner, and foreigners had cheated the Indians mercilessly. Was it possible that this man was free from evil designs upon them? A native friend answered that, as far as he could tell, all that the translator knew or believed was in one book. "I will get the book and bring it to you," he said, "and you may decide."

He brought the book to the council meeting the next night. The local chiefs expected to find in it all sorts of magic lore, and perhaps even diabolical incantations. It was in Spanish; a few of them could read a little in that language, and interpreted for those who could not. Very soon the anxious and unfriendly looks disappeared. Far from being the book of the Devil, this book was the book that talked about God and his Son, Jesus Christ. Here were the names of many of the saints and stories about them. Such a book could not be an evil book. The charges against the translator were dropped.

This Book is one which tells the truth about man and about God. Men come to it for light and often flee from it when its message exposes their evil deeds. No man can read it sincerely and be the same man again. However, there are still at least one thousand (3) tribes of people who cannot read it because no one has ever translated it into their own language.

The following chapters deal with the technical problems which are encountered in the task of translation. They are serious problems, but in sincere consecration to the task to which the Church has been commissioned by our Lord, they can and must be solved.

Chapter 2

PRINCIPLES OF TRANSLATION

THE principles of translation may best be treated under (1) methods used, (2) basic requirements to be met, and (3) fundamental factors of meaning.

2.1   METHODS EMPLOYED IN TRANSLATING

In general, there have been three principal methods in translation. These may be classed as (1) literal translations, (2) translations of ideas, and (3) translations based upon the closest equivalents.

2.1.1   LITERAL TRANSLATIONS

There are several degrees of literalness in translation. An interlinear translation from one language into another is a type of literal translation. There are many interlinear translations of the Greek New Testament, but these are difficult to understand unless a freer translation accompanies them, for the order of the Greek words is quite different from that of English words. However, despite the obvious fact that interlinear translations are never adequate to represent the full meaning of the text, many missionaries have been content to make almost interlinear translations of the Bible into various aboriginal languages. The results have been discouraging and practically useless.

Some well-known translations have been very literal. For example, in many passages the Septuagint Greek translation of the Old Testament translates the Hebrew almost word for word. The Greek is very poor when judged from the standpoint of the form of expression, but the translators were bound by a traditional literalism in linguistic usage. The Septuagint was of great importance among the Greek-speaking Christians and Jews, but it probably failed to attain wider acceptance because of the awkward and unnatural form of expression.

Some Bible students have attempted to translate in what they feel is a consistent manner by always rendering the same Hebrew or

11

Greek word by the same English word, and similarly for many types of grammatical constructions. This type of translation, which has been called "concordant," makes an immediate appeal to those uninformed about the problems and principles of linguistic usage. But no two languages correspond throughout in their words or grammatical usages, and such a literal type of translation actually distorts the facts of a language rather than reveals them.

2.1.2　　TRANSLATIONS OF IDEAS

Words are merely vehicles for ideas. They are symbols, and as such they usually have no special significance over and above the actual objects which they symbolize. Accordingly, some translators have adopted as a basic principle a formula which may be stated as follows: "What would the author have said if he had been using English instead of Greek or Hebrew?" This type of approach to the problem of translation is very valuable at times, but it has some serious handicaps. The translator is often inclined to be more interpretive on the basis of such a formula than if he attempts to stay closer to the actual wording of the original. Such a translation is likely to be based on the translator's idea of the "gist" of the text and consequently reflects his personal interpretation of it. For example, one translator changed "I am the bread of life" to 'I am the true life.' This is a rather extreme example. Nevertheless, the translator should be reminded constantly that it is necessary to translate precisely what the text says.

2.1.3　TRANSLATIONS BASED UPON CLOSEST EQUIVALENTS

A translation based upon the closest equivalents in the two languages represents a middle ground between two extremes: (1) literal translation and (2) translation of ideas. The principle of closest equivalence is designed to avoid awkward literalness on the one hand and unjustified interpretations on the other. The translation should be in the regular idiomatic form of the language.

Natives have failed to use many translations because the linguistic forms employed were so unnatural and strange. This is particularly the case when the native religion makes use of linguistic forms as a part of an elaborate ritual. Such natives are very sensitive to and appreciative of proper language forms, and any awkward literalism on the part of the translator is either openly denounced as not being the language or is apathetically received.

The principle of closest equivalence in translation also implies the avoidance of interpretive renderings, e.g. 'made different by holiness' for "transfigured"; and 'I should take sin away from them' for "I should heal them."

The principle of closest equivalence will be discussed throughout the rest of the book. It is not easy to define, but one may summarize the various aspects of this principle by the statement of a situation, namely, "The recognition by the native bilingual person of the translation as being the closest 'natural' equivalent to the statement of the text." This indirect definition will become plainer as more data and illustrations are presented, particularly in Chapters 8 through 14, dealing exclusively with various aspects of this principle. However, some features of the 'definition' should be explained here:

1 By "native bilingual person" is meant one who has from childhood spoken the two languages, namely, the language of the text and the native language. From a theoretical standpoint only the person who knows both languages and both cultural backgrounds as a *bona fide* member of such linguistic and cultural groups is able to understand the complete denotative and connotative values of the translation. However, from the practical standpoint one can postulate the problems and degrees of equivalence and attempt possible solutions.

2 By "natural" is meant the form of the expression. There are some unavoidable 'foreignisms' in any translation, e.g. transliterations of proper names; but, in so far as is at all possible, the translation should be in the natural form of expression of the people. At the same time it must be the closest equivalent to the text.

The implications and meaning of this definition may be more fully understood by an analysis of the basic requirements of translation.

2.2   Basic Requirements of Translation

To obtain the closest equivalence in translation it is necessary to consider three basic requirements: (1) the translation must represent the customary usage of the native language, (2) the translation must make sense, and (3) the translation must conform to the meaning of the original. It is not always easy to satisfy all three of these requirements, for they seem to overlap and at times to be contradictory. However, they must be carefully considered at all times in making any good translation.

2.2.1   USAGE OF THE LANGUAGE

We naturally expect a translation into English to be correct as far as grammatical form and the meaning of words are concerned. We are very ready to recognize "translationisms," forms of expression which are not natural to English. The same is true of any language. A natural form of expression must be attained in both the words and the sentence structure.

2.2.1.1   WORDS

In seeking to use those words of a language which represent the actual language usage, one must be concerned with four principal problems: (1) the derivation of words, (2) the grammatical forms of words, (3) classes of words, and (4) the connotative values of certain types of words.

2.2.1.1.1   DERIVATION

In many languages it is possible and very valuable to construct descriptive compound words. This is one of the most frequently employed methods of dealing with certain types of problems in which there do not seem to be corresponding words in the two languages. Some translators, however, have attempted to construct long compounds formed in a manner at variance with the one in which the particular language forms compounds. In other instances the translators have overdone the tendency to form compounds to a point where the usage is completely unnatural. Many times the native has extreme difficulty in understanding what is meant. For example, the compound word for "church" employed in one translation in an aboriginal language may be literally translated as 'where they all worship God gathering together, repeatedly meeting.' This compound is entirely out of proportion to normal compounds. The natives actually call a church 'a place where people go in.' This latter would probably be completely satisfactory in many contexts if used consistently.

Some translators have been involved in considerable difficulty by their failure to check with actual usage the meaning of their own word creations. One translator constructed a word for "glory" in accordance with the native pattern, with the literal meaning of 'the quality of greatness.' This word was actually in use by the people, but with the somewhat shifted meaning of 'haughtiness' and 'boastfulness.' The passages which concerned the "glory of God" actually spoke of the 'boastfulness (or haughtiness) of God.' If words are to be manufactured or created for the native language, they must be designed in accordance with the native patterns, and the meaning must be correct as well as immediately evident.[1]

2.2.1.1.2   GRAMMATICAL FORMS

In some languages certain categories which we have in various Indo-European languages are lacking. One category which is often missing is the form for the passive. Some translators have thought that they could construct such a form artificially, but they have succeeded about as well as a Hindu would if he tried to make the turban the common headdress for the average American farmer. Certain languages manage very well without passive voice forms, and it is absurd to attempt to construct them artificially.

Other translators have felt that the grammatical forms of a language needed systematizing and have proceeded to 'regularize' them, usually in terms of the Latin grammar which they studied in school. Nothing could be more disastrous for a translation, for nothing so destroys naturalness of expression as incorrect grammatical forms. Note, however, that correctness and incorrectness may be determined only on the basis of the actual usage of the language, not in terms of so-called logical categories.

2.2.1.1.3   CLASSES OF WORDS

Two languages are rarely found to agree as to their classes of words. For the Indo-European languages, which include English and Greek, grammarians usually speak of eight classes of words, namely, nouns, verbs, adjectives, pronouns, adverbs, prepositions, conjunctions, and interjections. This is an exceptionally high number of types of words as compared with most languages in the world. Some languages have only three classes: nouns, verbs, and particles. Not only are the total numbers of classes different, so that the types of grammatical constructions must of necessity be

---

[1] In citing words and meanings of Biblical expressions, double quotes indicate the English form in the traditional texts, and single quotes reflect the meaning of expressions used in foreign languages.

somewhat different, but actions or states which in one language may be nouns are treated as verbs in another language. For example, in the Mazatec language of Mexico such English nouns as *food, faith, love, baptism,* and *repentance* must all be translated by verbs. It is impossible to say, "God is love." Rather one must translate, 'God loves people [indefinite object].' In the Aztec language it is possible to construct nouns corresponding to "purification," "justification," and "regeneration," but they would be as awkward in construction and as unfamiliar as *mesoderm, ectoplasm,* and *gastropod* are in English. In many instances where English employs nouns, Aztec normally employs verbs. A correct translation will use the natural expression of the language.

2.2.1.1.4   CONNOTATIVE MEANINGS

The meaning of a word must be defined in terms of (1) what it denotes (this is the denotation of a word) and (2) what it connotes (this is the connotation of a word).[1] The connotative meanings, which define the ways in which people react to certain words, are important in matters of (a) literary styles and (b) vulgarity.

2.2.1.1.4.1   LITERARY STYLES

Some languages, particularly some of those in the Orient, have very highly specialized literary styles. In such literary dialects (for they are just that) the words used are often very rare in the colloquial speech, and the grammatical forms are different from those which people normally employ. At times the uneducated person cannot even understand something read in this literary style. In other instances he can do so but only with considerable difficulty. Such a style is looked upon by the educated, and often by the uneducated as well, as being the correct formal vehicle for religious subject-matter. This is because their own religious literature is in this form of speech. The translator may employ some of the forms of the literary style in order to add dignity to the translation, but any radical departure from the colloquial usage usually fails in achieving the best results. A literary style should never be followed to the point of making the translation unintelligible to an uneducated native when he hears it read. It should be carefully borne in mind that the Greek New Testament was

---

[1]The differences between denotation and connotation are discussed on p. 138 ff.

written in a colloquial form of speech. For the most part it was written in the style in which the average unlettered man of the Hellenistic world spoke. Because of this 'unliterary' quality it was frowned upon by the trained writers and critics of the Greek world. Its appeal was, however, to the man in the street, for it spoke clearly a language which he understood. Any translation which does not speak the language of the masses generally fails to reach the masses. The principal objective in style should be toward dignity and simplicity. The combination of the two is the highest art.

The translator may make use of some special styles to good advantage in translating. For example, many languages possess certain chant forms. These may be profitably employed in translating the Psalms. It should be noted that a failure to employ native prosodic patterns (features of stress, pitch, and length) has often seriously crippled the effectiveness of translations. For example, among the Totonacs of Mexico the native chant forms preserve the length of the vowels in the language. When some hymns were translated into the Totonac, the translator overlooked the matter of agreement between the long and short vowels of the language and the long and short notes of the music. One young Totonac Indian objected rather strongly to this oversight and so proceeded to translate some hymns which made this correspondence. The results were excellent.

The difficulties of translating hymns to fit our types of melodies are a constant problem to translators who are working with tonal languages. One translator found that what she had thought meant 'sinners' actually meant 'fat people,' for the tones of the language were almost the exact opposite of the tune. The native forms of music are a part of the cultural heritage of the people which should not be overlooked or slighted. They should be employed unless such literary patterns pertain distinctively to the pagan religious system. Such a situation is much rarer than is usually imagined.

2.2.1.1.4.2   VULGARITY

A word may have a proper denotative meaning, that is to say, it may point out the right object; but at the same time it may be used only in certain vulgar contexts. Words having such undesirable connotations should be avoided at all costs. In one instance the unwise use of such terms made it necessary to recall a translation by buying up all copies from the natives and burning them.

The translator had not been sufficiently careful about the connotation of some words. Words dealing with sex and procreation must *13.* be examined carefully. For example, it was necessary in one language to change "lame from his mother's womb" to 'lame since he was born,' for the literal translation was very vulgar. On the other hand in some languages there is nothing vulgar about words describing certain parts or functions of the body, and yet the mention of one's grandmother by name is regarded as being hideously immoral. The usage of the particular language must be carefully examined.

2.2.1.2   SENTENCE STRUCTURE

All the words of a language may be correct, and yet the translation may not be understood by the native speakers because of the sentence structure employed. Greek is an exceptional language in the extreme length of certain sentences. Few languages permit sentences of such length. Many of the long sentences of the Greek must be broken up into shorter ones if the translation is to be understood. In several instances natives have been observed to read a translation in their own language quite well and yet fail to understand the meaning because the grammatical structure was so unnatural and complicated that they could not follow.

Not only must the length of the clauses and their subordination be adjusted in many instances, but the order of the words and phrases must be carefully considered. Nothing seems to throw the *14.* reader off more than an unnatural order of words.

2.2.2   MAKING SENSE

It may be thought strange to insist that making some sense should be a basic requirement of translation. It seems too obvious to be necessary, but many translations are left unread because they do not make sense. It is not so much that they say the wrong thing, but that what is said has practically no meaning. To overcome this tendency it is important to observe two important rules: *9.* (1) the use of as few transliterated and newly borrowed words as possible and (2) the avoidance of phrases which are meaningless.

2.2.2.1   USE OF TRANSLITERATION

It is necessary to transliterate many proper names, for which there is no possible translation. However, it is not necessary nor advisable to transliterate such words as "centurion" or "apostle." One can always employ a phrase such as 'a leader of one hundred soldiers' for "centurion" and 'a sent one' for "apostle." Transliterated words are empty words as far as meaning is concerned. The reader will understand in exactly inverse proportion to the number of such words. The fewer empty words a translation has, the fuller the meaning will be to the reader.

A newly borrowed word is somewhat in the class of a transliterated word in that it has practically zero meaning to many of the native speakers. Some translators have assumed that it is easier to teach a new vocabulary than it is to find native words. Considering the high proportion of borrowed words which are sometimes employed, it is puzzling why such translators should have undertaken to translate in the first place. On the other hand, there is a legitimate use for some types of borrowing. Such problems are discussed somewhat fully in Chapter 8, which deals with principles of alternate choice of words. The translator should, however, make it a practice to be conservative about introducing words with which the native speakers have only a very limited experience.

2.2.2.2   USE OF MEANINGLESS PHRASES

Perhaps it may be said that no combination of words is completely meaningless, and yet many combinations which have been used by translators do approximate this point. For example, a literal translation of "it came to pass" is completely meaningless in its context when translated literally into Aztec. For the Mazatec language the phrase "fruit of his loins," Acts 2:30, has no intelligible meaning. In the Yipounou language of Africa the expression "having soldiers under me," Matthew 8:9, would imply that the centurion of the story was a gigantic man standing upon other soldiers, for in the Yipounou in order to designate the official relationship of leader to subordinates one must say, 'having soldiers behind me.'

Whether an expression is meaningful or not often depends upon the native's interpretation of natural phenomena. For example, the expression "from the uttermost parts of earth to the uttermost parts of heaven" is meaningless to the Totonacs, for the two sets of points described are identical in the Totonac cosmogony. As the Totonacs explain the universe, it is shaped like half of an orange. The earth constitutes the plane surface and the heavens constitute the curved surface. The uttermost parts of each are located at the extended horizon and hence are identical. For the Totonacs the translation must be made to read 'from all over the earth and the heavens.'

It must be understood that in any translation the native will be unable to understand all that is meant by the text. We certainly do not understand all that is meant by the English and the Greek or Hebrew texts. If we did, there would hardly be the basis for so many differences of opinion. Many items in the translation will be obscure, and it is necessary for the missionary to do a considerable amount of teaching. The translator should not, however, consider that in translating the Bible he is writing a commentary on it. This has frequently been the case. As a result, the substituted words and the paraphrasing have not been careful and faithful renderings of the text. For example, one translator, in an effort to interpret the first chapter of the Gospel of John to his constituency, translated, 'In the beginning was Christ, and Christ. . . .' (John 1:1). This is an unjustified rendering of the original text, and though the immediate gain in understandability may seem great, the ultimate loss to the reader of the Bible is much greater.

Where the AV reads, "That which is born of the flesh is flesh; and that which is born of the Spirit is spirit," John 3:6, one translator has paraphrased it, 'That which a woman bears is an earth-creature, and that which the Spirit changes the heart of is the child of our great Lord.' Not only has the translator departed widely from the text, but it is very questionable whether the translation is any the more forceful by virtue of the restatement.

The translator must constantly be on guard against meaningless or totally obscure phrases. One of the best ways in which these can be checked is to have the translation read to illiterates who have not been under the influence of the missionary's teaching and then to have these people tell back to the missionary parts of the account. One cannot expect complete understanding or the inclusion of all items, but if various people consistently misunderstand a passage, then there certainly must be something wrong with the translation. Some missionaries have found great difficulty in explaining certain facts about God and the gospel, only to find that the difficulty lay not in the dullness of the listeners but in the obscurity and confusion of the terms which had been employed to teach those facts.

In many instances missionaries have fallen into the habit of using a specialized vocabulary and the natives at the mission station have learned to mimic it to perfection, so that the translation may seem perfectly understandable to this small group but quite inadequate for more extensive distribution and use. Non-Christians may not understand all of the Bible, but it should make some sense to them. *The real test of the translation is its intelligibility to the non-Christian,* who should be reached by its message.

2.2.3 CONFORMANCE TO THE ORIGINAL TEXT

The problems which are involved in conforming as closely as possible to the original text are considered somewhat fully in Chapters 6 and 8 on Translation Procedures and Principles of Equivalence. Some introductory and fundamental considerations may be noted, however. These include the following:

1. The use of the most commonly accepted interpretation.
2. The use of an interpretation which does not contradict the exegetical position of any mission in the field.
3. The correspondence of lexical units (meaningful forms) wherever possible.
4. The use of the translation giving the fullest meaning.

2.2.3.1 COMMONLY ACCEPTED INTERPRETATION

The Bible is the heritage of the entire church and should not be made the means of propagandizing one's own special theories of interpretation. Incalculable damage has been done in the mission field by the insistence of those who felt called upon to wage interchurch conflicts over some passages dealing with prophecy or certain ordinances. Every translation will to some extent represent the theological views of the translator. It is impossible to avoid this. But such features should be kept at a minimum. Much more common, however, than wilful specialization of interpretation have been renderings which represent the translator's chance interpretation, for which he has never taken the time nor thought necessary to check with any authorities. One translator rendered "The zeal of thy house hath eaten me up," John 2: 17, 'The jealousy which thy people have has devoured me.' This latter interpretation is held by only a comparatively few people and should be replaced by the interpretation held by most scholars. One should constantly check the translation with reliable commentaries. One cannot be too careful in being assured of the best and most generally accepted interpretation of the Bible and should retain as a basic principle the recognition that no one group, including his own, has a monopoly on the truth. In any event the truth is to be preferred to hallowed falsehood.

2.2.3.2 AN INTERPRETATION NOT CONTRADICTORY TO THE EXEGETICAL POSITION OF ANY CHRISTIAN CONSTITUENCY ON THE FIELD

It is quite difficult to maintain a principle of not adopting an interpretation which is contradictory to any Christian constituency on the field. Certain Christian groups have widely differing viewpoints with regard to many phases of Christian teaching. It would be impossible to conform to all, and yet within certain limits it is wise not to make the translation of the Bible an arena for theological controversy.

One point on which translators are asked to reach a satisfactory agreement with all Christian groups represented in a given area involves words for 'baptism' and 'baptize.' If both immersionists and non-immersionists are represented among the missionaries and the native constituency, no translation should employ a word which would rule out one or the other of the interpretations as to the mode of baptism. If at all possible, one should obtain a word *16.* which may be applicable to all types of baptism. At this point it is important that a careful distinction be drawn between the etymological meaning and the actual meaning of the word. For example, among the Mayas of Yucatan the regular word for 'baptism,' which has been in usage for centuries, is *ok-ja'*, literally 'to enter water.' This would seem to rule out the use of this word by non-immersionists, and yet this word was used first by non-immersionist groups in Yucatan. Such a word no longer has its literal etymological meaning but now designates the rite of baptism as practiced by non-immersionists. If such non-immersionists are perfectly in accord in the use of such a word, there can be no objection to its use. To force the use of another, unfamiliar term would be quite unnecessary and unwise.

2.2.3.3. CLOSEST CORRESPONDENCE OF LEXICAL ITEMS

Much will be said in Chapters 8 through 14 on principles of equivalence relative to the necessary adaptations which must be made in the translation. However, one must not lose sight of the fact that underlying the adaptations is the basic principle of the closest possible correspondence of the lexical items (the words, parts of words, and combinations of words). For example, one translator rendered "denies me" in Luke 12:9 by 'fails to make me known.' It is true that 'denying' and 'failing to make known' are related somewhat in meaning, but denying that one is acquainted with a person and failing to reveal this same person are quite different situations. The translation must render in so far as is at all possible the precise meaning of the text.

2.2.3.4 THE FULLEST MEANING

It is possible to translate the bare outlines of the narrative or to represent in as full a way as possible the meaning of the original text. It is possible to translate the last part of Mark 8:36 as 'gain the whole world and die,' for the word 'to die' is somewhat equivalent to AV "lose his own soul" or the Greek *dzēmiōthēnai tēn psuchēn autou*, but the Greek idiom means much more than 'to die.' It actually means 'to pay the penalty (for some wrong) with one's life.' A translation which includes the meaning of 'paying the penalty' conveys the fuller meaning of the Greek and represents a richer religious significance.

2.3 FUNDAMENTAL FACTORS OF MEANING

The fundamental semantic[1] factors involved in translation may be conveniently treated under (1) the meanings of words and (2) the correspondence of meanings of words.

2.3.1 THE MEANINGS OF WORDS

By training in so-called precise usage of words, we are often led to believe that words represent points or at best very small areas of meaning, and that these points of meaning are arranged in some sort of stellar pattern, clearly separated from each other and having well-defined relationships to other words of similar meaning. This is only a part of the truth. Words are not points or small areas of meaning which are neatly separated one from the other. Some words have large areas of meaning and other words have small areas of meaning, but all of these words cover some area of experience. There is no part of our experience which is not covered by some

[1]*Semantics* is the science of meaning. *Semantic* is the corresponding adjective.

word or combination of words, except perhaps momentarily, when some new feature comes into our culture and we have no word to designate it. But every language possesses the potentialities of creating such designations. In English we have such new words as *radio, saxophone,* and *television.* There is nothing in the experience of any people which cannot be described and named by means of their own language. When a new situation arises, there may be a slight difficulty at first in describing it, but some way of symbolizing it is soon devised. It is reported that when one of the Indian groups of the Middle West first saw a bicycle, they named it by means of a compound word meaning literally, 'White man sits down to walk.'

One frequently hears of languages which are reported to have only a few hundred words in their vocabularies. Upon investigation all these reports have been found to be false. All languages are adequate to describe and discuss every phase of an aboriginal people's life, and such cultures are far more complex than most naïve tourists, or even some missionaries, ever suspect. For some time it was reported that the language of the aboriginals of central Australia was almost completely lacking in any adequate lexical structure. This was assumed, evidently, on the basis of the very simple material culture of these aboriginals. Further investigation has revealed, however, that these aboriginals have one of the most elaborate social structures that has ever been encountered in the world. Perhaps the Central Australians cannot name fifty parts of an automobile or an airplane, for these items may not be in their culture, but they have names for more than seventy different classes of relatives. There is no such thing as an inadequate language. Every language is adequate in terms of the culture of which it is a part. Every culture, however simple, which has been thoroughly investigated, has been found to have a language with at least 15,000 to 20,000 words in the vocabulary, if words are counted in a manner similar to that in which we count words in English. Moreover, it should be noted that such investigations have been made on the basis of comparatively limited written texts, and there are certainly many words in all languages which have not been included in such lists. The problem of the translator is not one of the sufficiency of the language but one of the equivalence of lexical items. For this he must understand the problems of areas of meaning.

Words differ greatly as to the areas of meaning which they cover. Some words such as *get* and *have* in English have very wide areas. Consider *get* in such expressions as: *to get hurt, to get up, to get a cold, it gets me, she gets the letter,* and *she gets a promotion.* It is, however, somewhat more difficult to realize the area of meaning covered in an English word, for we are so used to the area of meaning that we consider it more or less restricted because it is so familiar. A glance at English equivalents for a foreign word is more illustrative. For example, in the unabridged Liddell and Scott Greek Lexicon the Greek word *logos* is listed as having the following meanings: 'computation,' 'reckoning,' 'public accounts,' 'account,' 'measure,' 'tale,' 'esteem,' 'consideration,' 'value,' 'relation,' 'correspondence,' 'proportion,' 'ratio,' 'analogy,' 'rule,' 'explanation,' 'plea,' 'pretext,' 'case,' 'statement of theory,' 'argument,' 'principle,' 'law,' 'reason,' 'formula,' 'term,' 'continuous statement,' 'narrative,' 'fable,' 'story,' 'speech,' 'legend,' 'report,' 'tradition,' 'mention,' 'notice,' 'description,' 'section,' 'division,' 'oracle,' 'proverb,' 'maxim,' 'saying,' 'assertion,' 'word of command,' 'subject-matter,' 'event,' 'utterance,' 'phrase,' 'word,' and 'language.' None of these English words is exactly equivalent to the Greek word *logos,* but the area of meaning of the Greek word covers an area of meaning which includes, in certain contexts, at least parts of the areas of meaning of all these English words.

Most words do not have as wide an area of meaning as this Greek word. Some words are in fact comparatively restricted; for example, the English words *osmosis* and *nightingale.* But whether the area is small or great, the translator must know the entire area and not just some peripheral usage, for unless the context expressly forbids it the native will automatically take the word in its central meaning rather than in a peripheral meaning. For example, in Maya the word *pak'aj* has a peripheral meaning of 'to contaminate,' but the central meaning is 'to plant seed.' The peripheral meaning may be employed only where the context expressly indicates this specialization of meaning.

We are accustomed to speak of 'synonyms,' as though certain words were the exact equivalents of certain others. But there are no true synonyms. By this we mean that there are no two words which have exactly the same area of meaning. Conventional lists of synonyms are actually lists of closely related words, not identical words. Some words appear to overlap in meaning; for example, *peace* and *tranquillity*—but these words are not by any means identical. We may speak of *a peace conference*, but we do not speak of *a tranquillity conference*. These words *peace* and *tranquillity* may in some instances denote the same untroubled state of affairs, but our 'feeling' (the connotation) for these words and the range of usage are quite different. The expressions *boy* and *male child* may denote the same objective referent, and yet one does not say *Oh male child!* but rather *Oh boy!* Such expressions are not identical.

In defining words we attempt to state the area of meaning. This is usually done in the dictionary by (1) giving another name for the object, e.g. scientific names for specimens of plant and animal life, (2) describing a situation in other words, (3) giving close synonyms which will enable us to understand the approximate area of meaning indicated, and (4) citing instances in literature where the particular word occurs. Dictionaries are, however, rarely adequate. The clumsy translationisms which foreigners make in using English are evidence that they have not thoroughly understood the areas of meaning of the words. A recent grammar of English for Italians has such sentences for the students to study as: "I love the summer with his dry weather and beautiful sun that puts a joyful sign on everything" and "The baby raises that it is a pleasure." Such sentences are translationisms which reflect an inadequate knowledge of areas of meaning of English words as well as the grammar.

The area of meaning of any phrase, word, or meaningful part of a word may be defined by the situations in which such a linguistic form may occur. The situations are of two types: (1) <u>linguistic situations</u> and (2) <u>practical situations</u>. In defining the meaning of the word *boy*, we may state that it may occur in the linguistic situations in which a class of words called 'nouns' may occur. There are further subdivisions of this noun class of words to which *boy* belongs, but normally we are content with listing the principal class of forms to which such a lexical item belongs. *Boy* may also be defined by certain practical situations. The word *boy* may be used in a strict sense when speaking of a male *homo sapiens* before the age of puberty. In a more general usage it may also occur as a symbol for any male *homo sapiens* before the age of approximately twenty. It may occur in a further usage to denote a male *homo sapiens* who is an adult, but for whom there is a favorable interest or regard on the part of the speaker, e.g. in such an expression as *He is a great old boy.* The word *boy* may be used as a symbol to denote a male servant of any age, particularly when applied to Orientals or Negroes. *Boy* may occur with exclamatory intonation in expressions of general exclamation or surprise, as in *Boy, how I liked it!* and *Boy, it was terrible!*

In acquiring a full understanding of the meaning of words in any aboriginal language, we do not have the advantage, or possible disadvantage, of being able to consult a dictionary. We have to make our own dictionaries. In some cases this is an advantage, for we may do a scientific job and not have to undo the work of some-one else who may not have been fully aware of the matter of areas of meaning. However, to make such a dictionary we must call upon native source material in the form of texts. It is quite in-sufficient to take out a long list of words and proceed to ask a native what the meaning of each word is. Usually he will give the central meaning, but sometimes a peripheral one will come to his mind first. The only way to be assured of the area of meaning is (1) to collect instances of the use of such a word in a great number of different contexts and (2) by means of these situations, both linguistic and practical, to define and describe the area of meaning of the word.

Despite the translator's long experience with a language it would be unwise for him to undertake translating without the con-stant help of an informant, a native speaker of the language, to help him with the language form. Some translators have preferred to work alone and then to check results with informants, but the difficulty with such a procedure is that many lexical mistakes get into the text, and it is seemingly impossible to weed them all out. The constant use of an informant will prevent many lexical errors.

One frequently hears of missionaries who are reputed to have a better command of the language than the natives themselves. This is almost always an exaggeration of a situation, for seldom do foreigners attain the same facility in a language which native speakers possess. Aboriginals are often greatly impressed by the fact that anyone can possibly speak their language, for so few people attempt to do it. Then again they are more often astounded than edified at the types of words which the missionary manu-factures, though out of respect for his superior status they accept these expressions with rather dubious meanings as being phenomenal utterances. On the basis of these words, the missionary is often given this grossly exaggerated reputation for language ability.

2.3.2. THE CORRESPONDENCE OF MEANINGS OF WORDS

In learning a new language one has to learn the area of meaning of the various words in only one language, but in translating into another language one has to recognize the area of meaning of the words in at least two languages. It is of fundamental importance to realize that two corresponding words in two different languages never have exactly identical areas of meaning. That is to say, such areas will not be found to coincide when superimposed. The vocabulary of each language covers all phases of natural phenomena significant to the particular culture, but the vocabularies of any two languages never cover these phenomena in exactly the same way. For example, in the Maya language there are two words which may be used for 'pouring liquid on the head,' but one of these implies that the liquid is poured on with considerable force and in quantity. The other word is more closely descriptive of the action in Mat. 26:7. Maya likewise makes a distinction in the area of meaning covered by the English word *peace*. Maya has two words. One of these designates an inward peace of the heart and the other denotes the lack of strife between people. In translating the expression "search the scriptures," John 5:39, it was found that there were three words for 'search.' The first word means 'to search out a bad object from an assortment of good objects, or vice versa.' The second means 'to search out in a disorderly fashion,' and the third word means 'to search out in an orderly fashion and with regard to minute details.' The last word most appropriately fits the context.

Where English would probably use only one word, for example, *noise*, the Totonac language makes a distinction between six different stems for 'noise.' These have the following meanings: (1) 'the noise of children yelling,' (2) 'the noise of people talking,' (3) 'the noise of people arguing or turkeys gobbling,' (4) 'the noise of people arguing in great anger,' (5) 'a noise which becomes increasingly louder,' and (6) 'the noise of a funeral.'

In the Mazatec language a clear distinction is made in some of the area of meaning covered by English *in*. One word denotes the relationship of an object which is inside of an area; for example, 'in a shoe,' 'in a dish,' etc. The other word means that the object is mixed in with other ingredients. On the other hand, though the Mazatec makes such a distinction in the area of meaning corresponding to the English word *in*, the areas of meaning of the two English words *know* and *see* are covered by one Mazatec word. To our way of thinking, the distinction in 'in' is unnecessary, but the failure to distinguish between 'to know' and 'to see' appears inexcusable. The difference is only a matter of viewpoint, and in dealing with such problems we must not let our own language habits prejudice our understanding or use of another language.

On the basis of the above analysis of areas of meaning there are two facts which should be evident. One of these is that there can be no completely concordant translation, and the second is that the more translations which may be consulted in the making of a new translation, the more likely one is to define correctly that part of the area of meaning of a word which is to be understood in the particular context.

In checking any translation the Versions Secretary of the Bible Society notes the usage of certain key words. A comparison is made between (1) the Greek and English words and (2) the native word or words used to correspond to these. (See the sample page of a word check list in the Appendix.) It is not meant that the words should show automatic consistency in agreement. In fact, if this situation does exist, one knows immediately that the translation is not a good one, for no two languages could possibly show such correspondence in the areas of meaning of related words. The purpose of such check lists is not to force artificial conformity but rather to check for differences of usage and to inquire as to the validity of such differences. The check lists are just as important in helping the translator make the proper changes in the words used, as they are in creating consistency in usage. Consistency in itself is no virtue, for translations may be consistently wrong almost as often as they may be consistently right.

The more translations consulted, the greater the possibility of the translator's being able to identify that particular area of meaning of a text word which is to be understood in the specific context. For example, the Greek word *logos* has a very wide area of meaning, but if the translator compares the way in which this word is translated in (1) the various languages which he may know or (2) the various English translations to which he may have access, he will be able to restrict the area of meaning intended in the particular context, and may then more readily find that word in the native language which most closely approximates this area. The more one may superimpose areas of meaning represented by corresponding words in various languages, the more easily may one discover, by comparing the common area of meaning, that limited area which is intended for the particular context. Only such an orientation in the problems of semantics will enable one to translate correctly and idiomatically.

Chapter 3

LANGUAGES AND DIALECTS INTO WHICH
TRANSLATIONS SHOULD BE MADE

THE question as to which languages and dialects warrant translations represents two fundamental problems. The first of these is, "Should a particular language group have a translation?" The second is, "If there are dialect differences within the language group, what should then be done?" These questions will be discussed under (1) language groups for whom translations should be made, and (2) problems of dialect differences.

3.1 LANGUAGE GROUPS FOR WHOM TRANSLATIONS SHOULD BE MADE

It should be a basic principle of missionary endeavor that everyone should have at least some part of the Word of God in a language which he can read. The problem should not be primarily one of numbers, though this is often, and perhaps too often, considered as being a vital issue. However, the Bible Societies are not concerned primarily with the matter of numbers, but of need. For example, the American Bible Society published a Gospel in the Mohawk language for a group of about 1,000 Protestant Mohawks, of whom approximately three hundred live in the Borough of Brooklyn, New York. Portions of the Bible have also been printed for very small tribes numbering only a few hundred. The expense per person is not the primary consideration. The primary factors are the need which the people have for the Bible and the assurance that the books published will be used.

The need which people have for the Word of God may be defined in terms of (a) linguistic and (b) religious factors. — 22.

3.1.1 LINGUISTIC FACTORS

It should be a foregone conclusion that everyone should have the Bible in a language that he can read, but a great difference of opinion exists relative to the use of (a) related dialects and (b) the

31

trade language (the *lingua franca* of the region). However, one
thing is certain, namely, the closer the form of the Bible is to the
native speech of a people, the easier it is for them to understand it,
and the more readily the message may become a part of their life.
The Bible in a people's own idiom has a dynamic appeal to the
inner thought and life. As Edwin W. Smith of the British and
Foreign Bible Society has said, "Every language is a temple in
which the soul of the people who speak it is enshrined."

It has often been found that people can use the translation of a
related dialect. In fact, this is often easier than many missionaries
have at first realized. Not being thoroughly acquainted with the
language, they immediately are impressed with the great differences between the dialects. Yet the natives often speak with each
other with comparative ease and soon learn to overlook the differences. Of course, it has been discouraging to attempt to teach
natives to read by employing primers or written material based
upon another dialect. At all events, people should be taught to
read in an alphabet and with reading material which is designed for
their own dialect. However, after they have learned to read, they
can often make the adjustment to another dialect with amazing
ease. It has been found that translations of small portions of the
Bible in the various local dialects in order to acquaint the people
with reading and with the Bible vocabulary have been a means of
introducing the natives to a more extensive translation made in
the dominant dialect of the region.

In many instances the missionaries have insisted upon the use
of the trade language of the area. In some cases it is a native language such as Hausa or Swahili in Africa. In other instances it is
a language such as Spanish, Portuguese, or French, the language of
a foreign and politically dominant group. Regardless of the language, it has usually proved to be the case that the missionaries
have overestimated the ease with which the natives have understood the trade language. Usually the missionary learns the trade
language first and better than any of the other dialects or languages. Such training often prejudices him in favor of the trade
language. This may be a case of following the path of least resistance, but it is seldom given as the reason for the use of the trade
language. Usually missionaries declare that the only way to unify
the people is to insist upon the almost exclusive use of the trade
language. The prohibitive costs of publication in the various

languages and the lack of adequate personnel are also frequently given as reasons for the use of the trade language. Some of these reasons are valid, but very careful attention should be paid to the problem. In many instances it has been found that the use of the trade language has not produced the results which the missionary imagined or hoped for. The failure of a work to take hold and for an indigenous leadership to arise has usually been traceable to a large extent to the failure of the missionary to use the native idiom and to provide the people with a translation in their own language.

It has often been found that the trade language is too foreign to the people. They do not understand it sufficiently in those parts of the vocabulary which are essential for discussing spiritual truths. People may be able to carry on a good deal of commerce in a language and yet not understand words which deal with the emotional and religious life.

One important solution to the problems of the varied languages and dialects on the one hand and the trade language on the other is the publication of diglots. Those who learn to read their own language (they can do this in an amazingly short time provided the language is scientifically written) soon learn to read the trade language. By means of the diglot they are then able to extend their use and understanding of the trade language. Such diglots are actually a means of introducing the native populations to the use of trade languages more rapidly than would otherwise be the case. The reduction of the native language to writing and the publication of such diglots actually results in most instances in a more rapid adoption of the trade language by the people than would be the case were the native language never used for publication. It may safely be said that there are one hundred instances where there is too little translation in the native idiom to one instance where there is too much use of the local dialects. Few people have realized, as the Russians have, the importance of the native languages. The use of the many native languages within Russia during the last ten years of intensive literacy campaigns has revealed amazing literacy gains. In order to accomplish a record of change from a pre-1918 figure of some 33 percent literacy to a present 93 percent literacy, the use of the more than eighty indigenous languages of Russia has been an important factor.

To those who are informed as to the linguistic problems of missionary work it is becoming more and more evident that considerably greater emphasis needs to be placed upon adequate use of the native idiom. Missionaries who fail to give this sufficient consideration are likely to be defeating their own purposes in evangelism and development of native leadership.

3.1.2   RELIGIOUS FACTORS

A translation of the Bible or parts of it should be produced to fill a religious need. There is no point in publishing books in exotic languages so that collectors of such rare items may be able to fill their shelves. The expense and labor involved are entirely too great for this purpose. The Bible Societies do not object to the cost of production provided they are assured that the translation will fill a religious need.

In order to fill a religious need of the people an intensive and extensive reading campaign must be undertaken, to teach the populace how to read. In fact several missionaries have estimated that the translation and publication of the Bible is only a small percentage of the entire problem of getting the written page to the native. The reading campaigns must be given a prominent position in the entire evangelistic and educational program. Highly improved techniques of teaching people to read have been developed, among the most publicized of which are the methods of Dr. Frank Laubach. Missionaries should avail themselves of information outlining such programs and explaining the methods which may be employed in various circumstances to obtain the best results.

The translator must also be aware of the fact that in order to make the use of the printed Bible a vital part of the culture and life of the natives, he must also provide other printed materials. For any large constituency the Bible should not be the only book to be published. Other Christian books do not detract from the use of the Bible but rather increase the so-called 'reading complex' in the culture. All publications tend to increase the extent and effectiveness of the printed page. However, whether further publications come out in the language or not, if the people do have the Bible in their own language, they will enter into the society of the more dominant and complex cultural group on a literate level. Reading will have broken the chains of intellectual slavery, and the Bible will have brought them the eternal truth without which men cannot truly live.

The Bible in the language of the people has proved to be the primary and fundamental prerequisite for an indigenous church. In fact, so far as is known no really successful indigenous work has ever been accomplished without some of the Bible in the native language. The history of the churches in North Africa is significant in this regard, for during the time of the great Mohammedan conquests the only churches of North Africa which were able to maintain an existence were the Coptic and the Ethiopic Churches. These were also the only ones which possessed the Bible in the indigenous tongue.

A man's mother tongue is the one which speaks with strength and conviction in the difficult and perilous experiences of life.

3.2   PROBLEMS OF DIALECT DIFFERENCES

In attempting to solve the problems of the dialect or dialects into which a translation should be made, there are two types of factors. One of these includes a survey of the linguistic and practical aspects of the problems and the other concerns the technical solutions to such dialect differences.

3.2.1   LINGUISTIC AND PRACTICAL CONSIDERATIONS
OF THE DIALECT PROBLEMS

The problems involved in the linguistic and practical considerations of the dialect situation in various languages are almost unlimited. However, for a summary and brief consideration they may be treated under the following heads:

1 Linguistic center
2 Geographical center
3 Cultural center
4 Communication and transportation
5 Living facilities
6 Established Christian communities

These factors differ greatly in various localities, and the relative importance of the various factors may not be predetermined. The human factors are especially important and difficult to judge. There is no fixed formula for establishing the correct answer to a complex situation. Nevertheless, a translator should carefully consider all of these factors before undertaking any major translation work.

3.2.1.1   LINGUISTIC CENTER

Before discussing the techniques for determining the linguistic center of a language area it is important to define the terms *dialect* and *language*. These are sometimes used interchangeably. Often a language spoken by only a few people is called a *dialect*. A language may be defined as a speech community in which everyone understands some other speaker (barring, of course, the use of foreign languages). On the basis of this definition all those who are considered as speaking English may be considered as constituting a 'speech community,' even though this community includes many millions of speakers. The definition does not say that every speaker within this community must be able to understand every other speaker, but only that he must be able to understand some other speaker who is a member of the speech community. For example, there are dialects of Scotch English which the writer, who speaks general American English, cannot understand. This does not mean that the writer does not speak English or that Scotch English is not English, for between these two dialects there are several grades of difference, that is to say, several dialects. The speakers of each of these dialects are able to understand other contiguous dialects. There is, therefore, a continuous unbroken line of speakers who are able to understand each other when they are using their normal form of speech. Accordingly, this draws together mutually unintelligible dialects into one language. However, the speaker of any one dialect of English cannot understand a person speaking Spanish, unless, of course, he has learned Spanish as a foreign language. If he does, he actually becomes a member of two speech communities. English and Spanish are mutually unintelligible to all the members of the respective language groups. They are two languages.

Dialects may not be so easily defined as languages, for there are many different grades of dialect difference. In fact, no two individuals in any language speak exactly alike. We could say that each individual's speech constitutes a dialect, and yet this type of definition is not very practical. In every speech community there are groups of people who recognize that their own speech differs in some degree from that of others in the speech community. This subjective recognition is sufficient to establish a dialect area. The differences may be very great, so that the people have considerable difficulty in understanding each other; or the differences may be only slight. However, such dialect differences have been culturally and politically important since time immemorial. The story of the *shibboleth* in Judges 12 is one of the most famous instances of the recognition of dialect alternates.

In the case of any aboriginal language the translator must expect to be confronted with certain dialect problems. One of the first things which he should attempt to do is to determine the linguistic center of any given language area in which he intends to work. The linguistic center of such an area is characterized by having the greatest number of language features in common with the greatest number of speakers in the total area. This is to say, the speakers of the central linguistic area may be understood by more people than anyone else, for their speech has more features which are similar to the speech of other dialects. In determining speech centers the important practical consideration must be the number of speakers rather than territorial distribution.

The linguistic investigator often determines the approximate linguistic center of a language area by inquiring as to which people in the area can be understood most readily. If one can get his informants to give valid information on the subject, the results may be approximately correct. There are, however, two factors which are likely to distort the data obtained from questioning informants on the subject. The first is their habitual tendency to answer in the way in which they think the missionary may want them to answer. This is usually considered by them as being the polite way to act and speak, but it can be extremely tantalizing to one who is not so conditioned by training. The second factor is the conviction held by most people, aboriginals and civilized peoples alike, that their own form of speech is the superior form of the language; and even if not historically the more dominant, it is thought to possess the unmistakable marks of superiority which would commend it for use in any translation to be used over any large language area. Usually, therefore, the translator must supplement and correct his information, based on rather subjective impressions of his informants, by collecting and classifying actual data on the dialect differences within any language area.

In order to make a scientific analysis of the dialect differences in any language area one should select certain key points which experience has indicated represent certain dialect differences.

For example, in the following map of a hypothetical Papawapam language area, there are five centers.

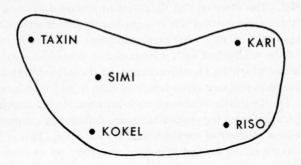

—— Marks the limit of Papawapam speech community. The five centers are municipalities which include a central town and the adjacent territory. They have the following population:

Municipality	Population
Taxin	500
Simi	2,000
Riso	1,200
Kari	600
Kokel	1,050

In order to make the most adequate check of the dialect differences it is important to select for comparison items which the investigator has found to represent rather important distinctions. Also, such items should be representative of all types of linguistic structure: phonology (the sounds), morphology (the word structure), syntax (grammatical constructions of phrases and sentences), and lexicon (the meaning of the words and phrases).

In any actual analysis one should have fifty to one hundred items to compare. For this Papawapam illustration only four items have been selected, but they are representative of the various classes of data. These are:

1. The palatal and velar series.

Some dialects have two series of back consonants, a palatal and a velar series. The other dialects have only one series, namely, a velar one.

2. Formation of the passive.

Some dialects have a passive suffix used with verbs. Other dialects employ a phrase to express a passive.

3. Order of the subject, object, and verb expression.

Some dialects employ the order of subject-object-verb, and other dialects have a subject-verb-object order.

4. *Taat* vs. *diil* for 'father.'

Some dialects employ *taat* 'father,' and other dialects *diil*, with the same meaning.

If lines are drawn so as to separate the areas which distinguish these four features, the resultant map of isoglossal lines would perhaps look much like the following:

Map of Papawapam Dialect Differences

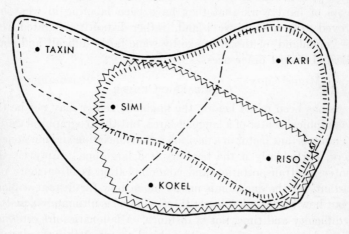

Key to Map

	Within Isoglossal Lines	Outside Isoglossal Lines
1	Double series of back consonants	Single series of back consonants
2	Subject-verb-object order	Subject-object-verb order
3	*diil* 'father'	*taat* 'father'
4	Periphrastic passive	Suffixial passive

It is, of course, impossible on the basis of the limited amount of data to get a fair idea of the relative importance of the various dialect areas. If several more factors were added, there would no doubt be several isoglossal lines which would be parallel. Such groups of isoglossal lines would represent important dialect differences. Nevertheless, on the basis of even such limited data it is possible to see that the municipality of Riso, which is not geographically central to the region, is nevertheless linguistically the center, for it has more features in common with the other areas than does any one other area. It is the only municipality included within every isoglossal line. Accordingly, a translation made on the basis of the dialect in Riso could be understood by more people than could one made on the basis of any other dialect. In this instance the data are so limited and the relative difference between Riso and Simi so comparatively slight that the problem is not too acute. However, this type of analysis should be conducted in every dialect area. Too many translators have found after several years of hard work that they have been laboring in what has proved to be a linguistic 'island,' rather distantly separated from the 'mainland' of the language by some fairly difficult and complicated dialect differences.

3.2.1.2   GEOGRAPHIC CENTER

As has been noted before, the linguistic center may not be the geographical center of a language area, but the geographical center is an important factor in a decision as to translation and missionary work, particularly if the territory is a large one. However, the center for transportation and communication is often more important, for the question is not so much how far distant a place is but how long it takes to get there. Travel is ultimately a matter of difficulty and time, not of distance. Missionaries are often inclined, however, to choose geographical centers rather than transportational and cultural ones.

3.2.1.3   CULTURAL CENTER

The isoglossal lines discussed under the linguistic center of a language area are not accidents. These differences of linguistic form are due to a definite set of circumstances. Such lines represent areas of weakness in the density of communication. They may represent either (1) man-made language barriers or (2) natural barriers. Political and social boundaries are man-made barriers to intercommunication. People carry on conversation more with those with whom they form a political or social unit than with those who belong to another unit. The more people talk together, the more their languages tend to be similar. Natural barriers such as mountains, canyons, lakes, rivers, and deserts also interrupt the density of communication, and, accordingly, isoglossal lines tend to coincide with these natural barriers.

In speaking of the cultural center we mean that locality from which go out most of the cultural influences and to which most people in the region look for political and social leadership. The principal market center in any area often serves as such a place, for most of the new products as well as new ideas come through such a center. Moreover, normally more people come to the market center than to any other one place. Usually, a government post or some local authority is located at such a point so that the commercial and political centers coincide.

In the era in which the dialect differences have arisen in a language, the cultural center has usually been a dominant factor in the determination of such differences. For example, the municipality of Riso would be such a center in the Papawapam area. Quite frequently the cultural center has remained the same for many centuries, so that the missionary will find that ease of communication is almost in direct proportion to the distance from the cultural center. However, it often happens that with (1) the intrusion of the white man and foreign government domination and (2) the opening up of new lines of communication and transportation, a new cultural center is formed. This new cultural center is in the process of creating new language changes and redistributing the dialect differences. The translator is then compelled to choose between (1) the former cultural center as indicated by the distribution of the dialects and (2) the new center, which may have the advantage of better transportation and communication.

3.2.1.4 COMMUNICATION AND TRANSPORTATION

The factors of communication and transportation are of utmost importance to the translator. In the ancient culture the cultural center was usually the most accessible to the rest of the tribe. Its very accessibility tended to make it a center. But this may not be the case at present. The introduction of other political and commercial factors has completely altered many earlier cultures. The present facilities are after all the important consideration and will tend to be increasingly more significant in the language area.

Communication and transportation must be considered from two standpoints. The one deals with getting into the area from the outside. The second has to do with itinerating over the area from some central point. Both situations are of utmost importance.

3.2.1.5   LIVING FACILITIES

The adequacy of living facilities must be considered in determining the desirability of a location for translation work. If there are dangers to health which may not be adequately coped with, there is little point in attempting to stay in such a locality. One cannot make a translation in a place where one cannot live long enough to learn to speak the language. It is reported that one translator went among an aboriginal people, spent a few months gathering a vocabulary and an introductory grammatical knowledge of the language, and then returned to his home in Europe to translate the New Testament without any further check with the native speakers of the language. This type of translation cannot be correct nor useful.

Under some circumstances it has seemed wise to bring an informant out from some particular region and work with him in a more favorable place, where the health of the missionary will not be impaired and where there will be more uninterrupted time for translation work. This type of practice has some value but should be employed only where necessary, for *so much of the value of the translation depends upon the personal life and ministry of the translator among the people. Despite the remarkable character of the printed gospel, it is seldom accepted and believed with any strong conviction unless the message is lived faithfully by the translator before the people.*

3.2.1.6   ESTABLISHED CHRISTIAN COMMUNITIES

It is important to consider the location, need, and potential leadership of the established Christian communities. Such communities usually provide the best informants for translation work, for the experience of those who have been Christians for some time is of utmost importance in finding the words to describe the spiritual experiences of the Christian life. Moreover, the established Christian communities have an immediate need for the translation if they are to increase appreciably in size or to grow in spiritual understanding. The promptest acceptance and use of the translation is among those who are already Christians. [3]Such people have the greatest motivation for learning to read and for assisting in reading campaigns designed to reach a non-Christian population.[4] Such Christian communities are likely to provide the most active and intelligent leadership for any indigenous work. The possibility of training them by means of a translation in their own dialect is an important factor to be considered in any analysis of the dialect problem for a language area.

There can be no formula for stating the relative importance of the various linguistic and practical factors in dialect problems. The significance of each must be determined for every new situation, for each language area represents a unique set of circumstances. The proper value to be given to each factor cannot be stated in advance of an examination of the particular situation. One can, however, be sure of the necessity of considering each factor and attempting to weigh the relative importance of each.

3.2.2   POSSIBLE SOLUTIONS TO DIALECT PROBLEMS

Having surveyed the linguistic and practical factors involved in any problem of dialect differences, one must next consider the possible solutions to such dialect problems. If the translation work is designed to cover more than one dialect area (it is often valuable to attempt to do so), there are several methods which may be employed. In general these methods may be classified under four principal types: (1) a composite translation, which does not represent the precise form of expression of any one dialect, but combines in so far as possible the usage of all dialects within a given language area, (2) a translation which attempts to employ predominantly the usage of one dialect, but contains some consideration in the text for other dialects, and by the use of footnotes and a glossary indicates all the principal differences of words, (3) a translation which represents only one dialect, and (4) translations into more than one dialect. Under each method of translating will be discussed the procedure and the evaluation.

3.2.2.1   THE COMPOSITE TRANSLATION

A. Procedure

In making a composite translation the translator attempts to combine the linguistic usage of more than one dialect. The problem is complicated in proportion to the number of dialects

(38) use of words and form which will be understood by the greatest number of people

included. Let us suppose, however, that one wishes to make a composite translation including five almost equally important dialects. This is, of course, rarely the case, for dialects will differ considerably in importance, depending upon the numbers of speakers and their relationship to the linguistic center. In attempting to check the usage of a translation with five dialects, one must have informants representing each area. In the case of every word or grammatical form one must determine the extent of the usage. Let us suppose that in the matter of some point of word order three of the dialects are agreed as over against two, but that in the matter of certain important words, e.g. 'Holy Spirit,' 'love,' and 'sin,' the division is likewise three to two, but in the second instance the dialects are lined up differently from what they are in the matter of word order. A composite translation will endeavor to employ those words and forms which are understood by the greatest number of people and the most important dialects. In each case it is a matter of determining the usage of the majority. In some matters there are alternative ways of saying things. If one way is understood by only three dialects and another by four dialects, then the form understood by the four dialects is used. In many instances the form employed by the minority may be inserted in a footnote if this is absolutely necessary for the meaning.

This type of translation is infinitely more difficult than anyone imagines who has not endeavored to produce such a composite work. It should never be undertaken by anyone who does not have a thorough grasp of the dialect situation and a comprehensive training in comparative methods of linguistic research.

It will also be found that it is quite difficult to reach an accord on many items in the translation, for it is difficult for informants, or the translator for that matter, to be completely objective about language usage. One's own form of speech appeals so much to one's private sense of logic and esthetics that any other form seems to represent a compromise with the truth. Many an attempt to harmonize dialects has resulted in total dissatisfaction and mutual ill will.

39-a B. Evaluation

1. Disadvantages

    a. The difficulty in reaching an accord on certain (if not many) points of the translation carries over to those who

are supposed to accept it. Ill will created in the making
of a translation seldom changes to enthusiasm upon the
completion of the printing.

b. Natives may react badly to a composite translation in
contending that no one actually speaks in the manner in
which the translation is written. This is of course true,
and it is difficult to explain to uneducated people the
purpose and methods of such a translation. If, on the
other hand, the translation conforms to at least one dialect, even though it may not be the native's own, he will
usually recognize the fact that some people speak in that
particular manner.

2. Advantages

    a. A composite translation can probably be understood, at
least to a certain extent, by a greater number of people
than any other form of the language. This is of course
the entire reason for the effort given to such a translation, apart from the possible thought of the translator
that by such a composite translation he will be establishing a form of the language which will be accepted
and used by all the people.

    b. A composite translation is sometimes advocated as a
possible means of unification of the language usage.
Despite what appears to be a logical situation, such a
unification of language usage on the basis of a composite
type of translation has not been observed to occur. The
actual situation seems to be that literary products in the
dominant dialect set the norm of usage, and other dialects tend to conform to this usage.

3.2.2.2 THE TRANSLATION INTO ONE DIALECT WITH CERTAIN ADAPTATIONS

A. Procedure

In making a translation which is basically in the form of one
dialect, the translator should choose that form of the language
which is understood by as many people as any other dialect.
The translation is made to follow this dialect so that in every
instance the words and grammatical constructions are those
employed by the speakers of this one dialect. However, the
translator does bear in mind the usage of other dialects. For

example, in the case of alternate usage, one word may be understood only by the one dialect in which he is translating. Another word, perhaps not quite so good, is understood by several dialects, including the principal dialect in which he is translating. In such a case, the translator will choose a word which may not be so idiomatic for the principal dialect in order that the translation may be more readily understood by people in the related dialects. When, however, there are no such alternate choices, the translator may give the word employed in the related dialects in a footnote, or he may list all the important word differences in a glossary. In the text a small star may be used before the word to indicate that its meaning is explained in the glossary.

It is much easier to handle the dialect differences which involve the meaning of words than the grammatical forms or the phonemes. Nevertheless, some accommodation may be made if the translator is careful and weighs all the factors.

This type of translation is much easier to make than a composite translation and has the obvious advantage of not incurring quite so much ill will over the non-inclusion of certain dialect forms. Nevertheless, extensive and thorough comparative study of the dialects must be undertaken if the translation is to be correct.

B. Evaluation
  1. Disadvantages
    a. Footnotes and glossaries seem quite legitimate and useful to us who are book-using people, but by those who are first being introduced to the use of printed material, such so-called 'helps' are rarely appreciated or used.
    b. If the dialect differences are important (they hardly need to be listed unless they are important), they are usually numerous. Accordingly, a thorough comparative analysis of the language is likely to bog down in the innumerable details, with the resultant footnotes and glossary being too extensive to be practical.
  2. Advantages
    a. The usage conforms to at least one dialect and thus provides a basis for the psychological reaction that the translation is in the language of the people. Only one who has

seen the delight registered in the expression of the native reader or listener when he recognizes a completely idiomatic translation can ever appreciate the importance of this psychological factor. All the patient efforts of the translator are repaid when the natives exclaim to each other, "That is just the way we speak!"

b. The readers from all dialects can obtain the meaning of any passage, if not from the text, at least from the footnotes and the glossary. This is a distinct advantage. The New Testament in the Mam language of Guatemala was recently published in something approximating this form and has been reported as meeting with very favorable reception.

3.2.2.3 TRANSLATION INTO ONE DIALECT

A. Procedure

In making a translation into one dialect, the translator is concerned only with making the best possible translation into the exact idiom of the dialect. Such a dialect should be the most important one for any given speech community, for the acceptance of such a translation by speakers of other dialects depends upon the prestige of the dialect chosen. No translator, however, should be completely neglectful of the usages of related dialects, but in many instances he may not care to go so far in accommodating his translation as one who attempts to follow the method explained above.

B. Evaluation

1. Disadvantages

   a. The reading public is likely to be more limited.
   b. A rather strong psychological barrier must be overcome before people of other dialects are likely to accept the translation with any great enthusiasm. These people will find it especially hard to read such a translation if they have not had some previous experience in reading, preferably in their own dialect.

2. Advantages

   a. The translation is in complete idiomatic conformity to the usage of one dialect. This is likely to be an important factor in the enthusiastic acceptance of it by the speakers of the dialect in question.

b. Given the proper choice of the dialect into which the
   translation has been made, the spread of its usage may be
   expected to be sure. In fact, this has been the method in
   which the standard literary forms of language have developed in almost all the countries of Europe. Standard
   German, Italian, French, Spanish, and English (to cite
   only a few) were all originally only the dialects of a
   limited, but strategically important, area. A similar
   development may be expected in other language areas if
   the same types of factors prevail, but in most instances
   one cannot duplicate the centralized control and influence which have existed in the various European
   countries.

3.2.2.4 TRANSLATIONS INTO MORE THAN ONE DIALECT

A. Procedure

For any one of several reasons it may not be practicable to
employ any of the previous methods of translating so as to
reach more than one dialect. The dialects may be too different,
and there may be no one dialect which has the possibilities of
being used as has been described. There is also the added
problem of teaching people to read a form of a language in
which, because of phonemic differences, there is not a one-to-
one correspondence between the symbols that are employed
and the sounds which are used. In order to meet these problems
it has seemed wise in some instances to translate into more than
one dialect. However, dialects are seldom of the same importance, and a coordination of the work usually aims at some type
of language unity. This is particularly to be desired if the dialects are spoken by limited numbers of people. It is often quite
impossible to give the people in each dialect the advantages of
the translation of any considerable portion of the Bible. The
expenses and problems of personnel are sometimes prohibitive.
Accordingly, for the most important dialect group one should
translate the New Testament, or entire Bible if this is possible.
For the other related dialects one may wish to translate only
a Gospel. Having made the principal translation in the most
important dialect, it is often not too difficult to undertake the
translation of smaller portions in other dialects. In each
instance the choices of words and grammatical forms should be

influenced by the most extensive dialect usage, but one should retain the principle of not employing anything which is not actually used in the particular local dialect.

B. Evaluation
1. Disadvantages
   a. Putting out several translations, even though of limited size, necessitates considerably more work than putting out only one translation.   43. R
   b. Several different translations may occasionally foster sectionalism.
2. Advantages
   a. Translations of even limited sections of the Bible make it possible to use the translation with the maximum effectiveness in any reading campaigns. There is great value in being able to introduce the Bible to people as one of the first pieces of literature in their own language. Often the desire to read the Bible is the only incentive which is strong enough to induce people to become literate.   43. b
   b. Having once learned to read and having become somewhat familiar with the religious vocabulary, the people are able to adjust themselves more rapidly to the use of a related dialect than if this dialect were forced upon them from the first.
   c. The message of the Bible speaks with singular effectiveness when in the precise form of the native's speech. Even though it might be impracticable for each dialect to have the entire New Testament, it may be found quite valuable to have a Gospel or at least a part of one in the exact form of each dialect.

One of the most frequent problems of any translation work into an aboriginal language is that of dialect differences. The solutions are in no case easy, but careful consideration of the problems and thorough treatment of them, by whatever method one is finally led to employ, have been found to yield rewards far beyond the expectation of the translators.

Chapter 4

TEXTS OF THE BIBLE
TO BE USED IN TRANSLATION

THE subject of texts to be used in the translation of the Bible is very adequately and succinctly stated by the following quotations taken from the *Guide for Translators, Revisers, and Editors*[1] published by the American Bible Society and following closely the rules of the British and Foreign Bible Society.

4.1   TEXTS TO BE FOLLOWED

"7 The Board desires that, wherever practicable, versions should be made and revised from the original Hebrew, Aramaic, and Greek, advantage being taken of any previous translations in the particular language, and of versions in cognate languages.

"8 For the Old Testament, the use of Ginsberg's edition of the Old Testament (published by the British and Foreign Bible Society) or of Letteris' edition is strongly recommended both as regards consonants and vowels, but any other standard edition may be used, liberty being given to translators and revisers to follow the Kethib or Qeri or renderings sanctioned by the English Authorized Version or the English Revised Version (1885) or the American Revised Version (1901) or by their marginal readings. In using the English versions preference, however, should be given to the readings given by the text rather than the marginal readings.

"9 For the New Testament, translators and revisers are recommended to follow the text of the original Greek edited for the British and Foreign Bible Society by Dr. Eberhard Nestle, but are at liberty to follow that underlying the English Authorized Version (edited by Dr. F. H. A. Scrivener, for the

---

[1]This *Guide* is reproduced in the Appendix to this volume.

Cambridge University Press), or that underlying the English Revised Version (edited by Archdeacon Edwin Palmer, for the Oxford University Press).

"10 Translators who are unacquainted with the originals are desired to follow the text or margin of the English AV or ERV (1881, 1885), or the ARV (1901), or, in the case of translators unacquainted with English, some other version sanctioned by the Committee."

Several items in the above quotations should be noted:

1 Previous translations in the same language should not be overlooked. This is too commonly the practice. Out of ignorance of work which has gone before or out of a desire for novelty of expression and independence of production, translators have frequently neglected to investigate previous translations. It may be that such translations have been made by religious groups having widely differing doctrinal positions, but this fact should not prevent one from investigating the usage. Where the previous translation has been correct, it should be adopted, and where it is faulty, the usage should be avoided. One should be able to detect and thus avoid such errors more easily by having examined them in another translation. Special attention should also be paid to catechisms, which, though they may not employ the Biblical text, are often full of Biblical vocabulary.

2 The usage in cognate languages is often overlooked because the translator feels that nothing can be taken over directly from the other translation, and so should be avoided. There are many times, however, helpful suggestions as to certain idioms and word formations, which may be incorporated with appropriate changes into the translation. As has been noted before, the more translations one consults, the more closely may one approximate the proper area of meaning for the particular context.

3 Before undertaking to translate from the original Greek or Hebrew, it is of utmost importance that the translator be qualified for the work. A little learning is sometimes a dangerous thing even in the hands of a translator. Before adopting an interpretation which does not conform to the AV (Authorized Version, better known as the "King James Version"),

the ERV (English Revised Version), or the ARV (American Revised Version), one should be able to present adequate authority for any such deviation. This does not mean that the English versions cited are necessarily to be the basis for the translation into an aboriginal language. This would be to defeat the purpose of the Bible Society in emphasizing the use of the original languages. It does mean that when the translator's interpretation of the Greek differs markedly from the more accepted English versions, such an interpretation should be checked with the utmost care.

4.2 PROBLEMS CONFRONTED
IN THE USE OF TEXTS OF THE BIBLE

The translator is usually confronted with three important problems in connection with the use of certain texts of the Bible. These are (1) additions to the text, (2) deletion of doubtful texts, and (3) alternative readings and renderings.

4.2.1 ADDITIONS TO THE TEXT

The additions to the text are of two types: (1) additions of material not to be found nor necessarily implied in the text and (2) additions necessary to make sense. The first type of additions may be termed unwarranted additions and the second type may be termed warranted additions to the text.

4.2.1.1 UNWARRANTED ADDITIONS

Unwarranted additions to the text are usually made by (1) those who attempt to introduce apparent consistency into the text and (2) those who attempt to explain some feature so that it may be understood more easily by the reader.

Illustrative of the first type of unwarranted addition was the insistence of one translator that the Luke form of the Lord's Prayer should have the same final verse as occurs in the Matthew form of the prayer. Such an addition, even though prompted by a worthy motive of attempting to produce uniformity, is not legitimate. The translator must restrict himself to translating the actual text.

It is often a temptation to a translator to make a slight addition to the text in order to make the meaning clearer. There are many passages which are obscure, and a few extra words may be very helpful. Note the translation of 1 Cor. 11: 10 by Goodspeed: " . . . she ought to wear upon her head something to symbolize her subjection, out of respect to the angels, if to nobody else." The last phrase helps to make the meaning plainer, and yet this phrase is not in the original text. Such an addition should be avoided, even at the expense of less clarity.

A moderate number of additions might be tolerated in certain situations, but the tendency is to elaborate on those particular passages which represent special doctrinal interests of the translator. The safest guide is to eliminate all additions which are not expressly in the text from which one is translating. There will be a greater number of obscure passages, but if they are obscure in the text itself their clarification should be left to teaching and to a commentary.

4.2.1.2   Warranted Additions

In translating from one language to another it is impossible to match the form of expression word for word. One language may use a pronoun, while another language may necessitate the repetition of the noun object or subject. One language may have a passive construction without an agent, as in Greek, but another language may not have such a passive construction, for example Aztec.[1] Accordingly, in such a language one cannot say, "Judge not, that ye be not judged," Mat. 7:1. There is no passive form in Aztec to correspond to the second verb expression. In Aztec one must turn such a passive expression into an active one, but both the subject and the object must be expressed. The translation in Aztec must read either 'Do not judge, in order that people may not judge you' or 'Do not judge, in order that God may not judge you.' Whether one is to insert 'people' or 'God' as the subject of the verb 'to judge' is dependent upon one's interpretation of the context. The general context, however, seems to point to the interpretation which would employ 'God' as the subject. In Aztec it is impossible to be ambiguous. The structure of the language will not permit it.

Warranted additions to the text are those items which must be (✗) added because of the linguistic structure of the languages involved. These problems will be discussed much more fully in Chapter 14.

---

[1]Unless otherwise stated, references to Aztec designate the Eastern dialect spoken in the State of Puebla, Mexico.

Warranted additions to the text have usually been indicated by placing such words in italics. These may be noted on almost any page of the AV and ARV. In some instances words appear to have been italicized quite unnecessarily and inconsistently. In other instances, rather considerable additions have been made which are not in the better manuscripts nor necessitated by the linguistic forms of the language. One of these textual additions occurs in the AV in John 8: 6, where the words "as though he heard them not" are added to the text.

The value of italicizing such additions is open to serious question. If the additions are necessary in terms of the equivalence of the linguistic forms, then there is actually no addition, in the sense of the inclusion of extraneous material. Moreover, italics often produce much misunderstanding. The average reader of the English Bible does not understand the significance of the italics. Any attempt to explain the italics to those who do not understand the essential problems of translation (this includes most people) almost always meets with unsatisfactory response. This is especially the case where the translation is made for people who are just becoming literate and for whom the translation is the first one published. In instances of major lexical and grammatical adaptations (see, for example, pp. 167, 171, 214, 258, and 266), it may be valuable to employ partial brackets, e. g. ⌞. . . . .⌟ (Cf. Appendix, *Guide for Translators*, p. 9.)

4.2.2   Deletion of Doubtful Texts

In connection with the deletion of doubtful texts one should note rule 11 of the *Guide for Translators:*

"Words and sentences for which the English and American Revisers in their marginal notes declare that there exists ancient authority should find a place either in the text or in the margin. The committee deprecates their entire omission."

The omission of certain passages on the basis of their doubtful textual authority involves many difficulties. If more than one full verse is omitted, and the numbering of the verses indicates this type of omission, the native, who normally has no knowledge of textual problems, is immediately suspicious of the content of the omission and the motivation for making such an omission. The problem is even more complicated if the translation is published as a diglot. In such a case the translation must include all that is included in the text language.

The translator who desires to omit John 5:4 (the angel's disturbing of the water in the pool of Bethesda) on the basis of some textual difficulties and because the passage is otherwise difficult to explain, should also be aware of the fact that John 7:53 through 8:11 (the account of the woman taken in adultery) involves similar textual problems. One cannot very well omit one without omitting the other. By all means the best solution lies in following the ruling of the Bible Societies as given above.

4.2.3   ALTERNATIVE READINGS AND RENDERINGS

Relative to alternative readings and renderings, rule 13, sections (a) and (b), of the *Guide for Translators* reads as follows:

"Rule 13, section (a), *Alternative readings.* These would include those instances in which there may be various readings of the original text which are of generally accepted authority. It is permissible for the translators to put in the margin a translation of an alternative reading in cases which seem to them to be of sufficient importance.

"Rule 13, section (b), *Alternative renderings.* In important passages where the original admits of more than one meaning, or where the meaning cannot be expressed adequately in one word or phrase, translators may put the preferred rendering in the text and alternatives in the margin."

Alternative readings and renderings are of great interest and importance to the advanced Bible student. They are of somewhat more questionable importance and value in a translation which is the first publication of any of the Bible in the language of an aboriginal group. Without a sufficient background to understand the significance of such alternative readings and renderings, the readers are more likely to be confused than to be instructed. In general it would seem that the best translation follows closely a simple text which is least marked up by problems and interruptions which the native may be at a loss to understand. Later editions may profitably contain certain critical material which the first translation may better do without.

Chapter 5

PREPARATION FOR TRANSLATING

THE type of preparation needed for translating is of utmost importance. The quality of the final product is usually in direct proportion to the quality and extent of preparation. This preparation is fundamentally of two types: (1) pre-field and (2) field preparation. The pre-field preparation includes the studies undertaken before going to the 'field'—the actual geographical location of the language area to be covered by the translation. The field preparation includes the work done in the language prior to undertaking the actual translation work.

5.1   PRE-FIELD PREPARATION

The pre-field preparation should include three types of studies: (1) Biblical, (2) anthropological, and (3) linguistic. A proper combination of all three of these studies is of absolute importance to the translator. A failure to be properly prepared in any one of these studies usually results in unfortunate mistakes in the translation.

5.1.1   BIBLICAL TRAINING

Biblical training must include at least three branches of study: (1) the meaning of the individual texts, (2) the relationship of such individual texts to general Biblical truth and (3) the natural and cultural environment of Bible times.

Translators often have a hazy idea about the meaning of certain passages which they have never taken the time to investigate or which they have only superficially investigated. For example, one translator thought that in Luke 7:2 it was the Centurion whom Jesus loved, rather than the servant whom the Centurion loved. In schools students are often taught to read more than to think. They may be like the young man who was asked to read a paragraph aloud to the class, but upon being questioned by the teacher as to the meaning of what he had read, he commented, "I wasn't

56

listening." Failure to read and study the Bible carefully is the basis of a great many errors in translating.

Even with the most careful reading of the Bible there are many obscure and ambiguous passages. The Gospels alone contain more than seven hundred ambiguous readings in which the Greek may be translated one of two different ways. One of the most famous of these ambiguities occurs in John 1:9, where the phrase "coming into the world" may be construed as going with "every man" or with "the true light." The translator should have some training in such problems of exegesis and should make his decisions on the basis of the most adequate information and the best authority.

Many students are inclined to overlook the value and importance of the study of general Biblical truth, in other words, systematic theology, but the competent translator can not afford to neglect for a moment the relationship of any translation to general theology. For example, in one instance the translator had used 'God does not choose whom he loves' for "God is no respecter of persons," Acts 10:34. The translation, however, involves rather serious theological problems as to the sovereignty of God. A translation such as 'God does not receive people because of their appearance' more closely conveys the idea of the Greek *prosōpolēmptēs*.

The study of the natural and cultural environment of Bible times is especially important. In order to find the closest equivalence in native culture one must be acquainted with the form and function of such an item in the Biblical culture. The translator *10 —* needs to know, for example, that the "steward" of AV New Testament corresponds almost exactly to the *mayordomo* of the larger estates of Latin America. All the problems of management and trusteeship are practically the same. The translator must be able to recognize immediately the setting of "kicking against the prick" when he sees the peasant driving his oxen with an ox-goad. To the average reader of the English Bible the feat of the newly restored lame man who was admonished by Jesus to take up his bed and walk seems Herculean, but to the one who has seen the bed-roll of an Indian laid out under some thatched portico, the cultural parallel is more immediately obvious. Adequate preparation in Biblical studies forms an essential prerequisite for all types of Bible translation.

5.1.2   ANTHROPOLOGICAL TRAINING

As one continues to investigate the problems of translation, particularly in the matters of principles of equivalence, it becomes increasingly evident that the translator must have an adequate preparation in cultural anthropology. In fact it may safely be said that more mistakes are made in translation because of failure at this point than for any other reason. The translator is always able to avail himself of adequate commentaries and dictionaries of the Bible, but except in rare cases there are no thorough ethnological studies available concerning the people for whom he is translating. Even if there are such ethnological helps, the translator is often at a loss to understand them or to appreciate the significance of the data which they contain.

Anthropology is the study of the whole life of any people and of all people, and cultural anthropology is the study of the social or cultural life, as contrasted with the biological. Cultural anthropology includes the study of cultural traits and complexes: what people eat, wear, and build; how they organize themselves consciously and unconsciously into a working society; what they think about supernatural phenomena. All these universal features are the proper study of cultural anthropology. In a more significant way than this, however, cultural anthropology is important for the perspective it gives, namely, the awareness of the factors which have molded man in space and time, and which mold us—from the wearing of ties to the reasons for which we kill.

Ethnology is that branch of cultural anthropology which deals with the description of any one society. Ethnological analysis specializes on the description of one society at a time, while cultural anthropology might be considered as the pigeon-hole cabinet into which this material is catalogued and the relationships made apparent. Both types of studies, which, of course, are supplementary to each other, are necessary for the translator. He must be able to analyze accurately the behavior patterns of the society in which he is working, but in order to do so he must understand the functional significance of any phase of culture, so that he may compare the cultural item of the Biblical account with the functional equivalent of the aboriginal society. The first requirement is a general understanding of the various phases of culture and some knowledge of the local content of these phases in the various cultures of the world.

One of the important features of the translator's training should be some study of the techniques for discovering the functional significance of given beliefs and practices. It is not always possible to ask people openly what a certain action means. For example, among the Mazatec Indians, an inexperienced missionary made the mistake of commenting to a mother on how pretty her baby looked. Instantly the mother rushed off screaming. She was not demented, nor even queer. She believed that anyone who commented on her child's beauty thereby attracted the jealous attention of evil spirits, and the child thereupon became the target of sinister influences. If it should die, the person who made the remark would be considered responsible. The mother's shrieking was an attempt to drown out the words of the missionary before they came to the attention of the evil spirits.

In other societies it is considered that one who asks for a person's name is not being polite, but rather has sinister motives; for by obtaining the name of a person one is in a position to work black magic and do great harm to the holder of this name. As a result, one often finds that people in such societies are known by two or three names. One may not find out the 'private' name of a man for many years. These same people may take great satisfaction in telling everyone their age, for the greater the age the greater the prestige in the society. In our own culture we tend to reverse the picture. We often demonstrate an eager desire for others to know our names, but we are somewhat more reticent about advertizing our age. The translator must be prepared to recognize the behavior patterns of people and to understand the function of these in the society. The native informant will not be able to furnish such socially self-conscious information, for his ignorance of final causes within his culture will be as great as would be the missionary's, were the native to inquire as to why the missionary wears a necktie.

The most important type of study in cultural anthropology which the translator should undertake concerns the problems of acculturation. There are three lines of study which he must follow: (1) the problems of acculturation in the language community to which he goes, (2) the adaptations which he himself as a foreigner must make to the culture which he is entering, and (3) the adaptations which the native is to make in accordance with the teaching of the Bible. Without an understanding of these three problems and a decision as to policy, much of the translator's energies will be spent beating the air.

The acculturation which has already taken place in a given society is often a clue to future policy. In some instances, the old religious pattern breaks down quite rapidly. This has been found to be the case in several African and American-Indian tribes. However, among the Zuñi Indians of New Mexico this is by no means the case. Although missionaries of various Christian faiths have worked among them for well over two hundred years, the percentage of those who have accepted the form and the content of Christianity is estimated by several as approximately one percent. The Zuñi religion is highly important in almost every phase of the community life, and the highly centralized and compact nature of the community life intensifies the religious significance of every social situation. The translator among the Zuñis is faced with an entirely different type of problem from that which one working among the Kiowas of Oklahoma has to contend with. Only the proper understanding of the acculturation problem will enable one to formulate adequate plans for the solution to such a situation.

The translator should be on the guard against wholesale destruction of the older patterns of culture in an aboriginal society. In an evangelistic enthusiasm for change he may be led to discount all forms of the existing culture. Unless he is able to make an adequate functional substitute, the social structure may collapse and a state of morbidity may result. One must remember that the aboriginal society has succeeded in establishing a system of organization which has made possible its continuing existence, often for many centuries. Such aboriginal peoples have often accommodated themselves to circumstances which the white man cannot cope with. To destroy the aboriginal patterns without providing a functional substitute may be disastrous. This is particularly true when one discredits a religious system without being able to provide another in its place. The loss of social controls which any religion tends to provide may result in social disintegration. This should be very evident in the distintegration in our own Western culture because religious convictions and fear of supernatural judgments have been largely eliminated from a considerable percentage of the populace, but at the same time no vital religious consciousness or set of social controls has taken their place. The breakdown of the old culture and the inadequacy of any new system have been the major features which explain the pathetic condition of some of the partially assimilated tribes in the Western Hemisphere.

The translator himself cannot ignore the effect of acculturation upon his own behavior patterns if he is to accommodate himself satisfactorily to the life of the people. In fact, he must make some adjustments if he is to be accepted by the natives as a 'cultured member of society,' in other words, a 'gentleman.' The translator cannot afford to continue to offend the natives whose notions of propriety may be quite different from his own. For example, it has been reported that in carrying handkerchiefs many missionaries have offended against the Hindus' sense of propriety and decency. To the Hindu the very thought of carrying about with one the discharge from the mucous lining of the nose has been considered exceedingly loathsome. Among the Tarahumara Indians of northern Mexico the translator who would be exceedingly talkative in public and who gesticulates to any great extent would immediately tend to lose prestige. There is a feeling that one's words must be weak and lacking in veracity if one must force his arguments upon others by excessive talk or by bold gestures.

Not only in the matter of personal habits but in the problems of translation the translator must make some adaptations. For example, one cannot ask the native speaker for a word for 'spirit' and then proceed to employ this native word wherever one would say "spirit" in English. In animistic cultures one will probably never find the type of usage of the word *spirit* which we have in English, e.g. *an evil spirit, a good spirit, the Holy Spirit, the spirit of a man, the spirit of a horse, a sporting spirit,* and *spirits of ammonia.* For such problems as these the translator must have an adequate background study in every phase of culture, but especially in the study of religion. He must be instantly able to recognize such factors as magic, animism, fetishism, totemism, polytheism, idolatry, and ancestor worship. The accuracy of the translation will be dependent upon the translator's understanding of these factors in the native culture.

The adaptations which the native must make to the Christian message constitute probably the most complicated part of cultural anthropological study. One must distinguish clearly between (1) the folkways (the customs) and (2) the morals of a people; in other words, those actions which are simply customs without any religious or ethical significance and those which do have such supernatural sanctions. For example, the translator must determine whether in translating hymns and the Psalms he can legitimately employ the chant patterns used for pagan religious ceremonies. He may find that he can use such rhythmic forms much more successfully than he has perhaps imagined.

Almost every sentence of a translation will bear the mark of the translator's anthropological training, for every sentence is a set of symbols for the behavior and thought patterns of one culture translated into another set of symbols representing different behavior and thought patterns.

5.1.3 LINGUISTIC TRAINING

The more experience the translator has with various languages, the more likely he is to be able to handle new linguistic problems successfully. However, there are some disadvantages in the traditional training and viewpoint with regard to languages. The translator who has been trained only in the grammar of Indo-European or Semitic languages is likely to want to reorganize the grammar of some aboriginal language in terms of the conventional grammars that he has studied. It is felt by many missionaries that the aboriginal languages are lacking in precise grammatical categories and forms. The result is that the missionary attempts to reorganize the language, but in actuality he is only making a mess of it. One who employs the techniques of descriptive linguistics does not attempt to reform the language but rather to describe what people actually say. He makes no attempt to systematize the language or to dictate what people should say. The language is a perfectly adequate instrument of expression, and so he contents himself with describing it and learning to use it.

Descriptive linguistics covers the study of all branches of language study: (1) phonology (sounds), (2) morphology (the words), (3) syntax (the arrangement of words), and (4) lexicon (the meaning of parts of words, words, and combinations of words). The translator cannot neglect any part of descriptive linguistic studies if he is to make an adequate translation.

In analyzing the phonological features of any language one must be able to identify all the phonetically different types of sounds. For this, phonetic training is essential. These phonetically different sounds must then be organized into phonemes, which are the psychologically significant units of sound. Only after making a thoroughly scientific analysis of a language is one able to construct anything like an adequate scientific alphabet or practical adaptation of it.[1]

A recent analysis of an alphabet constructed by a missionary with only the conventional language training revealed that he had failed to analyze correctly at least one third of the significant sounds of the language. The result was an orthography which the natives had great difficulty in reading. Accordingly, only a few went to the trouble of doing so. The effort and money expended upon the translation have been an almost total loss.

Many missionaries have been known to complain about a particular language because they thought that it was not correctly used by the natives. An aboriginal language rarely seems to function in a manner comparable to what the missionary has been accustomed in English or some other European language. Accordingly, he is convinced that the natives themselves do not understand how to use the language.

The missionary often tries to solve his problem by asking the natives what the various parts of some long words mean. When the natives are unable to tell, the missionary feels that he has conclusive evidence that the native language is a hodgepodge of inarticulate grunts. He seldom takes the time to realize that he would have great difficulty if he were called upon (1) to explain the meaning of the root *-ceive* in *receive, deceive, perceive,* and *conceive,* or (2) to describe just why the difference in order of the two constituents of *up-set* and *set-up* makes such a difference in the meaning of the two words. In languages which so freely combine suffixes and prefixes with stems that a verb stem may occur in well over fifty thousand combinations, the missionary finds that he needs some special techniques for analysis. Moreover, if he is to construct new words in the language, they must be made to conform to the native patterns of formation. In a recent translation into an African language the missionary constructed some compounds which had as many as a dozen syllables, although the native words seldom had more than three or four. No translator can afford to neglect the thorough study of word formation in the language.

The study of the syntax of a language is probably more neglected

---

[1] For a more complete discussion of these problems see Chapter 7 on Orthography.

than any other feature of language study. Often a translator has
all the words correct, but the manner in which the phrases are combined is so foreign that the native is scarcely able to understand
what is being said. The syntax of many languages is completely
different from English. For example, in Navaho in order to translate the sentence *the man hit the woman* one must say literally 'the
man the woman her-he-hit.' The last word of this sentence may
stand as a complete sentence in itself. The other words may be
described as being paratactically combined with it. Very special
care must be taken in syntax, for in no feature of a language can
one make so many telltale mistakes as in its syntax.

It should be obvious to everyone that the translator must make a
thorough study of the meaning of words and phrases in the language. This is not always done. Some translators may be comparatively sure that they are not saying something quite wrong.
But this is not enough. The aim of the translator must be to have
the words convey the precise meaning in the most idiomatic form
of the language. For example, in the Maya language it would be
possible to describe marriage by some term denoting the uniting
of a man and wife in a social contract, but the idiom in Maya for
marriage is 'to end one's road.' In other words, neither the
young man nor the young woman go their own ways any longer.
They 'end their own road' to join with someone else on a different
road. In the Yipounou language of the Gabon one who wishes to
translate idiomatically the expression "send away empty" will use
the native form 'send with one hand in the other.' With nothing to
carry, the servants have to go away holding their own hands. In
the Totonac language one may idiomatically translate "offend
these little ones" by saying literally 'show these little ones the
wrong road.' Only the thorough study of the lexicon of any
language makes it possible for one to use the language with the
utmost effectiveness.

5.2   FIELD PREPARATION FOR TRANSLATION

The description of various types of study to be included in the
pre-field training implies the application of these studies to the
particular language on the field. The actual stages and types of
preparation may be described under (1) collection of data, (2)
speaking the language, (3) analysis of ethnology, and (4) preliminary stages in the translation process.

5.2.1 COLLECTION OF DATA

In order to learn a language, and hence in order to do any type of translation work, the translator must collect the data of the language. The process of collecting such data differs somewhat, depending upon whether a native can be found who knows a language which the prospective translator also knows. For example, among most of the Indian tribes of Latin America someone in the tribe knows a little Spanish or Portuguese. The translator usually tries to get the assistance of such a person. First, he asks for the native words for various objects which can be seen and pointed out, e.g. 'a house,' 'a dog,' 'a man,' 'a bow,' 'an arrow,' 'the sun,' 'the moon,' 'the sky,' etc. After this he usually tries to indicate the possessor of such objects by obtaining forms such as 'my house,' 'my dog,' 'your bow,' 'his arrow,' etc. Following this, he may inquire for various expressions such as 'I am walking,' 'you are walking,' 'they were walking,' etc. These help to provide an understanding of the basic framework of the language.

Sometimes the missionary cannot find anyone who can assist in the capacity of an interpreter. If such is the case, the translator must point out objects, pantomime and employ all sorts of ingenious methods of getting at the meaning of words and phrases. However, after the initial few weeks the procedure is practically the same as when one has an interpreter.

In many cases it is quite impossible for one to find an informant who can give one the precise forms that are sought. For example, one may ask the native to say 'it is hot,' but he may object on the basis that it is actually cold. The translator may ask for 'your horse,' but the native may protest that he does not have a horse. Moreover, the idea of giving the complicated forms of the verb paradigms may seem foolish and meaningless to the native informant. One may find that it is quite impracticable to spend all the time seeking for someone who can give him the paradigms of the language. As convenient as such sets of forms may be for the learner of a language, they are often quite artificial in terms of the actual usage. What the translator must attempt to obtain as soon as possible are 'texts' in the idiomatic form of the language. Texts are anything which the native says which is not in response to a question of the translator as to how to say so-and-so. It is desirable to obtain stories of historical and mythological interest, for these often reveal many significant facts about the beliefs of the people. Chant forms used in religious rites are of utmost importance for one who wants to employ such forms in translating hymns and the Psalms. However, such special language forms are often difficult to obtain. Moreover, some of the most valuable texts are simple narratives of everyday events, e.g. "How one went to the market," "How one weaves a basket," and "How one makes a cornfield in the jungle." All these topics, that any native can talk about, are excellent material for texts. One should also be on the lookout for conversational texts. It is often quite difficult to take down conversation of natives, for it is uttered rapidly, and there are often many elided forms. However, the form of conversation is very important, for there are often many idiomatic features of conversational style which never come out in narrative texts. The Bible contains many important conversations which should be translated in a conversational form.

The importance of texts must not be overlooked. They are the source material for one's study of the language. From them one analyzes (1) the meaning of words in various contexts, (2) the order of words and the type of sentence structure, (3) the formation and function of various classes of words, and (4) the significant sound units of the language. No translator should attempt to do much final translating until he has analyzed several hundred pages of text material.

5.2.2   Speaking the Language

The facility with which one speaks a language is perhaps the best criterion for determining that stage in the study of a language at which some form of final translation work may be begun. The following may be considered as a fundamental principle of all translation, namely, *no final translation work should be undertaken before one is able to converse with the informants in the native language concerning all types of translation problems.* It may take one translator ten years to attain such facility. Another may acquire it within a year or so, but except under very special circumstances in which the native helpers have an unusual background of training in the Bible and in the text language, the translator's facility in speaking the language should be the basic index of his competence to undertake final translation work.

Facility in speaking the language is not adopted as an arbitrary criterion for translation work. It is of utmost importance that discussions as to form and meaning of words and phrases should be conducted in the native language. There are too many possibilities for misunderstanding if the text language or some other language is the medium. A thorough study of text material and an analytical knowledge of the grammatical structure cannot take the place of ability to speak a language. The converse of this is equally impossible.

No amount of analytical study of the language can give a person facility in speaking it, even as no amount of study of harmony, music theory, and the mechanical operation of the piano can make a piano player. The student must practice. The only way to learn any intricate technique is to practice. The only way to learn to speak a language is to speak it. There is no substitute for living with and talking constantly with the native users of a language.

Most persons learning a new language experience four principal stages in acquiring facility in it. At the first stage they are able to get the 'general drift' of statements of which they can more or less suspect the meaning. In the second, they find that they can carry on a conversation provided that they direct the topic of conversation. The third stage is one in which they can understand any conversation but can only participate adequately when more or less familiar with the vocabulary. The fourth stage is one in which they have comparative freedom in participating in any type of conversation. No translator should rest content until reaching the fourth stage of language facility, though he may find it advisable to undertake some translation work while still in the third stage.

5.2.3 ANALYSIS OF THE ETHNOLOGY

One may learn many customs and beliefs of a people through constant association, without any special methodological approach. With such a casual or 'amateur' methodology, however, large areas of culture will almost inevitably be overlooked; nor will one be able to analyze correctly the relationship of one feature of culture to another without some training and without carefully planned observation. For example, a Hottentot would have considerable difficulty in understanding the significance of Santa Claus in our culture without some rather extensive and systematic investigation.

There are four methods which the translator may use to good advantage in a practical analysis of the ethnology of the people: (1) field observation, (2) a diary notebook, (3) ethnological trait check lists, (4) analysis of texts containing ethnologically significant data.

The translator must learn to be all ears and eyes in every situation which he meets, for a translation of the Bible covers almost every phase of human behavior. There is nothing which will not be involved. For example, the instant the translator discovers that the people of his particular language group use a dibble stick for all planting of grain he should realize the difficulty which he will encounter in translating. A dibble stick is a long pointed stick used for making a hole in the ground into which seeds of corn or some other grain are dropped. Peoples who use the dibble stick for planting will find it almost impossible to conceive of the flagrant wastefulness of the sower in the famous parable who scattered the seed in an apparently profligate and senseless manner.

A diary notebook is an excellent way of analyzing the habits of a people. Many features of culture are spread out over many days' time and in casual observation no apparent set of relationships will appear. Only a written record will remind one of the series of events together with their proper sequence and spacing. For example, certain days of the lunar month may be taboo. No one is likely to tell the translator about it, perhaps because it is more or less a secret which the people do not want to tell the translator, or perhaps it never occurs to them that such would be important. However, if the informant refuses or fails to do certain habitual things on particular days, these facts should be noted. They may form an interesting story of good and bad times, so that when Jesus speaks of "my time" or "my hour," the native may interpret this to mean that Jesus was performing certain actions in keeping with a calendar of good and bad occasions.

The use of ethnological check lists may be an indispensable aid to the translator. Some lists are suggested in Chapter 13 for some of the more important words dealing with religious phases of culture. If one obtains the answers to these questions from observation, questioning, or native texts dealing with religious matters, he can much more readily choose those words which are going to be most applicable to the context. Obtaining the answers to a series of questions, however, will not always give one the answer to the problem. The question may not cover the precise point in question, for there are as many variations of primitive religious beliefs as there are primitive societies. Such questions should, however, lead one to the crucial points, and from there on one is dependent upon a general understanding of religious culture. For example, one may believe that the word for 'holy' is quite satisfactory, on the basis of its usage in many instances. Nevertheless, a more thorough investigation of this word may reveal that in its essential meaning it designates a taboo brought upon certain objects by the caprice of a spirit who has attempted to thwart the actions of a beneficent god by rather erratic meddling in supernatural things. An examination of the entire range of meaning of the word for 'holy' in another culture may reveal a long list of objects which have been tabooed and in which there is no basic moral or religious feature as judged from the standpoint of the Biblical usage.

The texts which have been taken by the translator are of inestimable value in analyzing the ethnology of a people. Some texts dealing with mythological matters are of utmost importance, but almost every text has some significance. For example, if in a story one learns that the people attribute success in a game of chance to the possession by the winner of a lion's claw, he will probably find that the natives are convinced that Matthias won the ordination in Acts 1 by a similar device. No detail is so insignificant as to justify its being overlooked if one is to understand thoroughly the life of a people.

5.2.4 PRELIMINARY STAGES IN THE TRANSLATION PROCESS

The translation procedure as a whole is treated in Chapter 6. It is well to note here, however, that in preparing for the final translation work there are some preliminary stages which are important.

It is often valuable for the translator to attempt some translation work within a year or so after he begins language work in a tribe. He may do this when he is in the second stage of the language study as described on page 67. It is not meant that such translation work is final or should even be used in making up a final draft. It is only a bit of linguistic exercise. It should give the translator an idea of the types of problems which he will encounter. He will know better what problems he must investigate more fully. It is best to discard completely this initial effort, unless sentimental attachment requires that it be kept as a memento of dismal failure. At any rate, such preliminary attempts should not be made the basis of final work. It is much easier to start with a fresh slate than to attempt to erase all the errors and correct them. It is particularly unwise to teach such verses to the natives with the idea that a final form has been established. If this is done, the translator may react as one did when asked to change an obviously false translation of the Beatitudes. She declared that such a change would be impossible, for the people had already memorized the passage. The literal inerrancy of an initial translation should never be made a working principle.

The translator will probably want to try a hand at translating in several different parts of the Bible, for the styles of writing and the words are very different. The greater the range of initial experience one can gain, the more likely will be one's success in the final translation work.

It is often wise for the translator to put out Bible stories or portions of the Bible in mimeographed form, for these can be used as a check of usage. Nevertheless, one should be careful about assuming that because these portions can be understood they are adequate as a final translation.

So much of the value of the final translation depends upon the pre-field and field preparation of the missionary that no one can afford to fail in carrying out a consistently thorough program.

Chapter 6

TRANSLATION PROCEDURE

THE proper translation procedure can make or break a translation. Just what procedure or set of procedures is to be followed differs greatly in individual instances. Perhaps the greatest differences depend upon whether the translation is to be done by (1) a non-native or (2) a native translator; in other words, whether the translator who is ultimately responsible for the form is a native speaker of the language or not. Since, however, the present book is designed especially as a help to the non-native translator, more emphasis will be given to this part of the problem. However, much of the procedure is applicable to both types of translation.

6.1 TRANSLATION BY A NON-NATIVE TRANSLATOR

The method of procedure to follow when a non-native translator is responsible for the form is dependent upon a great number of factors. Perhaps the most important of these are (1) the number of translators who are available, (2) the number and education of the informants, and (3) the types of consultants who are available to check on the translation. It is impossible to go into all the details of translation procedure or to chart all the modifications for various special situations. The following pages will attempt to list the steps in translation procedure in which there is one non-native translator. Important modifications of this general plan may be easily made for local situations. In some instances alternate suggestions are given. The problems and stages of procedure may best be treated under the following topics: (1) qualifications of informants, (2) handling of informants, (3) training of informants, (4) use of translation helps, (5) explaining the meaning of the text, (6) putting down the form of the translation, (7) revising the translation, (8) checking for general acceptance of the translation, (9) the use of the Bible Society check lists, and (10) the publication of limited portions.

6.1.1 QUALIFICATIONS OF INFORMANTS

Beyond the factor of the translator himself, qualifications of the informant are without doubt the next most important considerations in any translation work. At times, a good informant has actually made up for a poor translator. In fact, the informant in many ways is actually the translator and the so-called translator is only the collator and checker of the material. This relationship will become more obvious as one examines the procedure.

Good informants are rare, for their qualifications are high. There is no absolute rule or formula for deciding upon the necessary qualifications which an informant must have, but translators have found that the following characteristics are of great importance:

1 A CHRISTIAN

It is sometimes possible to translate by means of a non-Christian informant, but this is extremely difficult. Much of the religious vocabulary of the Bible describes subjective reactions of people. It is quite difficult to explain such phenomena to those who are totally ignorant of such experience. The translator must be sure, however, that the Christian informant, who has probably been trained by the translator himself, is not just repeating the errors in word usage which the translator himself has made unwittingly in his more elementary stages of language usage.

2 AN ADULT

In most instances the translator should be at least twenty years of age. A younger person rarely has had sufficient experience or attained sufficient intellectual maturity to be used with any great value.

3 A MAN

It is usually found that the men of a tribe have far more extensive knowledge of the world and affairs than the women. Their usage of the language is often better developed. There is a very important exception to the use of men informants. As a rule women translators should not use men informants, nor men translators use women informants, except under very special circumstances. In almost no aboriginal societies will the association of translator and informant of the opposite sex be understood or tolerated without deep suspicion. Translators have done irreparable damage to chances of acceptance of the translation by such action.

4 ADEQUATE EDUCATION

An informant may have a considerable formal education, usually in the trade language of the region. His ability to read the trade language is often very helpful. Such educational qualifications are usually a distinct advantage. They can, however, militate against his usefulness if he attempts to insert his 'superior education' into the translation by insisting upon the use of the trade language. He may also attempt to be overly rhetorical in a style which will only repel or confuse others. Far more important than the informant's formal education is his keenness of mind.

5 INTELLECTUAL ABILITY

This is without doubt the major qualification of the informant. If he has a keen mind, he can be trained by the translator. Nothing can, however, make up for mental dullness.

6 LANGUAGE EXPERIENCE

The more languages that an informant knows, the better he can grasp the problems of equivalence in finding forms of expression that fit in various contexts. One must be certain, however, that the informant is thoroughly familiar with his native language into which the translation is being made. This is the first prerequisite. The man who knows his own language thoroughly and yet may have difficulty with the trade language is of much greater value than the man who knows the trade language well and yet is not completely at home in the native language. In testing an informant's use of the native language, one should investigate which language he learned first and which he uses in his home and with his family. The use of the native language in these situations is of utmost importance.

7 WILLING ATTITUDE

The sincere desire on the part of the informant to assist in the work of translation is important. The principal motivation for the informant should not be his salary, for monetary gains are almost always inadequate to compensate for the tedious hours of work at something which is quite strange to the informant and for which he is probably laughed at by his friends, who may accuse him of being lazy because he does not do more strenuous work or of betraying his own society by friendship with the translator. An informant may be quite frequently accused of divulging the secrets of the language, which in many societies is considered the symbol of social solidarity. Sincerity of purpose on the part of the informant is one of the best checks against the incorporation of words into the text which have a wrong connotation.

6.1.2 THE HANDLING OF INFORMANTS

Many a good informant has been ruined by inconsiderate actions on the part of the translator. The keynote to any translation work must be that of collaboration. The translator and his informant must consider themselves as a team, working together to accomplish as perfect a translation as possible. Because of the superior knowledge of the informant in the matters of his own language, he must be considered by the translator as an equal. Only such a feeling of equality and companionship can weather the storms of differences of opinion and the arbitrary decisions that sometimes have to be made. In dealing with informants, translators have found it valuable to observe the following rules:

1 DO NOT ARGUE WITH THE INFORMANT ABOUT HIS LANGUAGE.

The translator must remember that the native language belongs to his informant, and between the two of them the informant is the authority. Of course, the informant may be wrong, even as we are often wrong in the usage of English. But arguments get nowhere. If the translator is right, he may want to *suggest* that possibly another form may be used, but if the informant is adamant, there is nothing gained in arguing. The matter should be dropped for the time being. Later evidence will decide one way or the other. The translator will often be amazed at how many times, when he would have been inclined to argue a point, the informant was actually right, though perhaps the informant did have some difficulty in explaining his position.

2 DO NOT FORCE YOUR OWN IDEAS ON THE INFORMANT.

Many a translator has browbeaten his informant into submission. As a result the informant lost all interest in trying to correct or to make suggestions. Some translators do not even attempt to argue their position but 'bully' their way along, regardless of the knowledge or feeling of the informants. One missionary had revised his translation with several informants and concluded that because they agreed with his form that it was correct. It had not occurred to him that he had consistently defied many suggestions that the various informants had first made. After such discouraging response to their suggestions they refused to say anything more. A person is not going to offer help on the translation of a verse, just to be intellectually scalped.

3 STOP WORK BEFORE THE INFORMANT IS TIRED.

Most informants cannot work more than approximately an hour at a time and continue to do good work. They may after some experience be able to extend this time, but it is better for both informant and the translator to take off ten or fifteen minutes of every hour. A good, vigorous game will fill in the recess period to best advantage, and teaching people to play games should have a high priority on the translator's list of practical objectives.

4 DO NOT INSIST ON THE INFORMANT'S EXPLAINING JUST WHY HE SAYS SOMETHING IN A PARTICULAR WAY.

The descriptive linguist does not seek to explain the why's of linguistic forms. There is usually no reason. Any linguistic system is an arbitrary arrangement of analogical forms. The translator would be rather hard put to it to explain to a foreigner why the verb *to be* has five forms in the so-called indicative, namely, *am, is, are, was,* and *were,* when no other verb has more than three forms. There is no reason why this should be the case. It is just that way. An insistence upon an explanation of forms confuses the informant. The translator must discover the patterns of usage by an examination of the texts which he has taken. Very often the informant will have made a mistake, but instead of insisting upon an explanation of the reason for the form, the translator must be in a position to suggest an alternate form which he thinks may fit the situation better.

5 SHOW ENTHUSIASM FOR THE INFORMANT'S SUGGESTIONS.

This is the positive attitude which should correct the negative situations discussed under rules one and two. There is nothing which so stimulates an informant to do his best as honest appreciation for his suggestions. The translator's enthusiasm is often the informant's most satisfying compensation.

6 APPROACH THE WHOLE TRANSLATION PROCEDURE WITH A SPIRITUAL ATTITUDE.

There is absolutely nothing like sincere prayer and devout patience to convince the informant of the importance of the translation and its value in problems of human relationship.

6.1.3   THE TRAINING OF INFORMANTS

The training of an informant for translation work is largely a matter of practice with translation problems and procedures. However, there are some definite steps which one may take so that the best results may be obtained.

1 EXPLAIN TO THE INFORMANT EXACTLY WHAT IS WANTED.

One should go over the principles of translation in such a way that the informant can understand them. In brief, one must explain to him that the translation is to say what the text says, but that it is to say it in a form which seems perfectly natural to him as a native speaker. One should point out to the informant the problems of equivalence and make him conscious of the differences in various cultures. It is sometimes possible to introduce the problems of alternate possibilities in translating by showing him different translations in the trade language.

Most informants are inclined to be literalists when they are translating written material. In general they attempt to match the text word for word. The same informants may be excellent as interpreters of the spoken language, for in such cases they are dealing with the ideas which they attempt to reproduce in the native form of speech. The problem will be to help the informant strike a happy medium between word-for-word literalness and the style which he may employ in interpreting.

2 MAKE THE INFORMANT CONSCIOUS OF STYLISTIC DIFFERENCES.

The explanation of the principles of translation is important in conveying the meaning of style. However, it usually is necessary to deal with a good many actual sentences before the informant understands the problems of style. If the order of words is intelligible, he is usually inclined to leave them in the order which seems to parallel the usage of the trade language. One must, however, take sentence after sentence and suggest different orders of words and different syntactic usages until the informant understands that the translator is seeking to find that form of expression which is the most natural.

It is often possible to teach style by having several informants discuss the form of a sentence. The discussion of various possible orders of words will often suggest to the informant the problems and principles of procedure in discovering the best syntactic form. By commending the informant's good judgment when he has made a correct choice or suggestion, one will increase his sensitiveness to the problems. If in every instance the translator congratulates the informant for having discovered an error made by the translator, the informant's 'feeling' for style will be greatly stimulated. Nothing is so encouraging to the informant as to have the translator admit his own mistakes.

3 TEACH THE INFORMANT TO WRITE HIS OWN LANGUAGE.

After having learned to write his own language, the informant may be encouraged to do some translating by himself. Such translations are seldom in anything like a final form, but the informant learns by doing. The more he translates on his own, the more conscious he becomes of the problems and the possible solutions.

6.1.4 THE USE OF TRANSLATION HELPS

There are seven types of translation helps which all translators should employ: (1) translations of the Bible into English or other modern languages, (2) commentaries, (3) background studies of Bible life and times, (4) word studies, (5) lexicons, (6) concordances, and (7) grammars. The translator should be familiar with these aids from his use of them during the process of his Biblical training. Yet there are certain aspects of such translation helps which should be considered. The following suggestions, however, are very limited and are only intended to cover some of the more significant matters.

Of the translations in English there are two principal types: (1) the AV and its revisions—(a) the Authorized Version (AV), more commonly known as the King James Version, (b) the English Revised Version (ERV), (c) the American Revised Version (ARV), also called the American Standard Version, and (d) the Revised Standard Version (RSV), of which the New Testament was published in 1946, and (2) translations into modern English, of which most have been the work of individual translators, e.g. Goodspeed and Weymouth. The Twentieth Century translation, which deserves greater attention than it has been given, also falls generally into this second class, but was the work of "about twenty scholars representing various sections of the Christian church."

There are several factors which recommend the use of the ERV and ARV, rather than the AV, as the basic text for translation purposes:

1 The texts of the original languages employed for the ERV and ARV are much superior, since they represent, particularly in the case of the Greek, very important textual improvements.

2 The ERV and ARV contain the results of much extensive research in the fields of Biblical exegesis carried on since 1611, the date of the AV.

3 The ERV and ARV take into consideration some of the extensive changes which have taken place in the English language since 1611.

The RSV reflects more modern English forms of speech and a number of improvements in rendering. Because, however, it is freer in rendering and is less close to the original languages in form, as a basic text it is of less value to the translator than the ARV and ERV.

Of the many English translations of the second class, those by Goodspeed and Weymouth are probably the most helpful. Translators should, however, make use of any and all translations made by competent scholars. The advantages in the use of such translations may be given as:

1 The uses of different words and idioms are suggestive of various possibilities in translation.
2 The sum total of different usages in the various translations helps to define the area of meaning for the Greek or Hebrew word or phrase.
3 The diversities of rendering are an aid to the translator in obtaining the 'sense' of the passage.
4 The recognition of alternate possibilities makes one more aware of the problems of lexical equivalence and adaptation.

Because of the extensive interest in the Basic English 'version' and the attempts by some translators to employ it as an aid in translation work involving aboriginal languages, some brief consideration should be given it. Some translators have been able to find in the Basic English version some very helpful suggestions as to possible idioms and forms of expression. There are, however, some important linguistic features of Basic English which must be considered in order to understand the fundamental translation problems involved:

1 Basic English is an artificially restricted form of language. There is no language in the world which anywhere approximates the 850 basic word vocabulary. All languages have many thousands of words.
2 Basic English is not a means of precise statement. For the 850 words in the basic vocabulary there are more than 12,000 principal meanings given in the Oxford Dictionary. This means that for 850 'signaling' units there are more than 12,000 'objects' or referents which are 'signaled.'
3 Basic English is artificially constructed in that it possesses only 18 verbs, with the principal lexical units expressed by nouns. Linguists who have worked with various types of aboriginal languages are constantly confronted with the problems of languages in which nouns tend to be at a minimum and in which all processes, activities, and states (including many phenomena normally expressed by adjectives in English) are expressed in verbs.

Basic English may possess many distinct advantages in certain restricted linguistic situations, but as a basis for translation work it is likely to be far more confusing than it is helpful. The linguistic peculiarities of the artificially restricted system tend to complicate rather than simplify the task of the translator.

In addition to translations commentaries constitute the most useful helps for the translator. No matter how familiar a passage may be, one should not attempt to translate it without consulting at least one standard commentary. There is too great a tendency for one to take for granted the interpretation of familiar verses. Commentaries which concentrate upon the minutiae of exegetical interpretation are in general preferable to those which place greater emphasis upon the broader hermeneutical and homiletical aspects of Biblical truth.

Background studies of Bible life and times are an essential supplement to the translator's helps. Without a proper understanding of the cultural forms of the Bible it is impossible to determine accurately the possible equivalences which may occur in the native patterns of life. The writings of Adolf Deissmann are important helps to the translator in understanding the features of Hellenistic culture. Bible dictionaries and encyclopedias should be constantly consulted concerning problems of cultural equivalence.

Word studies are of very great help to the translator in understanding some of the more subtle distinctions between various closely related words. For the New Testament vocabulary the best known treatments are by A. T. Robertson, Marvin R. Vincent, and W. E. Vine. Vine's *Expository Dictionary of New Testament Words* is especially recommended. A good treatment of Hebrew synonyms occurs in *Old Testament Synonyms* (1871) by R. B. Girdlestone.

Lexicons are indispensable aids to the translator. Thayer's lexicon has been the standard and widely employed reference for the Greek New Testament. However, there are certain very helpful treatments in Abbott-Smith, *A Manual Greek Lexicon of the New Testament*. The widely used *Hebrew-English Lexicon of the Old Testament* (1906) by Francis Brown, S. R. Driver, and C. A. Briggs is highly recommended. The somewhat smaller Hebrew Lexicon (1901) by Alexander Harkavy may also be valuable. This latter lexicon represents Jewish scholarship. Where one lexicon may not provide the needed clue to the proper identification of the area of meaning, another lexicon may be quite satisfactory. The translator should have several.

Concordances may constitute valuable aids in determining the areas of meaning for various words. Strong's *Exhaustive Concordance* contains a cross-reference system which makes it possible to identify the Greek or Hebrew word in the original text and also includes a comparative concordance which indicates the differences between the AV, ERV, and ARV, but on the whole Young's *Analytical Concordance* is more satisfactory in analyzing areas of meaning, since the listings of passages under each English word are subdivided according to the Greek and Hebrew words of the original text. The indices in the revised edition (20th) are an invaluable aid to translation and the correct analysis of the meaning of the Hebrew and Greek words.

Grammars of Greek and Hebrew may be of considerable help to translators who attempt to translate directly from the original languages, but on the whole it is generally easier to refer to the treatment of grammatical problems in the commentaries, where they are discussed with reference to the particular passage being considered.

6.1.5 EXPLAINING THE MEANING OF THE TEXT

Many translators fail to obtain the proper form of translation because they fail to explain clearly to the informant the meaning of the text. This is often one of the most difficult parts of the work, for the informants are rarely well enough trained in the trade language to be able to use a translation in it with complete understanding. Moreover, the translator should remember that he himself may have spent several years in the study of the Bible, and still there are undoubtedly many passages which are obscure to him. He can scarcely expect the informant to understand the meaning of a passage in the text which is written in a language with which he is probably not too familiar. To increase the difficulty the translation is often in a form of the trade language which is not in common use by present-day speakers. Consider, for example, the form of the de Valera Spanish Version, which in many ways is further removed from the colloquial Spanish of Latin America than the King James Version is from present American English usage.

In explaining to the informant the meaning of the text, translators have found the following steps valuable:

1 THE TEXT SHOULD BE THOROUGHLY INVESTIGATED BY THE TRANSLATOR IN ADVANCE.

The translator should not depend upon his general idea of the passage or his memory of previous explanations. Before translating a passage he should refresh his mind by reading at least one commentary on the passage. He will also find it valuable to read other translations, either in English or in other languages. The more thoroughly he understands the passage and the more extensively he has investigated the usage in other translations, the easier it will be for him to explain the passage and to suggest possible ways of translating it.

2 WORK OUT BEFOREHAND IN SIMPLE TERMS AN EXPLANATION OF THE MEANING OF THE PASSAGE.

It is often not enough to understand the meaning of the passage oneself. It is valuable to have thought through the exact form of the explanation to be given to the informant. At times it will be valuable to work out a translation or paraphrase in the trade language or English, having in mind the possible form of the translation in the native language. Usually the translator does not know precisely the form which the translation should have. The work of the informant is to give the form. However, the translator knows the general mold of expression that a particular verse must take. He may then prepare an explanation of a passage by a translation which will follow the native pattern of expression. For example, in Aztec it is necessary to change almost all passive expressions of English into active expressions. A preliminary translation can anticipate the difficulties and suggest the appropriate pattern to the informant.

3 LET THE INFORMANT READ THE TEXT, OR READ IT TO HIM.

Whether the informant is to read the text or whether it should be read to him depends upon the informant. Some informants can do better if they themselves read the text. They are more likely to get all the words into the translation. On the other hand, informants who read the text and translate from the written text, following it word for word, are often much more stiff and literal in the form of expression than those who listen to the passage read and then give a translation back on the basis of only having heard the text language. It should be remembered that few natives are trained by eye learning. Their entire education, informal though it may be, has been based upon ear learning. Accordingly, their reactions are often better for having only heard the verse than for having read it, for reading often involves the use of a strange and only partially mastered medium of learning.

4 DISCUSS THE MEANING OF THE VERSE IN THE NATIVE LANGUAGE.

It is of utmost importance to discuss the meaning of the verse in the native language. One can never be sure that the native actually understands the verse if the trade language is used, for the informant may just be repeating automatically so many words, or he may be using the words in some strange sense. For example, one informant translated "this kind cometh not out but by prayer and fasting" by an expression which meant 'this generation cometh not out. . . .' The reason for this was that he mistook the Spanish *género* 'kind' for *generación* 'generation.' The informant did not understand the meaning of the Spanish, and probably no amount of discussion of the verse in Spanish would have revealed the mistake, while a discussion in the native language immediately revealed the mistaken understanding of the informant.

A discussion of the meaning of the passage is one of the best ways for the informant to get away from a word-for-word duplication of the trade language. If there are several informants present, they should be encouraged to discuss the verse, for in the process of the discussion the various parts of the sentence will fall into their natural native order and the selection of the proper words will be automatically made. The writer has observed several times that, when two informants are working, the first suggestions for a translation of a sentence will often be an almost literal rendering of the trade language. However, by the time the informants have discussed the sentence two or three times, the exchange of conversation concerning this has resulted in an almost automatic reworking of the translation in terms of natural native usage.

If the passage or sentence is extremely difficult and discussion of the idiom does not give very good results, it is best to pass the particular section up for the time being. One may briefly make notes as to the problems and some of the suggestions, but it is unwise to spend too much time on one section. Further experience and a similar problem elsewhere may shed light on the difficulty and make the solution of the problem relatively simple.

6.1.6 PUTTING DOWN THE FORM OF THE TRANSLATION

There are several different ways in which the first and basic form of the translation may be put down. In general, however, translators tend to employ one of three principal methods: (1) where the *-44* non-native translator writes out the form of the translation without the assistance of informants, (2) where the informants and the translator work together on the form, and (3) where native translators do a first rough draft which must then be considerably revised. This third method should not be confused with the translation process, involving well-trained native translators, discussed in section 6.2.

Translators may employ the first method with considerable value if they have attained an adequate mastery of the language. They should, however, make certain that everything which they have written is carefully checked by competent informants and thoroughly revised in terms of the native linguistic forms. In general, however, even expert translators find it more valuable to employ the second principal method of procedure, or to combine the second and the third. The following suggestions for a procedure in translating will in the majority of situations prove most valuable:

44 - 1 WRITE DOWN THE TRANSLATION AS THE INFORMANT SPEAKS IT.

The process of putting down the actual form of the translation is important. The form should in every case be the spoken form. The translator or the informant may write it down, but not while looking at the text language nor while attempting to compare all the items. After having written down the form as the informant speaks it, the translator may then compare it with the text to find if there have been any unnecessary additions or any deletions. The translator should not insist on writing down his own form of the translation. He should in all cases use the form suggested by the informant. It may be necessary to change the rendering, but the informant's suggestions should constitute the basic framework of the sentence. In such a case there is much more likelihood of its being in an idiomatic form than should the translator use his own rendering as the basis of the translation.

2 WRITE THE TRANSLATION OF EACH VERSE ON INDIVIDUAL SLIPS OF PAPER. *(different color of slips)*

The importance of using individual slips can hardly be over-emphasized. In working on any verse one should write down a brief analysis of each problem which is confronted. All alternative suggestions which are valuable should also be noted on individual slips. The final form should likewise be written down on a slip and then all the slips covering any verse be filed together. This means that everything applicable to any problem can be found in one place. One does not have to look back over a series of manuscripts and papers to find the items.

It is also valuable to use slips of different colors. For example, all discussion items may be written on white paper, but the final form of the verse may be written on yellow paper. This yellow slip should in each case be put at the first of all the slips dealing with this verse. If an extensive revision takes place while the translation is still in the slip stage, another color may be used for the slips showing the revision. It is true that after the translator transfers the material from the slips to the manuscript page there will be some adjustments to be made, because the immediate connection of some verses may have been overlooked. However, the inconsistencies may be cleared up quite quickly.

3 USE THE INFORMANT IN EVERY STAGE OF TRANSLATION.

At no stage in the translation should the translator work independently of the informant. The translator will find it inadvisable to make even a composite translation without the immediate assistance of informants. One translator asked several informants to translate certain passages on their own. The translations were not too good, for they were based upon too literal a rendering of a word-for-word correspondence. Nevertheless the translator then took these various translations and by selecting words and phrases from them made a composite translation which was as awkward as any of the others. Even after he has had considerable experience in the language, the translator should not trust himself for constructing the final syntactic or lexical framework of the translation.

6.1.7 REVISING THE TRANSLATION

No translation is ever made the first time in such a form that it does not need revising. In fact, most careful translators are amazed at the number of times they have profitably gone over the translation with the purpose of revising and polishing it. It is, however, not fundamentally a matter of how many times one has gone over a manuscript, but rather how thorough one has been in the process. Several weeks should elapse between the first translation and the revision. It is valuable to let the previous work have time to 'cool off.' Further experience and a fresh approach to the old problems will greatly enhance one's chances of satisfactory revision.

The use of several informants in the revising of the manuscript is very important. This often tends to create some difficulty, for one informant may not want to appear to be working against another, who may very likely be a good friend. At least the informants may feel much closer to each other than to the translator. On the other hand, by playing one informant off against the other the translator may unwittingly create a feeling of jealousy and competition between the informants. This situation has sometimes been rather disastrous to the Christian community. The best procedure is to tell all the possible informants from the very start that their help is desired. One informant may be good on the precise meaning of words, another on sentence structure, and another on word formation. The translator should take time to encourage each informant in his specialty, but to remind them all of the value of each other's work. Such training can constitute real lessons in Christian grace. Every effort must be made to create a feeling of teamwork if the informants are to be of the greatest helpfulness.

In the actual process of revision, the translator will find the following steps of practical value:

1 THE TRANSLATOR SHOULD STUDY THE TRANSLATION BEFOREHAND FOR POTENTIAL DIFFICULTIES.

In reading over the translation the translator will find words, phrases, and grammatical structures which do not appear to be in an idiomatic form. In some instances, the words will not seem to be adequate to convey the meaning of the original. All such points should be marked for further consultation with the informants. The translator should also have some alternate suggestions to propose in order that no unnecessary time may be wasted. The informants usually need to have something tangible to deal with in determining the validity of any form of expression.

2 THE TRANSLATION SHOULD BE READ OVER TO SEVERAL INFORMANTS.

These informants may be consulted in a group or individually. If they are in a group, one is less likely to obtain their individual opinion, for they will usually tend to follow the opinion of the one who has the greatest prestige in such language work. On the other hand, if discussion does arise, the differences of opinion as to the usage are of utmost importance. In every case, the informants should be asked what the translation of each passage means. They may not be able to give a very satisfactory reply to all details, and they may make some mistakes. This should not be surprising, but if all the informants make the same mistake in interpretation, then there is something wrong with the translation. The missionary who thinks that all the natives are ignoramuses because none of them seem to understand what he has translated is the victim of his own stupidity.

3 THE TRANSLATOR SHOULD OFFER SOME ALTERNATE FORMS OF THE TRANSLATION.

These alternate forms are not necessarily to be considered as final. They are designed primarily to obtain the natives' reaction to the meaning and style of the alternate possibilities. An alternate suggestion may often be rejected, but it may also result in some better suggestion on the part of the informants.

4 THE INFORMANTS MUST BE ENCOURAGED TO STOP THE READING OF THE TRANSLATION AT ANY POINT WHERE IT DOES NOT SEEM NATURAL.

This process may result in many interruptions. Some translators have thought that they could obtain better results by giving a copy of the translation to informants and asking them to write in alternate suggestions by changing the order of words and phrases so as to conform the translation more closely to native idiomatic style. This is usually, however, quite unsuccessful. Native informants very rarely have sufficient training in literary work to enable them to sit down and correct a written manuscript. Their reactions to the usage of the language come primarily by hearing it, not by seeing it written. The most valid analysis of the form must be based upon reactions to hearing the translation read.

At this point it should be noted that a translation must not have to depend too much on artificial punctuation to give the sense. The punctuation must be based upon the syntax of the native language. Important distinctions must not be left entirely to the punctuation.

5 Check the concordance of words.

Checking a translation for the concordance of words is a great aid in attaining consistency. One may use either the American Bible Society word check lists or a concordance. The *Englishman's Greek Concordance* is very helpful. It is valuable to know how, for example, the word "love" has been translated in its various occurrences. The translator will not always use the same aboriginal word, each time that "love" occurs in English. The translation would be almost sure to be inaccurate if this were done. Certainly, the English word "love" does not always stand for the same Greek word. The purpose in the checking of the concordance of words is only to call to one's attention the differences and thus to make one fully aware of the changes and the basis for the changes that have been made.

6 Check the agreement of parallel passages.

If the identical expression occurs in two different places in the New Testament, there is no special reason why it should be translated in two different ways. There should be a preferable form for such an expression, and it should be used consistently.

7 Check for mechanical consistency.

The forms of proper names, the use of periods at the end of sentences, proper indication of direct quotations, versification, and the numbering of verses and chapters should all be checked with care.

8 Prepare the manuscript in accordance with instructions in Chapter 15.

6.1.8 CHECKING FOR GENERAL ACCEPTANCE
OF THE TRANSLATION

Having gone over the problems of the translation with the informants and consultants (consultants are those who have had considerable experience in the language and in Christian teaching, e.g. native preachers), one should then check for the general acceptance of the translation. The translators and the informants may have been employing forms which have seemed quite appropriate to them, but have actually been rather stiff, formal, and difficult to understand, except by those who have been conditioned to the understanding of them by considerable teaching and experience with Christianity.

There are two general classes of people who should be consulted about such a translation. The first class includes the Christians. These should be asked to tell the translator what certain passages mean. Their replies are important, for the readiness with which they are able to understand the translation is an index of its effectiveness in teaching. An even more important class of people on which to test the translation are the non-Christians. Many times the Christians have become thoroughly accustomed to the translator's strange expressions. The non-Christians who have had no contact with the translator will be able to give a more valuable criticism of the translation. It is true that these people will not be able to understand so much of the meaning of the Bible as the Christians, who have presumably been given considerable instruction in Christianity. Nevertheless, the translation must make some sense to the non-Christian. It must not be a strange combination of relatively unknown words. One of the principal purposes of the translation should be to reach the non-Christians with a written statement of the truths of Christianity. A translation which is not in the native form of speech will fail to accomplish this purpose. Those best qualified to judge this fact are usually the non-Christians.

It should be obvious to the translator that the value of the translation is directly proportionate to his willingness to accept criticism. It is not always easy to obtain fair criticism of a translation from natives. They will usually answer exactly what they think the translator would like to have them answer. Since the apparently logical thing would be for the translator to have them approve the translation which he has made, this is usually done. Actually such people are only being polite in terms of their own standards of politeness. The translator must go about the entire task as one who is helping in a work, not directing it, if he is going to obtain the helpful criticism of the people.

The missionary must also be careful not to be deluded about his own knowledge of the language nor unduly elated by the compliments of the natives as to his speaking knowledge. The better the translator knows the language of the native, the less likely is the native to compliment him on his use of it. The nearer he conforms to the native idiom, the less the people will call attention to the fact that he is a foreigner attempting to master a difficult language. The missionary should not be flattered by kind compliments as to his usage of a language but, rather, relieved when he no longer receives such comments. Silence will indicate one of two facts: either he has successfully learned the language so that his usage no longer calls for sympathetic encouragement or his usage is so atrocious that no native wants to discuss such an embarrassing subject.

It may appear to some from this description of the procedure in translating that the non-native translator has very little to do with the actual translating and that he functions more or less as an umpire in the determination of usage. This is somewhat the case, but not exactly. The quality of the translation is usually almost directly proportionate to the translator's ability in the language, for it is he who must check the informant's usage, be sure of the proper meaning, and suggest the alternate possibilities. The procedure which has been outlined is not, however, primarily for those translators who have an inadequate knowledge of the language. Actually, the non-native translator who is extremely proficient in the use of the native language will generally be the first to acknowledge his own inadequacy. He will also be the one to check each usage most closely and carefully with the native speaker. The really skilled translator will make constant use of the native informant.

6.1.9　　　　　BIBLE SOCIETY CHECKS

Before publishing any part of the Bible, the American Bible Society attempts to make a thorough check of the translation. The purpose of this check is twofold: (1) to be assured that the translation is an accurate rendition of the original texts and (2) to assist the translator in making what improvements are possible. Translations which are not accurate can do almost irreparable damage. In one instance in Africa the word used for 'virgin' also designated a girl who participated in certain lascivious puberty rites. When the missionaries protested against these practices, the natives defended their ritual by claiming that the Bible declared that Mary the mother of Jesus was a member of this cult. Such a mistake in a translation must be avoided if at all possible. In many instances checking with the Bible Society has resulted in many improvements for which the translators have been very thankful, for it has made the book a more usable one.

There are two principal types of checking which the American Bible Society undertakes. When possible the Secretary for Versions attempts to check directly with the missionary. In other instances the checking is done entirely by means of examining the text without the assistance of the missionary.

6.1.9.1 DIRECT CHECKING WITH THE MISSIONARY

In checking directly with the missionary the Bible Society Secretary makes use of all the written checks described below. In addition to this he works directly with the manuscript by having the missionary or preferably a native speaker translate the rendering of the manuscript literally into English or some other modern European language known to the Secretary. The Secretary then follows carefully, noting the usage of (1) the English text (or of other modern European language texts which have been used as a basis for the translation), (2) the Greek or Hebrew text, and (3) the translation in the native language. By this means the Secretary has been able to check the meaning quite carefully, and in the cases of difficulty suggests certain possible improvements and corrections. Actual discussion with the missionary, and if possible with the native informants, has in many instances resulted in solving translation problems which would otherwise require many months of correspondence. If the Secretary cannot visit the field himself, it has proved valuable to have the missionary bring his manuscript of a translation with him when he returns on furlough. The Secretary can then go over matters in detail with him and, instead of simply noting some discrepancies and inconsistencies, can often be of practical help.

6.1.9.2   Checking on Written Material

The following types of checks have been developed by the American Bible Society, largely through the work of Dr. Eric M. North and Dr. James Oscar Boyd. They have proved of great aid to missionaries and should be used extensively in the checking of the translation. It should be noted, however, that these checks are based primarily on the principle of consistency. This is valuable, but has its limitations, for a translation may be consistently wrong as well as consistently right. Only direct checking with the missionary and native informants is adequate in some instances. Nevertheless, on the basis of the examination of the written material the Secretary is often able to point out difficulties, even if he cannot in every case suggest solutions. The American Bible Society employs five types of checks: (1) word check lists, (2) parallel passage check lists, (3) proper names check lists, (4) verse-by-verse analysis, and (5) native texts. The first four have been used for some time. The fifth has been used in some instances and with very good results.

6.1.9.2.1   Word Check Lists

A sample page of the word check lists may be seen in the Appendix. As has been noted, these checks lists are not designed to force conformity but to call attention to usage. If the missionary fills in these word check lists before submitting a manuscript to the American Bible Society for checking, he should be sure that the forms in the word check lists compare exactly with the forms in the text.

Because of syntactic differences in the use of a word it may appear in several forms in the word check lists. The forms in the text should not, however, be made to conform artificially to some standard form which has been selected for the purpose of filling out the word check lists. For example, one translator made out the word check list correctly but found that the forms which were listed showed considerable variation of suffixial form. He did not understand exactly the syntactic reasons for such differences, although he had noted that the natives were more or less consistent in the usage. Nevertheless, he went back and changed all the forms in the text, by eliminating the final suffixes, in order that the forms listed in the word check lists might appear the same. This was most unfortunate. A later check of the material made it necessary to reinstate all those suffixial forms. In linguistic work one cannot afford to cheat against the facts in order to produce conformity. One's linguistic sins will always find one out.

6.1.9.2.2 PARALLEL PASSAGE CHECK LISTS

There are two types of parallel passage check lists. The first type are the intra-Gospel parallel passage lists and the second are the inter-Gospel lists. A sample of a single page of the first of these lists may be found in the Appendix. These lists are designed to enable the translator more easily to phrase consistently those verses or parts of verses which are identical within the same book. The second type of tests, the inter-Gospel tests, comprise a large book of 'coupons.' Each coupon contains a passage which is parallel to one or more passages in the other Gospels. Both the ARV and the Nestle Greek texts are given. A series of numbers makes it possible to find all the parallels in the other Gospels. The coupons are arranged in a loose-leaf folder so that they may be taken out for filling in on the typewriter. These check lists may not be purchased, but they are loaned by the American Bible Society to translators who have need for them and for as long a period as this need may exist. These coupons, properly filled in, constitute an important help to the translator in obtaining consistency of usage. Consistency is no virtue in itself, but when combined with excellence of usage it can be of real help and value.

6.1.9.2.3 PROPER NAMES CHECK LIST

A sample copy of a page of the proper names check list occurs in the Appendix. The list, which must always be supplemented by a concordance to find the references, is a help to the missionary in making sure that the same transliterated form of the name is used in each instance. Nothing is quite so confusing to natives as to see a name written in several different forms. The problems of transliteration will be discussed on p. 243 ff.

6.1.9.2.4 VERSE-BY-VERSE ANALYSIS

The Versions Secretary attempts to make a verse-by-verse analysis of the text. He compares usage so that he can identify the general area of meaning of each word or phrase. He cannot, of course, check for peripheral meanings or connotative values, unless the parallel usages of the words make these quite obvious. He tries to be sure (1) that the words mean what the Biblical text means, (2) that there are no unnecessary additions, (3) that there are no deletions, (4) that the numbering and division of verses are correct, and (5) that the general grammatical structure is consistent and idiomatic. In checking for idiomatic usage the Secretary can only compare the translation with the text which has been used as a basis for it. If the agreement is automatic and word-for-word, the Secretary knows that the translation cannot be good, for no two languages in the world have the same grammatical structure. Only consistent variation from the text language can indicate anything like an idomatic translation.

6.1.9.2.5 NATIVE TEXTS

In order to make an adequate check as to the stylistic usage in the translation, it is very important for the Secretary to have some fifteen to twenty pages of narrative text in the native language. If this can be supplied with an interlinear literal translation and an accompanying free translation, one can check more adequately for the native sentence structure, length of sentences, word formation, word order, and types of subordination. Such texts, to be of any value at all, must be written in exactly the form in which the natives speak.

Having examined the written material, the Versions Secretary corresponds with the translator, listing each item in the translation which seems wrong or doubtful. Each item is numbered, and the translator is requested to reply to *each* item. If there is sufficient reason for the usage as in the manuscript, the Secretary is interested in knowing about it. If a change is desirable this should be listed. The Secretary cannot claim always to be right, by any means. He is desirous, however, of having satisfactory explanations on all points which have appeared dubious.

The checking of a translation and the ensuing correspondence always take some time. In general, however, missionaries have felt that it has been very worth while. The improvements which have been made have generally been considered to justify the time spent. It is impossible to be too careful with the Word of God.

6.1.10 PUBLICATION OF LIMITED PORTIONS

It has been suggested previously that the publication of small portions of the Bible in mimeographed form is valuable. Such material may be mimeographed on cheap paper, for in addition to its cheapness it will wear out sooner. It is better to have one's early efforts disappear rather than to have them haunt one because of the mistakes which have been corrected in succeeding translations. When one reaches the stage of wanting to have printed editions, there are three suggestions which have been found important to follow:

1 PUT OUT ONE BOOK BEFORE COMPLETING THE NEW TESTA-
MENT.

The best check of a translation is the usage and acceptance by the native speakers of a language. The translator may have called a church 'an organization of called out ones' in an attempt at etymologizing a Greek word. The natives may insist on calling it 'a gathering together.' If this is the usage which the people insist on having, then the translator should conform to this usage. After all, an *ekklēsia* was only an 'assembly' to the Greeks, and the etymology of 'called out' would have been as far from the thinking of the average Greek, as 'break the fast' is far from the English speaker's immediate understanding of 'breakfast.'

In matters of style, orthography, dialect geography, and general understanding, there is no test equivalent to usage by the native. No translator can afford to complete an entire New Testament without testing the acceptance of at least one book.

2 THE BEST GOSPEL TO PUBLISH FIRST IS MARK.

The Gospel of Mark is the shortest Gospel. It has the simplest narratives and thus is most easily understood by those who have just learned to read. One of its very important values is that it does not begin with great difficulties. The Gospel of Matthew starts with an almost 'impossible' genealogy. It is impossible in the sense that the names are all strange and meaningless. It is a discouragement to anyone who has just become literate. The Gospel of Luke begins with some very difficult historical and poetic portions. The introduction is often rather a stumbling-block to the new native reader. The Gospel of John begins with the discourse on the Word. This discourse is very difficult for anyone to understand who has not had considerable training in Christianity. The best guarantee that a reader will continue reading is that the subject-matter be easily understood. For this, the Gospel of Mark has been found to be the best. The Gospel of Mark has a full story of the ministry, death, and resurrection of Jesus.

3 THE TRANSLATOR SHOULD PLAN TO PUBLISH PORTIONS OF THE NEW TESTAMENT AT VARIOUS INTERVALS.

If the format is the same for all portions, these may be bound together into an entire New Testament when all the portions have been completed. The value of such spaced publications is that they keep up reader interest. The failure of many reading campaigns has been due to the inability of the translators to continue to supply reading matter.

6.2   TRANSLATIONS BY NATIVE TRANSLATORS

Translations by native speakers of a language are usually in the form of revisions. Few native speakers are sufficiently well qualified by education and Bible training to undertake the first translation of the Bible into their own language. In most cases at least, these native translators have some portions of the Bible to use as a basis for translation. In some instances the New Testament is put out first by non-native translators, and then it is revised and the Old Testament is translated by native speakers. The problems with such translations usually concern (1) personnel and (2) procedure.

6.2.1   PERSONNEL

Matters of personnel involve the qualifications of (1) translators and (2) consultants.

6.2.1.1   TRANSLATORS

The translators must have a thorough knowledge of both languages: the text language and the native language. If possible, the translators should have a working knowledge of Greek and Hebrew, but this is frequently not the case. It may be that some of those who would like to undertake translation into what they consider their native language have so grown away from their original language by contact with the speakers of the trade language that they are no longer qualified to translate adequately.

Native translators cannot be qualified to do a very thorough and accurate piece of work unless they have had some rather intensive theological training. This is usually more than they get in the average missionary Bible school. Native translators should show some literary ability. The fact that they are good speakers does not mean that they are able to put ideas on paper. On the other hand, they may be creative in their thinking and yet not sufficiently meticulous to do the job well.

6.2.1.2   CONSULTANTS

A very important part of the success of a translation done by native translators lies in the qualifications of the consultants who are available. Usually such consultants are missionaries who know the language well enough to check for the adequacy of the meaning and the consistency of the usage but who do not have a sufficient knowledge of the language to undertake translation in it. Consultants should by all means have some knowledge of the Greek or Hebrew.

Biblical Training, Knowledge of native language

6.2.2   METHODS OF PROCEDURE

The following suggestions, based upon the practices employed in various translations, may prove helpful:

1. The work should be done by a committee if at all possible. The use of a committee is important in gaining wider acceptance for the translation and in eliminating errors. However, members should be admitted to the committee because of their qualifications and not because their presence would satisfy some religious clique.

2. Various portions should be assigned to each translator.

3. The translations which have been made by each member of the committee should be typed or mimeographed and distributed to the other members of the committee for criticism.

4. The differences of translation and the types of criticisms should be examined and classified so as to solve problems as rapidly as possible. Any problem should be examined in the light of all its occurrences and not repeatedly for every instance in the text.

5. The problems should be submitted to the translators and consultants for examination.

6. At a meeting of translators and consultants, the solutions of such problems should be discussed and voted upon.

7 The final results should be mimeographed and submitted to native pastors, church leaders, and missionaries for their general comments.

8 These comments should be considered and weighed by the committee. The purpose of step (7) is to prevent unnecessary reaction after publication by those who felt wronged at not being consulted.

9 The manuscript should be prepared in accordance with instructions in Chapter 15.

It is quite impossible to treat all the various types of circumstances under which translation and revision work is undertaken, and it is also impossible to define rigidly the various procedures which should be employed. There are always many local situations which demand adaptations.

One of the most difficult translation tasks is the revision of some standard translation. In the first place, the tendency is to use a venerated translation far longer than its linguistic form justifies. This prevalent traditionalism constitutes a very practical problem, since the revision, in order to be acceptable, must generally conform to at least the fundamental outlines of the previous translation. Revision committees frequently feel that there is a need for change, and proceed to make changes, but their work is often less valuable because they do not consider carefully in advance the principles and bases for change, nor do they make decisions to cover types of problems, but rather, they consider each word and phrase as an individual, more or less isolated, item. To prevent some misunderstanding and to promote the work more successfully, the following suggestions may prove valuable as supplementary to the previous list:

1 The revision committee should include certain specialists. In addition to men who are trained theologically, it is valuable to have those on a revision committee who have (a) special linguistic training (such men can be consulted as to dialect usages, orthographic matters, and problems of formal structure), and (b) literary ability in the native language. Note, however, that literary and stylistic ability in one language is no guarantee of similar ability in another language, for the stylistic patterns change from language to language, and proficiency in writing can only be gained by considerable ex-

perience in the particular language medium. Only a well-trained native speaker is generally adequate to pass upon stylistic matters.

2 The revision committee should decide in advance the particular types of changes which they consider necessary to make in a given text. Revisions generally include such changes as (1) modifications of word order, (2) substitutions of different important words, and (3) the avoidance of obsolescent forms. Whatever the types of changes are, the committee should attempt some formulation of procedure before beginning, in order that the resultant translation may possess some fundamental formal unity. During the process of working on the revision, the committee may wish to modify considerably some of the original proposals, but such problems should be treated as representative of types of problems, not as unrelated individual items.

3 The work of each translator on the committee should be copied, circulated to the other members of the committee, and returned to the secretary of the committee with the notes of each committee member. Someone should then go over all the comments made by the members of the committee and classify the types of suggestions, so that when the committee is in session the problems may be treated as classes of items. The committee should have copies of all the significant alternative suggestions made by the various members in order that decisions may be made promptly and in light of the most adequate presentation of the possibilities. This involves a good deal of paper work, but in the long run it is a tremendous saving in time and energy. If everything is down in black and white there is considerably less of a tendency to haggle over unimportant details or to spend a lot of time on impromptu suggestions which may not have been thought through sufficiently in advance.

Chapter 7

ORTHOGRAPHY

PROBLEMS of orthography are in many instances the most troublesome features of the translation work. These problems may be most conveniently considered under (1) the alphabet, (2) the writing of word units, and (3) the punctuation. In terms of the scientific analysis of the language, the alphabet represents the phonological system, the writing of word units concerns the morphological features of the language, and the punctuation entails an analysis of the syntactic structure.

7.1   THE ALPHABET

The particular alphabet to be used for a language may constitute a very complex problem. The traditional usage and the pressures exerted by the usage of the trade language or languages add greatly to the difficulties encountered in reaching any satisfactory solution. In adopting any alphabet one must consider (1) its scientific basis, (2) the symbols to be employed, and (3) the practical modifications of the scientific alphabet which must be made in some instances.

7.1.1   SCIENTIFIC BASIS OF THE ALPHABET

Stated briefly, a scientific alphabet is a phonemic alphabet. A phonemic alphabet is one in which there is one symbol for each psychologically significant sound unit, in other words, a sound which is significant because it makes a difference in the meaning; e.g. p and b are different psychologically significant sound units in English because *pat* and *bat* are different in meaning. The word *phonemic* is not a synonym of *phonetic*. The distinction is very important, though it is not always easy to understand. An illustration may help clear up the matter.

In English there are several different varieties of the k sound. For example, there are k sounds which are pronounced relatively far front on the hard palate, e.g. the k as in *keel*. This k is much further front (from a phonetician's viewpoint) than the *k* sound in the word *call*. In fact, the position of articulation (where the tongue meets the palate) of the *k* sound differs appreciably, depending upon the vowel which follows the *k*. For example, compare the position of articulation in the *k* sounds in the following words: *keel, kill, Kate, kettle, cattle, cot, call, cold,* and *cool*. Phonetically these *k* sounds are somewhat different, but note that they are in each case automatically conditioned by the vowel which follows. As a result, we are not normally conscious of any difference at all. In fact some persons might be inclined to deny that there is a difference.

Compare some other *k* sounds in English. The *k* in *kill* is uttered with a considerable amount of aspiration (breath) following it. Accordingly the stop is called an aspirated *k*. But compare the *k* in *skill*. When an *s* precedes the *k*, there is practically no aspiration. Compare the following words: *take* vs. *steak*, *peak* vs. *speak*, and *Kate* vs. *skate*. In each case the voiceless stops *p, t,* and *k* are aspirated (i.e. occur with noticeable breath) when initial, but when preceded by *s*, they are unaspirated (i.e. lack this breathiness). Phonetically, here are two different types of stop sounds. One is aspirated and the other unaspirated. A phonetic alphabet would have to indicate this difference. Nevertheless, to us as English speakers, it would seem an unnecessary distinction to make, for the alternation is automatic and as such is not psychologically significant. That is to say, we do not distinguish between words by means of this difference in aspirated and unaspirated consonants.

Consider another example. The *k* is released in *kill* and *skill*. In other words, the tongue comes down from the palate before the next sound begins. In the word *act* this is not the case. The middle of the tongue stays in place till after the tip of the tongue comes into place for the *t*. The *k* sound in *act* may be called an unreleased variety. It is similar to the first *k* sound in the sequence *Dick killed*. Phonetically, the *k* sound here is a doubly long consonant, for there is normally no open transition (break) between the first *k* sound and the second.

It would be possible for us to analyze many other sounds in English and to discover that there are many different phonetic varieties of what we as native speakers consider as identically the same sound. Phonetic writing, if it is to be an 'accurate' phonetic alphabet, would attempt to indicate all the fine shades of distinction in sounds. But to us as native speakers, such an alphabet would seem very clumsy. In fact many of the distinctions would confuse us rather than help us in reading our language. For us, the phonetically different *k* sounds that we have just considered are all 'identical,' for they appear to us to have the same functional significance. We prefer to write just one symbol which would indicate this psychologically pertinent sound unit. Actually, as we have seen, this unit (for this is the way we 'think' of it) is made up of several different, though related, sounds. But to us the psychologically significant feature is the sound unit, not the phonetically different sounds, which may be called 'phones.' We generally prefer just one symbol to represent all these related phones and not a dozen or more symbols or several different diacritical marks added to a single symbol. This correspondence of one symbol for each one of the psychologically significant sound units is what may be called the *phonemic principle* in orthography. Each one of these units is called a phoneme. The phonemic alphabet, one made up of phonemes, is quite different from a phonetic alphabet in that it eliminates all those differences which are not psychologically significant in the language.

It will be valuable for us to consider a little more fully the scientific basis for the phonemic alphabet, for no adequate alphabet may be constructed without a thorough understanding of the principles upon which such an alphabet is based. The phonemic alphabet may be said to rest upon four fundamental principles. These may be stated briefly as follows:

1 The phoneme is composed of phones which are phonetically similar. (This fundamental principle underlies those which follow.)

2 The phoneme (the psychologically significant sound unit, made up of different phones) includes phones (the phonetically different types of sounds) which vary freely within certain limits. This is known as *free variation*.

3 The phoneme includes phones which differ according to the situations in which they occur. This is known as *conditioned variation*.

4 The function of a phone in the structure of the language may determine the phoneme to which it belongs.

These principles of phonemic theory are of little value apart from some illustrations of how they are applied.[1]

7.1.1.1   Phonetic Limits of a Phoneme

In saying that a phoneme is composed of phones that are phonetically similar, we are simply stating a general principle. For example, we can readily unite all the *k* sounds (phones) in English together into one phoneme, for they are quite similar. They include a complete stopping of the air for an instant by the closing of the nasal passage and closing of the oral passage by the middle or back part of the tongue placed somewhere along the hard or soft palate. Also, the vocal cords are free from any vibration. This last condition is not the case in most pronunciations of the *g* phoneme in English. Note also that in English there is a minimally different word pair, namely, *kill* and *gill*, which establish the phonemic contrast between the *k* and the *g* phonemes. Nevertheless, there are different sound units in English for which we cannot get such a minimally different pair. Compare the *h* and the ŋ (written *ng*). The *h* phoneme only occurs initially in a syllable and ŋ never occurs in this position. It is, therefore, impossible to find two words that differ by these two sounds only. However, we would not want to consider *h* and ŋ as members of the same phoneme, for they are so dissimilar in sound.

One may well ask just how similar or dissimilar sounds must be, to be included or excluded from any one specific phoneme. There is no absolute answer to be given to this. No one has ever been able to determine the criteria for it. However, if one carefully follows out the other principles of phonemic analysis, those problems which depend upon the degree of similarity of phones are much fewer than one may anticipate. The nature of this introductory analysis will not permit a more comprehensive treatment of this technical and theoretical problem.

7.1.1.2   Free Variation Within a Phoneme

The phones which belong to a phoneme never have exactly the

---

[1]It is impossible in so short a space to outline the principles adequately. For this one should consult *Phonemics*, by Dr. Kenneth L. Pike, published by the Summer Institute of Linguistics. The following explanation is only an attempt to introduce the significance of the phonemic alphabet and to suggest how it is arrived at. The methodology is quite complicated in many instances and should be thoroughly studied. Dr. Pike's treatment is by far the most adequate for the missionary translator.

same pronunciation. This means that in saying the word *kill* no one ever pronounces it twice identically the same. Our ears are not able to pick up the differences, but instrumental recordings of various pronunciations indicate that we do not say words exactly the same. From a practical standpoint, however, various pronunciations of a word may sound exactly the same to us. The trained phonetician will no doubt pick up differences that the untrained listener will not hear. But if he tries to, even the untrained person is able to hear differences in the pronunciation of *kill* uttered at various times. In some instances there may be a slightly different quality. In fact, if we listen very closely to various pronunciations of *kill* by the same person or by different persons, we may be able to distinguish several different qualities. But despite the rather wide range of vowel differences, the vowel in *kill* varies freely only within certain limits. It does not become as high and fronted as the vowel of *keel*. The vowels of these two words may become quite similar, but they are not interchangeable, nor do the qualities overlap.

The range of variation in a sound is entirely determined by the structure of the particular language. In the Quechua language, there are basically three vowels, *i*, *a*, and *u*. In certain situations the *i* and *u* change automatically to *e* and *o* respectively, but apart from this type of conditioned change (which is considered under the next section) one must note that the three basic vowels of Quechua have a much wider range of free variation than the vowels of English. There may be wider variation without running into other qualities of vowels, for there is not so much competition from closely similar vowels. The Quechua *i* vowel may sometimes sound like the vowel of *keel* and on other occasions like the vowel of *kill*. The *u* vowel varies also, sometimes sounding like the vowel of *pool*, and other times like the vowel of *pull*. The *a* vowel also covers quite an area of sound, varying from the vowel sound of *cat* through the vowel sound of the second vowel of *sofa*. The three vowels of Quechua have a wide range of variation.

No one language can ever be reduced to writing on the basis of the usage in another language. The areas of significant sound units will never be exactly superimposed, any more than the areas of the meaning of the words. Each language is a system unto itself. Even as we must respect the individuality of a language in determining the area of meaning of its words, so we must learn to respect its individuality in determining the area of variation of its significant sound units, the phonemes. In order to solve the problems of meaning in a language we must know how the language divides up all types of phenomena under certain word symbols. In order to solve the problems which concern the phonemes, we must know the significant divisions of sounds which the language itself makes. A distinction made in any other language constitutes no criterion for setting up a similar distinction in the language being analyzed. This fact must be borne in mind at all times.

7.1.1.3 CONDITIONED VARIATION WITHIN A PHONEME

As we noted above, there are phonetically different sounds (different phones) which are definitely conditioned by surrounding sounds. The different *k*'s which we noted as occurring before certain vowels, after *s*, and before other stops in certain combinations are all conditioned variants. The native speaker is not conscious of these differences and is confused by any attempt to force such distinctions of symbolization. For example, in the Tarahumara language there are two different *s*-like sounds. One of these is similar to the *s* in English. The other is similar to the English *š* (written usually *sh*). In the Tarahumara, however, the *s* variety occurs before the vowels *e*, *a*, *o*, and *u*, but the *š* variety occurs only before the vowel *i*. These different sibilant (*s*-like) sounds are conditioned by the vowels which follow. The conditioning is automatic. There would be no point in trying to teach the Tarahumara two symbols for one sibilant phoneme. To insist on such a distinction would only be confusing. The Tarahumara speakers have only one *s* phoneme. The phonetically different variants are psychologically meaningless. In other words, they never make a difference in the meaning of words in the Tarahumara language. The situation with English aspirated and unaspirated stops is practically identical. The difference between an aspirated *k* as in *kill* and an unaspirated *k* as in *skill* is psychologically meaningless, for the difference between aspirated and unaspirated consonants never makes a difference in the meaning. In other languages, the difference between an aspirated and an unaspirated consonant may make a difference, e.g. in the Mazatec, where the difference between *ti* 'boy' and *thi* 'round' is only a matter of aspiration.

7.1.1.4 FUNCTION OF THE PHONE IN THE LANGUAGE STRUCTURE

The particular function which a phone has in the structure of a language may determine the phoneme to which it belongs. Let us say that in a particular language the only diphthongal combinations (sequences of vowel-like sounds) are made up of the phonemes *a*, *i*, and *u*, plus an *i*-like or a *u*-like sound. In this same language the second vowel-like sound of each diphthong is more constricted, in other words, more consonant-like, than the first part of the diphthongal combination. The problem is whether these combinations should be considered as combinations of vowels or combinations of vowels plus consonants. A look at the general structure of the language will help. Let us suppose that this language has only such combinations as CVCVCV or CVCCVCCVC (C stands for any consonant and V for any vowel) if we eliminate all instances in which the diphthongal combinations occur. Also the language has a *y* and a *w* phoneme which occur initially in syllables. If, on the other hand, the second part of the diphthongal combinations, namely, the *i*-like and *u*-like sounds (which are phonetically very close to the initial *y* and *w*, except for slightly less 'consonant' quality) are written as *y* and *w*, then the system of the language is perfectly regular. One can state that (1) any consonant may be initial to the syllable, (2) any consonant may be final to the syllable, (3) each syllable has a single vowel, and (4) clusters of more than two consonants never occur.

Whether one is to write the possible diphthongal combinations as *ii, ai, ui, iu, au,* and *uu* with the second member as a vowel or as *iy, ay, uy, iw, aw,* and *uw,* is not dependent so much upon the phonetic quality of these combinations as upon the function which these second elements have in the language. If in the system of the language they function just like consonants in making certain consonant clusters, they should be written as consonants.[1] In other words, the function which a phone has in the structure of the language may determine the phoneme to which it belongs. The importance of the general structure of the language in making such phonemic distinctions has been called *pattern pressure.*[2]

---

[1] This is almost exactly the situation which exists for the most part in the Quechua language of South America.

[2] This is the most complicated principle of phonemic procedures. Only an extensive analysis of the many factors involved makes it possible to apply the principle correctly. There is no room here for such a consideration. See Dr. Pike's book.

7.1.2 The Symbols Used in a Phonemic Alphabet

The symbols used in a phonemic alphabet may best be discussed under the headings of (1) segmental phonemes (the consonants and vowels), (2) the suprasegmental or prosodic phonemes (indications of length, tone, and stress), and (3) the junctures (means of indicating significant points of combination within words and between words).

7.1.2.1 Segmental Phonemes

The segmental phonemes (the consonants and vowels) of a language are usually represented by roman letters and with values assigned to each more or less in accordance with the usage of the trade language of the area. It is not necessary by any means to use the roman alphabet. If circumstances dictate another usage, it may prove important to use some modification of the symbols of the trade language, e.g. Russian, Amharic, Thai, Hindi, etc. The use of the roman alphabet is, however, spreading, and it is much easier to obtain materials printed in the roman alphabet than in almost any other, unless such material is to be printed in the country in which another alphabet is in use. In any case, one should use an alphabet and not an orthography which has a special symbol for each syllable—as Japanese, Cree, and Cherokee, for example.

In using the roman alphabet one often finds that there are not enough correspondences. That is to say, the native language has more phonemes (or entirely different ones) than can be easily represented by the common roman letters. In such an instance, one may choose to employ diacritical marks which may be written above or after the letter. For example, instead of using some strange-looking p for a glottalized p in order to contrast it with an unglottalized one,[1] the translator may use p alone for the unglottalized phoneme and p' (p plus the single apostrophe) for the glottalized p phoneme.

On the other hand, it may not be possible to employ diacritical marks which may be printed after the symbol. Some diacritical marks are combined with the basic form of the symbol, for example š, for the English *sh*. For the most part, translators draw these

---

[1] Glottalization means the simultaneous closing of the glottis. The type of release gives a popping-like sound to the phoneme.

extra symbols from the International Phonetic System; the Americanist Symbols, used by American scholars in the writing of Indian languages; and the symbols recommended by the International Institute of African Languages and Cultures. One should not, however, use a complicated form of a symbol if it is possible to use a simple one. For example, a language may have the phoneme *č* (the sound of the initial and final affricatives in English *church*) and the phoneme *ǰ* (the sound of the initial and final affricatives in English *judge*). There would be no point in using the comparatively rare symbols *č* and *ǰ*, if one could use the simple forms *c* and *j*. This can be done if there is no other use made of the symbols *c* and *j*. The symbols should be the simplest that one can use. There are, however, some practical factors which must be considered, and these will be discussed in the next principal section.

It has been found valuable in some instances to eliminate the use of capital letters in the language. This may seem rather strange on first thought, for we are so used to capitals. But it should be noted that we do not speak with capital letters. When we pronounce divine names, we do not normally change the phonemic character of the consonants and vowels. If we get along perfectly well without such distinctions in speech, we can also do so in the written form of the language. Capital letters usually require a considerable amount of time to teach and always seem to present more or less difficulty. The capital forms of several letters of the roman alphabet are quite different from the small forms, e.g. *G* vs. *g*, *B* vs. *b*, *R* vs. *r*, *Q* vs. *q*, *E* vs. *e*, *A* vs. *a*, *D* vs. *d*, and *H* vs. *h*. There are other sets of symbols which exhibit minor differences.

It has been a general practice, however, to capitalize (1) the first letter of each verse, (2) the first letter of each sentence, (3) the first letter (all of the letters in some instances) of names of Deity, (4) the first letter of proper names, and (5) the beginning of direct discourse. Even though people are greatly helped in learning to read if they do not have to master the capital letters at the very start, the pressure of the usage of the trade language and the convenience of indicating proper names by a special type of symbol usually weight the evidence in favor of the use of capital letters. It is quite unwise to adopt an arbitrary position in regard to such matters. Careful attention must be given to the particular circumstances in each situation.

7.1.2.2   PROSODIC PHONEMES

The prosodic phonemes include (1) stress, (2) length, and
(3) tone. There are several ways to indicate these features:

7.1.2.2.1   INDICATION OF STRESS

Stress is indicated either by an accent mark over the vowel of a
word, e.g. *tolúka*, or by an upright bar (a single quotation mark in
typing) preceding the syllable, e.g. *to'luka*. The use of the bar
before the consonant is important in some languages where it is
necessary to indicate the point of onset of the stress; whether, for
example, in the word *tikraka* the stress is *ti'kraka* or *tik'raka*. If
such a difference exists in a language, the use of an accent mark
over the vowel would not indicate this important syllabic feature.

7.1.2.2.2   INDICATION OF LENGTH

There are three principal ways of indicating phonemic length.
One of these is to double the vowel. For example, long *a* may be
written as *aa*. This is the regular usage in Finnish and several other
languages. In a language where there are no ambiguities that result
from such doubling of vowels, this usage has been found very
valuable. There is something about seeing the vowel written twice
which is psychologically important to the factor of duration.
However, in many instances the phonological pattern will not permit this doubling of the vowel. In the Totonac language the doubling of the vowel produces ambiguity, while in the Eastern Aztec,
a contiguous language, it works very well. Where the vowel cannot
be doubled, one may place a single raised dot or colon following the
vowel, e.g. *a·* or *a:*, as in *kuma·ta* or *kuma:ta*. The single raised dot
has seemed preferable to the colon. Perhaps even better than the
use of dots is the use of a macron (a bar) over the vowel, e.g. *ā*.
Regardless of the system, one should always employ the same device to indicate length which affects the meaning of words. A long *a*
should not occur with a macron and a long *o* with a dot or accent
mark, as is done in some 'homemade' orthographies.

7.1.2.2.3   INDICATION OF TONE

If a language employs tonal differences to distinguish between
words, these differences should be marked throughout the translation. Many translators through lack of training or unwillingness

to pay attention to certain features of the language have omitted writing tone. In some languages this may be done without too disastrous results, for example, in some of the Bantu languages.[1] With the Navaho language of the southwestern part of the United States this is not possible. It is true that some natives have learned to read Navaho by means of a rather inadequate method formerly employed by Protestant missionaries. Many readers had continual difficulty and were observed repeating words several times. They would pronounce all the consonants and vowels, but could not identify words because they had not pronounced the words with the correct tonal pattern. By means of a more scientific system of writing Navaho, in which the tones and vowel lengths as well as some other previously neglected items are indicated, more people were reported by the Federal Government to have learned to read in a few months than had learned previously during a period of several years. In the case of several of the languages of Mexico, it has been absolutely necessary to indicate the tone. Omission of the significant tone on words is as incorrect as leaving out certain vowels and consonants.

In some instances translators have thought it was sufficient to put the tone marks only on words that would otherwise be ambiguous. This is usually quite inadequate. If tonal features are used to distinguish between words, they should be indicated wherever they occur. There is no more justification for omitting the tones except in minimally different words (words that differ only because of a tonal difference) than for omitting the vowels except in minimally different words. If a feature of stress, length, or tone is important, that is to say, if it makes a difference in meaning, *it should be indicated.*

The differences in the methods of indicating tone are dependent to a considerable extent on the type of tonal language under consideration. The two types are principally (1) register tone languages and (2) contour tone languages.[2]

7.1.2.2.3.1 REGISTER TONE LANGUAGES

Register tone languages are those in which the tones may be described in terms of the end points of the tone. Such languages

---

[1]In Africa practically all the languages south of the Sahara are tonal. The failure to analyze these tonal languages correctly has been unfortunate.

[2]See Kenneth L. Pike, *Tone Languages.*

have a basic stair-step pattern. Tones may be on these various steps or may be glides from one of these step levels to another. Of course, the tonal elevation of the steps changes with the general height of the voice. The thing that counts is the relatively different levels of the steps (the end points). Many languages of Africa and the Americas are register tone languages.

Register tone languages have been found with two, three, or four steps. The Navaho language is a two-register language; Mixteco and some dialects of Zapoteco are three-register languages; the Mazatec dialect of Huautla de Jiménez in Oaxaca, Mexico is a four-register language. The tones on vowels (in some languages tone phonemes occur on consonants also) may be on a single register, or step, or they may constitute a glide from one of these registers to the other. It is usually (but not always) found that the glides from one register to another occur on long vowels or diph-thongs.

In writing a register tone language one may use the following signs: *á* for a high tone and *à* for a low tone. If it is necessary to distinguish a third tone, one may use *ā* for the third tone. A fourth tone may be marked as *ȧ*. Note, however, that in any case one of the tones may be left unmarked. Hence, in Navaho, which has two registers, it is only necessary to mark the high register. The low register is distinctive because it is unmarked.

Sometimes it is necessary to mark glides on a single short vowel. This may be done by composite tone marks: e.g. *â,* high to low; *ǎ,* mid to low; *a̋,* mid to high, etc. Combinations with an upright mark may also be used, e.g. *a̗,* mid to high; *a̖* high to mid, but these markings with an upright bar have been found difficult to use. If glides only occur on long vowels and these long vowels may be written as two vowels, e.g. *aa,* instead of *a·* or *ā,* then the individual tone of each part of the long vowel may be indicated easily, e.g. *àá,* low to high glide. Note that it is quite difficult to employ complex glide marks over a vowel which has a macron, e.g. *ǟ.* Such a set of symbols would have to be cast especially for the language, for this is not a standard form.

7.1.2.2.3.2   CONTOUR TONE LANGUAGES

Contour tone languages are like sections of a roller-coaster. The principal characteristics are the direction and extent of the glide or contour, not so much where the glide begins and to what point it rises or falls, but that it goes in a certain direction and extends over a certain time. The speaker is not so concerned with where a glide starts or stops as with the direction which the glide takes, how steep it is, and how long it continues. The analysis of most of the tonal languages of the Orient would indicate that they are contour tone languages.

Many different devices have been used to mark the different contour tones of a language. In some instances periods (on the line and raised), commas, semicolons, and colons have been used before or after the syllable to indicate the tone of the syllable. This has sometimes proved quite effective and satisfactory. Some translators have numbered the tones 1, 2, 3, 4, etc., with small numerals preceding each syllable. The more common device is to use certain contour symbols, e.g. *á* for a rising glide, *à* for a falling one, *â* for a rising-falling tone and *ã* for a rising-falling-rising tone. The problem is essentially not so much a matter of the particular symbol but the phonemic accuracy of the system (the one-to-one correspondences) and the consistency with which the symbols are employed.

7.1.2.2.4 THE INDICATION OF THE JUNCTURES

When (1) parts of words are put together to form words, or (2) words are put together into phrases, or (3) phrases into sentences, or (4) sentences, combined in any discourse, there are certain significant features about the ways in which these units are combined. The points of combination are conveniently called *junctures*. The junctures between words are normally written with an open space. The important junctures between phrases are indicated by commas, semicolons, and colons. The junctures between sentences are indicated by periods and by capitalization of the first letter of the next word. These types of junctures between words are very well known to us. The junctures within words (so-called internal junctures) are not so well understood. In English we indicate some internal junctures by hyphens, but this is not carried out consistently in the conventional orthography. If we wrote English scientifically (and if we did, it would be much easier read), then we would want to indicate the difference between *nitrate* and *nightrate* (as for telegrams), for otherwise these two words would appear identical, as they have exactly the same consonants and vowels. What we must indicate in the orthography is that in *nitrate* the second syllable begins with the medial *t*, but in *nightrate* the second syllable begins with the *r*. The best way to indicate this is by using a hyphen. The sound sequence at the juncture of *night* and *rate* in *nightrate* is almost identically the same as that which may occur between words. Hence, when there is a so-called external juncture (a combination of phonemes that usually occurs between words) occurring within a word, then this external combination may be indicated by a hyphen.[1]

One must be careful that one's use of the hyphen corresponds to the regular word-constructing pattern of the language. In one recent translation from Africa the translator combined every phrase with hyphens which corresponded to a single word in English. For example, a "priest" was translated as a 'man-who-offers-sacrifice.' The construction was simply a phrase in the native language and should be written as such. There was no point in combining the phrase into one word by putting hyphens between all the parts; but, as a syntactic phrase, formal features (such as verb tenses) must be adjusted to the context.

7.1.3   Practical Adaptations
                of the Scientific Alphabet

When once the translator has made a scientific analysis of the language and has reached a satisfactory one-to-one correspondence between the symbols and the psychologically significant sound units, it is sometimes necessary because of practical circumstances to make certain modifications of the scientific alphabet. These problems will be discussed under (1) the practical considerations which necessitate changes in the alphabet and (2) the types of adaptations which may be made.

7.1.3.1   Practical Considerations in Making
                Changes in a Scientific Alphabet

There are many factors which may force certain changes in a completely scientific alphabet. Such factors may not be overlooked or brushed aside, for often the entire success of any reading campaign is dependent upon them. Even though the translator may be absolutely sure of the greater value and practicality of the scientific alphabet, he may find that he must modify it if he is to meet certain situations. His ultimate purpose is primarily to reach the

---

[1]For a more detailed analysis of juncture problems, see Eugene A. Nida, *Morphology*.

native people with the message of the Bible, not the championing of linguistic methods for their own intrinsic worth. Any adaptations should be made exclusively on the basis of the possible use of the orthography by the greatest number of people.

The factors which often dictate changes are the following: (1) available type and printing facilities, (2) present orthographic usage in the native language, (3) usage in the trade language, (4) future linguistic developments, (5) attitude of the governmental and educational authorities, (6) use in related dialects, and (7) attitudes of other missionaries and translators. The relative importance of these factors cannot be determined in advance for any situation. The translator must use his own judgment. On the other hand, he should be warned against making concessions in the name of practicality and because something may seem immediately expedient, when in the long run such changes may be costly in terms of the much greater difficulty in teaching people to read.

7.1.3.1.1 AVAILABLE TYPE AND PRINTING FACILITIES

If the translation is to be published in the United States, almost any kind of type can be secured if one is willing to pay the rather considerable prices. Very rare symbols often have to be specially cast. One should not have to depend on doing all printing in the United States. The Bible should be only a part of the literature of a people. An enlarging literature program will call for Sunday-school materials, tracts, Bible stories, and devotional books. One will want to adopt those forms of the letters which are most likely to be found in or available for local print shops. However, it would prove far cheaper to invest in some special fonts of type than to destroy the greater usability of an orthography because of too many accommodations to local facilities.

Certain features of printing should be noted:

1 It is very difficult to print underlined letters. (Underlining on the typewriter means italics in printing.)

2 All superimposed diacritical marks are cast with the letter and require special fonts. If one uses an accent mark such as ', it will be necessary to have special letters for all the vowels with such an accent mark.

3 The use of boldface type (thick, heavy type) vs. normal type in order to distinguish between phonemes is awkward to print,

very difficult to write and hard to read. This should not be used. The difference in the phonemes should depend upon the outline of the symbol, not the light or heavy quality.

4 The use of capitals (usually small ones) vs. small letters in order to distinguish phonemes is often quite confusing if the translation employs regular capital letters for titles, proper names, beginning of verses, etc.

5 Italics (underlined in typing) vs. regular letters are often an advantageous distinction, but should not be used too much.

7.1.3.1.2   PRESENT USAGE IN THE LANGUAGE

It is unfortunate that in many languages a very inadequate orthography has been employed for some time. The traditional prestige of such an orthography, plus the antipathy of the present readers to any change, makes it almost impossible to inaugurate any type of orthographic reform. For years such a reform has been advocated for English, but English-speaking people continue to subject their children to the arduous process of mastering an unscientific orthography, even though the results are often far from satisfactory. The failure of many students to attain fluency in reading after a considerable length of time is rather pointed evidence of the difficulties encountered in an unscientific orthography.

It should be remembered that any orthography may be taught, provided there is enough social pressure to learn such an orthography. Even Chinese has been taught and learned for many centuries, but the tragic waste of human energy that could better be expended in learning something more useful than an arbitrary orthography is seldom seriously considered by those who have once mastered, however imperfectly, the traditional forms. The strength of traditionalism seems never to be stronger than in language and religion. An alphabet becomes a cultural fetish to many people, and the translator is sometimes quite powerless to withstand successfully the pressure of such traditionalism. If the traditionalism is indigenous, that is to say, is a part of the native life, then the translator must usually depend upon the strength of this native cultural pressure to create readers for the translation. If, however, it is only the manufacture of a few years, the translator may find that other missionaries are the real champions of the orthography, not the natives. He must be careful not to capitulate to forces which would ultimately destroy the usefulness of the translation; but in withstanding such pressure, he must be wise as a serpent and harmless as a dove.

7.1.3.1.3 ORTHOGRAPHIC USAGE OF THE TRADE LANGUAGE

The orthographic usage of the trade language usually has considerable prestige among the native people. This is because the leaders of any group who have become educated have normally learned the orthography of the trade language. The usage of the culturally and politically dominant group is interpreted as being superior, regardless of its intrinsic merits. A power maintained by the possession of machine guns may be an unanswerable force in giving a certain usage, however unscientific, the prestige of correctness.

The reactions of the few educated natives to the new orthography are important. If they snub it as culturally inferior, or even 'unscientific,' because it does not agree with their own learning, the translator may find a considerable problem on his hands. The governmental attitude is often closely related to the reactions of the educated natives. The translator may find himself caught on the horns of a dilemma from which few people have been able to escape uninjured.

7.1.3.1.4 FUTURE LINGUISTIC DEVELOPMENTS

It is seldom profitable to act in the capacity of a prophet, and a linguistic prophet who prophesies scientific advance in linguistic usage is too frequently disappointed by the successes of traditionalism. However, in many countries, particularly of Latin America, there are groups of scholars who are working more and more toward completely phonemic alphabets. If there is a progressive linguistic element within a country, and if this element is working for scientific alphabets, it is important for the translator to make use of this potentially important contribution of scientists. The forces of religion are so often traditional and reactionary that it is unfortunate for the translator to add to any prejudice against the Bible by using a traditional and unscientific orthography, which may be interpreted as typical of the unprogressiveness of clericalism. The translator will often find it valuable to be in the forefront of linguistic usage rather than to lag behind, for in the latter case he may be accused by progressive elements of sabotaging the improved scientific procedures.

7.1.3.1.5 THE ATTITUDE OF GOVERNMENTAL AND EDUCATIONAL AUTHORITIES

It is of utmost importance to obtain the friendly cooperation and assistance of the governmental and educational authorities. A reading campaign of any great extent is usually beyond the resources in money and personnel of any one mission or group of missions. The most effective approach is through the combined efforts of the government and education offices. Moreover, it is usually only by permission of the government authorities that one is permitted to continue with one's work, and the continuity of any translation program is one which involves many years.

It is important to be able to demonstrate, at least with a limited group, the advisability of any orthography. One should prove by carefully conducted tests (1) that those who learn to read by means of scientific orthography can learn much faster and (2) that, if books are published as diglots, the translator can succeed in teaching the national or the trade language much more rapidly than by the more customary methods. Some translators have championed the use of the native languages and in so doing have opposed the government's insistence upon the use of the national language in the area. Had such translators presented a plan by which they could teach the national language (1) by employing the native language as the first basis of teaching people to read and (2) by using diglot literature, then both the translators and the governmental authorities would probably have been satisfied.

One must sometimes go a long way in accommodating an orthography to meet official demands, but the trained linguist is frequently able to win the confidence of officials and hence is rarely obliged to make so many concessions. He can usually find a compromise position which will make it possible to teach the natives to read their own language in an alphabet which is almost phonemic.

7.1.3.1.6 THE USE OF AN ORTHOGRAPHY IN RELATED DIALECTS

The use of an orthography in related dialects must be considered in judging the practical accommodations which may be made in an alphabet. Let us suppose that one dialect has two series of stop consonants. One of these series, including p, t, and k, is aspirated. The other series is unaspirated. This series that is unaspirated often sounds like b, d, and g in English. It would be possible in such a dialect to indicate the aspirated series as p, t, and k, and the unaspirated series as b, d, and g. However, let us assume that in another closely related dialect there is only one series of stop consonants. In other words, there is no difference between a p and a b, but all bilabial stops are voiceless and unaspirated. In words where the first dialect had p or b, this next dialect would have only one bilabial sound rather half-way between the two sounds of the first dialect. The people who speak the second dialect would have to learn that the signs p and b stand for the same sound in their dialect. Similarly t and d, and k and g, would be identical. It might prove easier, however, if in the first language the aspirated series of stop consonants were written ph, th, kh, and the unaspirated series written as p, t, and k. Those in the second dialect could then be told simply to ignore the h symbol. This would make it somewhat easier for both dialects. It would be easier in the first dialect to learn the single value of the h rather than learn the three other symbols, b, d, and g. At any rate, one should always be on the lookout for dialect differences in choosing a practical alphabet.

7.1.3.1.7   ATTITUDES OF OTHER MISSIONARIES AND TRANSLATORS

Without doubt some of the most tangled controversies that have ever arisen on the mission field have centered about orthographic problems. No topic can produce more heated arguments with less scientific basis than orthographic and linguistic matters. Such arguments frequently do not treat the facts of a language in a very objective manner. People rarely recognize that all symbolism is arbitrary and that no linguistic category is completely logical; in fact, the average one is usually quite illogical. When we apply our so-called logical arguments, which are usually based on prejudices of traditionalism, to language problems, which are never completely logical, then we are hopelessly entangled. We seldom see that we are arguing in circles, though usually we suspect our opponents of doing so. It is quite difficult for us to see that no aspect of any people's culture is completely 'logical.' In the study of culture one cannot say that one plus one equals two. There are no features of culture that can be reduced to such simple mathematical units. All features are extremely complex. Accordingly, until we have had some sort of scientific conditioning to linguistics and anthropology in general, it is best to avoid linguistic arguments.

The best approach for the translator is to demonstrate the validity of his methodology. The phonemic alphabet may be tested. However, in testing the value of one orthography over another, one must set up a test in which two groups of a similar number of people with similar backgrounds and mental ability are given similar instruction in the two orthographies. One must be careful to make such a test as fair and objective as possible. The validity of a one-to-one correspondence should soon produce results which will convince those who are interested in arriving at impartial conclusions.

7.1.3.2   TYPES OF POSSIBLE MODIFICATIONS OF A SCIENTIFIC ALPHABET

There are two principal types of modifications which are made in the scientific alphabet in order to make it suit certain pressure groups or practical circumstances. These include (1) the use of digraphs and (2) the indication of conditioned variants.

7.1.3.2.1   THE USE OF DIGRAPHS

A digraph is a combination of two letters to indicate a single phoneme, e.g. *ch* in English and Spanish. A trigraph is a combination of three letters to indicate a single phoneme.

The symbols that go to make up some digraphs or trigraphs often show very little or no relationship to the use of the same symbol when it occurs alone. For example, the *ch* in English is made up of two symbols which, when they occur alone, usually have little or no resemblance to the *č* (ch) phoneme. The *c* does stand for a sibilant sound in some instances, e.g. *city*. The *ch* is an affricative with a sibilant off-glide, but this is the only point of comparison. Apart, then, from this very faint resemblance, the *ch* digraph is made up of parts which do not correspond to the phones which go together to make up the affricative *č* phoneme. The *gh* digraph in *rough* is another example. There is no resemblance between the *gh* digraph and the *f* phoneme which ends the word *rough*, except that both *f* and *h* are usually symbols for voiceless continuants. The use of *ll* in Welsh to indicate the voiceless *l* phoneme is a type of digraph, but one which bears at least some resemblance to the usage of the constituent members of the digraph when they are used alone.

In some instances, there is a definite agreement between the members of a digraph and the constituent phones of a complex phoneme. For example, in some languages a dental affricative which sounds like English *ts* in *rats* may actually have the function of only one phoneme. Technically it should be written with a single symbol. The symbols *c* and *ȼ* are sometimes used for this. On the other hand, some translators have found it necessary, because of various circumstances, to employ a digraph *ts* for this complex phoneme. They have done the same with such other sounds as *dz*, *tš*, and *dž*. Complex phonemes which are composed of nasal continuants plus stop consonants, e.g. *mb*, *nd*, and *ŋg*, are often written as digraphs instead of as one symbol. Some translators have thought that it was easier to teach people to read such combinations than to teach separate symbols, e.g. small capitals such as B, D, and G. However, no comprehensive tests of this problem have been conducted.

In some few instances translators have used one sign to represent two phonemes in the native language. For example, they have adopted some sign such as *x* to stand for *k* and *s* as in English. This is not the best practice. One should use one symbol for each phoneme. There are some exceptions to this rule in actual practice. For example, in some languages the sound which is much like English *š* (written *sh*) is phonemically a combination of *s* plus *y*. That is to say, the *š* sound functions exactly like a combination of *s* and *y*, and technically it is this. On the other hand, some translators have preferred to write this single phone with one symbol rather than two. The value of one usage as over against the other should be tested thoroughly, but as yet this type of investigation has not been carried out fully.

7.1.3.2.2 THE INDICATION OF CONDITIONED VARIANTS

When the trade language makes a difference in the indication of certain sounds, which are, however, only conditioned variants in the native language, there is a tendency to force the pattern of the trade language upon the native language. For example, in the Quechua language of South America there are basically only three vowel phonemes, *i*, *a*, and *u*. However, *i* and *u* in combination with certain back consonants are changed to *e* and *o* respectively.

This is the conditioned variation which was mentioned on p. 104. This gives the Quechua language five rather distinctly different vowel sounds, and these correspond phonetically to the five Spanish vowel phonemes, *i, e, a, o,* and *u.* Since there are some Spanish words which have been borrowed into a small part of the Quechua-speaking area with the Spanish vowel qualities preserved, this has modified the pattern of the Quechua in this area. Those Quechua-speaking people who have learned to read Spanish in the area mentioned are acquainted with the five vowel symbols of Spanish. This knowledge of the Spanish orthography influences their interpretation of the automatic conditioning of the Quechua. Translators have considered it necessary to write five vowels in Quechua, even though for most of the Quechua language area it would be necessary to write only the three. However, because of the traditional methods of writing Quechua, the ardent supporters of the five vowel system, and the possible future spread of Spanish influence, the translators have considered it advisable to employ the five vowel symbols even in certain of the dialects where the three vowel symbols would be technically preferable.

The influence of the trade language often upsets the consonant pattern of the language. For example, in the Zoque language of Mexico there is only one basic series of stops. These are usually voiceless, but after nasal continuants they are automatically voiced. For example, *p, t,* and *k* become automatically *b, d,* and *g* in the combinations with *m, n,* and *ŋ* respectively. If it were not for the Spanish words coming into Zoque, it would not be necessary to indicate this change from voiceless to voiced form of the consonant, for the change is automatically conditioned. There are, however, some Spanish loan words which do not preserve this automatic-conditioned pattern, e.g. Spanish *cuando* 'when' and *cuento* 'story.' In these two words there is a contrast between *nd* and *nt.* There are other Spanish words which violate the regular pattern, and the chances are that this will be an ever-increasing situation. Accordingly, some consideration must be given to these problems created by the effect of the trade language, particularly when those who represent the trade language are usually the more dominant political and commercial group. No one can legislate for such situations in advance. Each one must be examined on the basis of its own merits. The decision should be made in terms of the greatest effectiveness of the orthography. However, one special note of warning should be given. The translator should at all times bear in mind the needs of the monolingual person, for whom the translation should be principally designed. The bilingual is able to use the translation in the trade language. The monolingual should be given the fullest consideration in any such orthographic problems.

7.2 The Writing of Word Units

The problems involving the writing of word units are of four types. The first of these has been discussed, namely, the symbolization of the phonemes. The second involves the length of word units. The third type involves alternate forms of words or parts of words. The fourth type includes certain orthographic devices of morphophonemic symbols and reconstructions.

7.2.1 The Length of Words

To determine what unit in a continuous stream of speech is to be considered as a word and written as such is often quite difficult. The procedures for solving such problems are usually quite complicated.[1] One cannot write the word units consistently without a thorough scientific analysis. One thing that the translator must not do is to form his opinions of how long a word should be before examining the structure of the language in question. Furthermore, he cannot tell what should be written as one word in a foreign language simply by comparing the usage in his own language. In Africa many missionaries have written Bantu in the so-called disjunctive manner, following the parallels of English or some other European language. Frequently the results have been unfortunate, for the units that have been written as separate words have absolutely no separate significance. They may not occur independently. To divide up Bantu words as many translators do is just as meaningless as to divide up an English word *ungentlemanliness* as *un gentle man li ness* or to write Spanish *comprábamos* as *comprá ba mos* because we may translate this word in English by three words 'we were buying.' It has been a great mistake in writing the Bantu languages to adhere to the usual disjunctive method of writing.

On the other hand, in some Indian languages of this hemisphere there has in some instances been a tendency to write too many separate words together as an individual word. The problem is not, however, basically one of the length of the words. If people

---

[1]See Eugene A. Nida, *Morphology*.

speak by means of large synthetically combined units, they can read by means of these. The writing must be based upon the spoken form. Any attempt to rearrange the language for the sake of writing it is purely artificial and only adds to the difficulty which the reader will have.

7.2.2 ALTERNATE FORMS OF WORDS

In any language there are words which occur in more than one form. These alternations are of three basic types. The first type represents differences between dialects. The second type shows differences within the same dialect, not conditioned by the speed of the utterance. The third includes differences which are usually conditioned by the speed of the utterance.

7.2.2.1 DIALECT DIFFERENCES

The differences of dialect must be treated as dialect problems. These have been considered to some extent on p. 36 ff. The best procedure to follow is that which employs those words and forms of words which have the widest usage in the language.

7.2.2.2 ALTERNATES NOT DUE TO THE SPEED OF UTTERANCE

The alternate forms which occur within the same dialect and are not conditioned by the speed of utterance may be illustrated by the alternate pronunciation in English of the verb *transfer*. The verb is now found to be accented either on the first or the second syllable. Historically, the verb was accented on the second syllable and the noun derivative on the first syllable. But on the basis of the pattern for deriving verbs from nouns without change of form, a new verb has been formed from the noun *transfer*. Now we have two pronunciations of the verb. In a scientific writing of English we would want to indicate the position of the stress. Anyone who has had to learn English as a foreign language will appreciate the value of such an indication, and those learning to read English would be immeasurably helped. In writing the accent, we would have to decide whether we would place the stress on the first or the second syllable of the word. The first inclination in finding a solution for such a problem is to follow the so-called historically correct form. But this is no criterion for writing a living language. What is historically the correct form may not be the more common form in usage. Historically *It am I* was correct in English, but this is no longer used. The decision as to form to be employed must be based upon the actual usage of the people. In order to determine how we would write the stress on *transfer*, we would have to find out the relative frequency of occurrence of the two different forms.

In a language such as English it might be possible to determine the so-called historically correct form (by which we mean that form which was formerly used), but for most aboriginal languages there would be absolutely no way of determining what the former usage was, and what is more, it is not important. A descriptive analysis of a language is an analysis of the language of today, not of yesterday. The use of the language of today will be the most effective means of reaching the people of today. For example, the translator may find that the word *traskat* means 'peace' and that it comes from the elements *trasa* 'to sit down' and *kat* 'heart.' He may suspect that historically this combination was *trasakat*, but that it has changed to *traskat*. However, if the native speakers say *traskat*, he must employ the form that people actually speak. Furthermore, he should not put in an apostrophe to indicate that a vowel may have been lost. If the phoneme is not pronounced, it is absent; that is all. There is little advantage in indicating that it was ever there. Despite the usage in English and some European languages, one should not clutter up a manuscript with apostrophes to indicate possible or actual omissions of phonemes. These are not indicated in speaking, and they should not be indicated in writing. There is no need of marking the exit of a phoneme by hanging up its 'hat' throughout the orthography. If the phoneme has gone, by which we mean that the phoneme is not actually pronounced, the hat should be thrown out too.

7.2.2.3 ALTERNATES DUE TO THE SPEED OF UTTERANCE

All languages have different forms of words, depending upon the speed of utterance. For example, in English we may say *did you* as [ˈdid yuw], but more often in fast speech and sometimes in comparatively slow speech we say [ˈdijə]. In the writer's own speech there are five different alternate forms of the first syllable of the word *believe*. In the first form, the first syllable has the same vowel as the vowel phoneme of *leave*. In this case the two syllables of the word *believe* have the same vowel phonemes. The second form is pronounced with the vowel of the first syllable like the vowel of English *bit*. The third form is pronounced with the vowel of the first syllable like the vowel of *bet*, the fourth form like the vowel of *but*, and the fifth form has no vowel at all in the first syllable. This last form is quite common in fast speech. The occurrence of any one of these five forms is directly dependent upon the speed of utterance. They occur in successively faster speech situations in the order in which they are here listed.

Translators who are appalled and confused by the alternate forms of words in an aboriginal language do not have to look far to see many parallels in English. The alternate forms of the so-called auxiliary verbs *will, would, can, could, shall,* and *should* are quite illustrative of alternates. But this does not answer the problem. Nor is it possible to give a hard and fast answer to all such problems. The best approach, however, is to write those forms which occur most frequently in the moderate speech, or perhaps moderate-to-slow speech. There are three fundamental reasons for this. (1) One who is learning to read will be reading slowly, and he should have the advantage of forms which are approximately at the speed which he will be using. (2) The translation will often be used for reading aloud in public worship. The forms which approximate such moderate speed will be most easily read. (3) The changes from the slow forms to the fast forms of speech are usually automatically conditioned. A person with the fuller form may automatically shift into the faster form with an increase of speed, but the reverse process is somewhat more difficult. For example, in the contraction *he's* we would not know before reading further whether this stood for (1) *he has* in *he's been helping me* or (2) *he is* in *he's doing well*. However, knowing the fuller form, which may also occur in moderate and sometimes comparatively fast speech, one can shift to the alternate reduced form much more readily. The translator is not to interpret this, however, as justifying artificial forms which are never or only very rarely used in modern speech. One must not attempt to lean too far forward or backwards. Ultra-conservativeness is much more likely to be injurious to the translation than ultra-progressiveness.

7.2.3   ARTIFICIAL ORTHOGRAPHIC FORMS OF WRITING

Morphophonemic writing and reconstructions of historical and comparative forms are from the phonemic standpoint artificial forms of writing. They sometimes have their strong adherents, so they should be considered briefly.

7.2.3.1 MORPHOPHONEMIC WRITING[1]

In making the grammatical analysis of a language one may often employ certain types of symbols to mark arbitrary classes of forms. This is called morphophonemic writing. For example, in English there are certain words, e.g. *wife*, *knife*, and *life*, which change the *f* to *v* before adding the plural suffix. Some other words, e.g. *fife*, *cuff*, and *bluff*, do not so change. Descriptive linguists have often found it valuable in a grammar to indicate the differences in such classes by writing one class of words with a capital letter, e.g. a final F for the first set of words and the other class with a small letter. This distinction is, however, only a part of the technical grammatical description and is only a symbolic method of indicating arbitrary classes of forms. In no case should one write morphophonemically in a translation.

7.2.3.2 COMPARATIVE AND HISTORICAL RECONSTRUCTIONS

By comparing different languages and dialects, one may sometimes arrive at a formula which may approximate what people originally said in a prior state of the language before the different dialects became differentiated. By comparing various known stages of the history of a language (such data is, however, very rarely available for aboriginal languages), one may reconstruct approximations of even earlier stages of a language. Some translators have thought that they could perhaps reconstruct from several dialects a common form of the language which would be considered historically correct. They have also supposed that by some means or other they could teach this form of the language to the people. Such attempts in almost all instances have either not gone beyond the stage of contemplation or have resulted in rather complete confusion. Only a person with a very comprehensive knowledge of historical and comparative techniques should ever undertake such a task. Even then the value of such work would be questionable, for the extra effort necessary to teach people to read such an artificial form of the language would not be compensated for by the advantage that a greater number of people might use it.

---

[1]See Eugene A. Nida, *Morphology*.

7.3   PUNCTUATION

The punctuation employed in a translation should represent the syntactic structure of the native language, not the syntactic structure of the text language. In no case can one employ the punctuation of the text language, phrase for phrase and sentence for sentence, for no two languages in the world will have the same types of syntactic structure.

In most instances it is necessary to simplify the complex sentence structure of the Greek text. The punctuation will accordingly be changed, for the punctuation is a set of symbols employed to indicate the extent and relationship of certain phrases and clauses.

It should be a basic principle that the simpler the punctuation one may employ the better it is, if it represents the sentence structure of the native language. Regardless of anything else, such punctuation should be consistently used. In keeping, therefore, with the principles of simplicity and consistency, one will find useful the following suggestions as to the use of various punctuation marks:

1 THE PERIOD

This should be used at the end of every complete sentence. It will probably occur more frequently than in the text language, for many of the longer sentences of the text language must be broken up into shorter sentences.

2 THE COMMA

The comma should be used to mark (1) pauses or (2) ends of certain intonation patterns which are employed to indicate the length of phrases and clauses within the sentence. Note that commas are to mark the phonologically significant units in the native language. If, for example, there is a pause in the native language to set off certain types of apposition, then the commas may be used to mark this pause, but if no pause occurs, the comma should not be used merely because it occurs in English.

3 QUESTION MARKS

The question mark should be used when and if it is necessary. If the language indicates questions by a special order of words or by some particles in the sentence, then it is not necessary to employ a question mark. If, however, the mark of a question is a particular intonation of the sentence, then the question mark should be used. If there are different types of intonations, depending upon whether the question is (1) a rhetorical one (not expecting an answer), (2) one implying a positive answer, or (3) one implying a negative answer, the translator may want to employ more than one kind of question mark if the only means of indicating such differences is by different intonations of the voice. One form of the question mark may be the same as in English, another may be written upside down, and another backwards. These may be placed either at the beginning or the end of the sentence (or both, as in Spanish), depending upon that part of the sentence which has the distinctive intonation. One must not limit himself to use of the traditional punctuation marks if in the native language there is something important to be indicated which does not correspond to the modern European language usage.

4 THE SEMICOLON

The frequency of use of the semicolon depends entirely upon the structure of the language. If two clauses, which are independent in form, are customarily combined in a paratactic manner, e.g. the English sentence *It's very late; I must go*, then one will have considerable use for the semicolon. If such independent clauses are not combined but each ends as a full sentence, then one will employ a period between such clauses.

5 THE COLON

The colon may be conveniently used to introduce direct quotations if quotation marks are not employed. There is little point in using the colon with the frequency and manner in which it is employed, for example, in the AV and the Spanish de Valera Version. It should be replaced, except where introducing direct quotations, by a comma or a semicolon.

6 QUOTATION MARKS

Quotation marks are sometimes a distinct advantage. They are used in some modern editions of the Bible and with very good effect. If, however, the native language has special particles or words to introduce or close a direct quotation, these should be used. In such a case the quotation marks are unnecessary. The use of quotation marks involves several acute problems of determining the limits of quoted material, e.g. John 3: 16–21.   The use of quotation marks borders dangerously on interpretation in some contexts.

7 THE DASH

To indicate a break in the syntactic structure, as for example that which occurs rather often in the Pauline Epistles, one may employ the dash to very good advantage.

Basic to the use of any system of punctuation in any language is the complete understanding of the syntactic system of the language. The punctuation must be designed to elucidate the native text, not to represent the propensities of Greek grammar.

Chapter 8

PRINCIPLES OF EQUIVALENCE

THE basic principles of translation have already been discussed in Chapter 1. The principles of equivalence have also been introduced and certain types of solutions have been suggested. This chapter is an attempt to formulate more fully these principles by an examination of certain significant problems and a brief classification of lexical problems.

8.1   FORMULATION OF PRINCIPLES OF EQUIVALENCE

Any formulation of principles of cultural equivalence involves two different types of problems. That is to say, the choice of words in any context is determined by two factors: (1) the cultural significance of the item to which the word refers and (2) the linguistic status of such a word, namely, whether it is native, borrowed, newly constructed, or archaic.

8.1.1   CULTURAL SIGNIFICANCE

The principles of alternate choices of words as based upon the cultural features may best be discussed under (1) outline guide for such alternate choices, (2) bases for adaptations, and (3) semantic factors in alternation.

8.1.1.1   OUTLINE GUIDE FOR ALTERNATE CHOICES

In all situations involving what we term 'equivalence' there is actually no exact equivalence. No corresponding two words in two different languages ever have identically the same meaning. The problem is not one of finding absolute equivalents, but of finding relatively close equivalents. There can be no absolute standard of conformance. It must always be a matter of degree. To those who are accustomed to insist upon absolute blacks and whites, this may seem rather strange. Nevertheless, to anyone who will take the time to examine the situation carefully, it will soon become obvious that we must work in varying shades of gray, not pure black and white. We attempt to approach an absolute standard, but we know from the start that it cannot be reached, for the language medium which we must use is not a set of exact mathematical formulas.

The equivalence which we seek to establish in speaking of any part of culture is twofold: (1) equivalence of objective form and (2) equivalence of functional significance. These two aspects often go together. For example, the *mayordomo* of the large estates of Latin America is almost the exact equivalent of the Greek *oikonomos*, the "steward" of the AV. He not only has the same responsibilities but is looked upon by the people in almost the same way as his ancient counterpart.

In many instances, however, there is not an agreement between the various cultural features nor a similarity in the function which these have in the life of the people. For example, two cultures may possess the same forms but attach quite a different functional significance to these forms. A snake was repudiated as an article for food in Bible times, Luke 11:11. But in some cultures a snake would be greatly preferred to a fish. The objects in the culture are the same, but their functions are quite different. In Bible times people habitually wailed at death. In the Maya culture, all such wailing is postponed for at least a year, for the living do not want to induce the dead to remain around because they have been attracted by the wailing. The expression "sons of thunder" may be translated literally into almost any aboriginal language, but the different functional significance of thunder, in that this natural phenomenon may be considered a god, may result in the phrase meaning that the god Thunder had two sons, namely, James and John. The fact that two forms may be the same in two cultures is no guarantee that they will have the same meaning, for the functional significance may be quite different.

On the other hand, two different types of objects or actions may have the same functional significance. In the Greek New Testament the word usually employed to indicate taking a position to eat means literally 'to recline.' The literal translation in Matthew 14:19 would be 'he commanded the multitude to recline.' But this is not done in most translations. We have made a transfer to another type of action, but one which has the same cultural significance. We say therefore, "he commanded the multitude to sit down."

Various figures of speech are illustrative of two different forms with the same functional significance. The Greek language employs a word meaning 'actor' to designate a hypocrite. In the Totonac language a word meaning literally 'a two-worded person' is the designation for a hypocrite. The linguistic forms are different but the functional significance (the meaning) of these forms is closely equivalent.

The primary objective in translating is to represent in so far as is possible both the form and the function of the Biblical account. There are no sets of formulas which may be followed in working out the problems of correspondence and equivalence. One must use "sanctified judgment." But such judgment may not be satisfactorily employed without a complete examination of the facts and an understanding of the basic principles.

When there is agreement between the Biblical and the aboriginal culture as to the form and function of some cultural item, there is no problem. When there is not this agreement, the following outline may be followed:

1 If the form is different or non-existent, one should employ
   a. The closest functional equivalent in the other culture, or
   b. A description of the Biblical feature.

2 If the function is different or non-existent, one should employ
   a. A different form having the same functional significance, or
   b. A foreign term with zero meaning, or
   c. A more or less literal rendering of the original text.

3 If both the form and the function are different, one should employ
   a. The word with the most nearly adequate formal and functional significance, or
   b. A foreign term with zero meaning.

This outline is quite meaningless apart from illustrations to point out exactly what is meant. One will not find exactly similar situations in any two languages. The illustrations are only designed to point out the principles. The translator must judge each new situation on its own merits.

1 If the form which exists in one culture is quite different from the form which has the same significance in another culture, there

are two things which the translator may do. He may choose (a) a word which designates an item which has a different form, but the same functional significance, or (b) some descriptive term which will convey something of the form and function represented in the Biblical culture.

Alternate 1, a.

In the Totonac culture there are no footstools, in the sense of objects about the same size and shape as footstools of Bible times. In fact, the chairs used by the Totonacs would be more like the ancient footstools. They do, however, have a special type of stick upon which they regularly place their feet in cold weather in order to keep them off the dirt floor. They themselves sit on low stools resembling our footstools. Instead of making up some word for footstool or using their word for chair, which resembles the form of the footstool of Bible times but not its function, the translator may use the word 'foot-stick.' The Totonac 'foot-stick' does have a different form from the corresponding Biblical item, but it is not too different in form and it is almost identical in function.

Alternate 1, b.

The native language frequently lacks names for cultural forms which are not specialized in the native society but which are functionally similar to features in the Biblical culture. For example, a culture may not have an army organized by companies of 100 men. Accordingly, there will not be a name corresponding to the word "centurion." There may be some military official who has approximately this number of men under him, and so a word such as English *captain*, Spanish *capitán*, or French *capitaine* may be used. However, if there is no military official even approximating the position of the centurion of the Bible culture (and it should be noted that, relatively speaking, the centurion was a much more important military figure than a captain in a modern European army), one may use a descriptive phrase such as 'the leader of one hundred soldiers.' In almost every culture there will be some term for soldiers or warriors. Unfortunately, war is a universal culture trait.

2 If the function of a particular form in a native culture is quite different from the cultural significance of this item in the Bibli-

cal culture, there are three principal alternates: (a) a different form, (b) a new word, or (c) a literal rendering of the text.

Alternate 2, a

In the first of these, one may adopt another cultural form, which has approximately the same functional significance. For example, the phrase "sons of thunder" is illustrative of this problem. This item in the culture is a linguistic one, a special figure of speech. In another language this form cannot be duplicated literally without an entirely different meaning. The functional significance of this type of figure of speech is different. Accordingly, in order to avoid having the expression mean to the native that some god named Thunder was the father of the two disciples of Jesus, it is necessary to change to some other cultural form which has the same function. The translator may therefore want to use some such expression as 'men like thunder,' for this is the essential meaning of the Semitic idiom.

Alternate 2, b.

The functional significance of a corresponding form may be so different that no adaptation can possibly be made. For example, there may not be in the aboriginal language any word which may be employed for God or Spirit. It may be necessary to introduce a new word which has practically zero meaning to the native speaker. This has been done several times in introducing foreign names for God. One should be cautious, however, in doing so, for every word with zero meaning is usually sooner or later equated with some other word which is better known by the people. A foreign term also has the disadvantage of representing a foreign cultural feature, and anything so intimate and important as the name of God should not have the disadvantage of being 'foreign' in its connotation. These problems will be discussed more fully on p. 204 ff.

Alternate 2, c.

Even though the functional significance of many features of a culture is different, it is not always possible nor advisable to make an adaptation. For example, though the Maya and the Palestinian patterns of wailing at death are quite different, yet the translation should represent faithfully the event which took place in the Bible culture. All people are familiar more or less with alternate modes of behavior in other tribes, and so the translator must explain to the native readers that other peoples had this special mode of behavior.

Cultural differences are always of interest to people. Many aboriginal people are amazed and not a little amused at some things recorded in the Bible. A man carrying a water jar, men with beards, garments reaching to the feet, crowns on the head, pinnacles on the temple, tents, fishing with nets, eating locusts —all these cultural features represent great contrasts to the mode of life of some peoples in the world. We cannot make all such cultural features conform. Moreover, we do not want them to conform in each detail. Our task is to represent in so far as is possible the Biblical culture. Note that in this section we are discussing the alternate possibilities of change. Immediately following this we shall take up the fundamental basis for undertaking such changes.

3 If for both the form and the function of any cultural item in the Bible there is no parallel in the native culture, one may do either one of two things: (a) employ the closest equivalent there is, even though this may be quite remote, or (b) use a foreign term with zero meaning.

Alternate 3, a.

In the Maya language and culture there is nothing which corresponds to a mountain of Palestine. The Maya country is extremely flat, except for some slight knolls, rising perhaps 100 feet at the most above the general level of the terrain. A 'mountain' in Yucatan bears about as much physical resemblance to a mountain in Palestine as a California bungalow does to the Empire State Building. Moreover, no one ever thought of gathering a crowd of Maya Indians out on the side of a 'mountain.' A *muul* 'a low hill' is the closest equivalent which the Maya language possesses. A foreign word would be meaningless, and a phrase which gives a description of the size of mountains in Palestine would scarcely be believed. Accordingly, in many instances, even though a particular feature in the Biblical culture has scarcely any formal and functional parallels in the native culture, it is necessary to employ some native word or expression, though it may need considerable amplification by means of teaching or footnotes.

Alternate 3, b.

When there are absolutely no similar forms in the two cultures nor items which have the same function, one is often obliged to introduce a foreign word which has absolutely no meaning. For example, the Eskimos have no sheep. Only a few Eskimos even have any idea of what such an animal might be like. In such a case, one must borrow the foreign word *sheep* from English or some other modern language. It would be necessary to place a footnote at the first occurrence of this word to explain it. Such a note might read:

> "Sheep are gentle domesticated animals raised for wool and meat."

Such a definition would explain something of the form and function of sheep in the Biblical culture.

The story has been widely circulated that the word 'seal' was used for sheep in one of the Eskimo translations. This is an intriguing story but without foundation in actual fact. A baby seal might be considered parallel to a lamb as far as general attractiveness and reputed 'innocence' is concerned, but after these features the parallel stops. Such an adaptation would be completely unsatisfactory.

8.1.1.2   BASES FOR ADAPTATION

The changes which have been proposed in departing from a literal rendition of the original text are not random changes, nor are they made purely for the sake of cultural adaptation. Such changes are not dictated by a desire to make the Bible seem as though it were recording some events which took place just yesterday in the next town. This would be quite impossible. Changes are made only on the basis of two situations: (1) when there is no possible equivalent in the native culture, and (2) when the literal translation gives an entirely wrong meaning.

When there is no equivalent, it is always possible to introduce a foreign, meaningless word, but it is unwise to use too many meaningless words if one wants to be understood. Among the people of the Ponape Islands near Truk there was no word for 'father' when the missionaries first came. The people possessed a type of communal marriage, so that no one was able to identify the father of a child. Since these people had no cultural feature of 'fatherhood' in the sense of the family unit, they had no word for 'father.' They did have a word for 'guardian,' for at a certain time in the child's life a particular man would take over the custody of the child; that is to say, he would stand responsible for the care of the child. The only word which could be used by the translators for 'father' was this word for 'guardian.' If a foreign word for 'father' had been used, it could only have been explained in terms of this word 'guardian,' for both the biological and social aspects of the word 'father' are significant.

On the other hand, the translator is not to make changes in the meaning of words just in order to make the cultural equivalence slightly stronger. One translator wanted to use 'beetle' instead of 'moth' in Luke 12:33. He insisted that the beetles where he was living did much more damage to the cloth than the moths. Nevertheless, the Bible text says "moth," and if there is such an insect in the culture at all, it must be designated, even though some other insect is more destructive.

The second principle governing changes in the translation includes those instances in which a close rendering of the original gives an entirely wrong meaning. For example, in one of the languages in Africa a translator had endeavored to stay very close to the original text, so he rendered "children of the bridechamber" as 'the children of the house of the man who marries the woman.' He had no doubt seen the marginal note in the ARV pointing out that the "children of the bridechamber" were friends of the bridegroom, so he attempted to compromise the translation in this direction. The result was entirely misleading to the native. For in a country in which polygamy was commonly practiced, who else could the 'children of the house of the man who marries the woman' be except the man's children by his other, former wives? There was no way of literally translating the expression "children of the bridechamber" into the particular African language without giving the wrong meaning. The translator must (1) adopt the marginal reading of the ARV, or (2) the interpretation which is preferred by some and followed in the de Valera Spanish Version, namely, 'the guests at the wedding.'

To recapitulate, the only two bases for extensive departure from the text are (1) the non-existence of some item in the native culture and (2) incorrect meaning of a close translation.

8.1.1.3   SEMANTIC FACTORS IN ALTERNATION

We have previously discussed the semantic principles in translation and have mentioned areas of meaning, pointing out the differences between peripheral and central meanings as well as denotative and connotative distinctions. It is important, however, that we go into this matter somewhat more fully in light of the problem of alternate choices and the principles of equivalence.

In instances where the close or literal translation of the text conveys the wrong meaning, one can do one of two things: (1) give the culturally equivalent item in the translation and omit any explanation or (2) give the translation of the text as it is and give an explanation of the culturally different situation in a footnote. In many cases, this latter method of handling the problem is preferable. For example, in one of the translations into Chinese where the text read 'sit on the right hand of God' the translation preserved the wording of the original. However, because in China the preferred place of honor is on the left and not on the right, a translation footnote is added saying that among the Hebrews the place of honor was on the right. This makes it possible for the reader to understand the cultural significance of an item without changing the actual reading of the text.

In many of the illustrations given throughout the following six chapters, the translator will find it valuable to follow the text closely and give in a footnote the alternate translation based upon cultural parallels. Whether or not the problems suggested in the following pages should be handled in the text or in the footnotes is largely dependent upon (1) how widely different the cultural items are and (2) the actual range of meaning of the words used. The individual instances will have to be decided for each translation. As a general policy, however, it is important to adhere as closely to the text of the original as possible, provided the translation makes some sense. The intelligent use of footnotes will make it possible to adjust many of the cultural differences without appreciably departing from the Biblical text.

The difference between the denotation of a word and the connotation of it is very significant in all translating. It is not always the problem of what a word points out (the denotation), but how people react to such words (the connotation). For example, the word *communism* denotes a particular political system. The connotation of this word, that is to say, the way people react to the word, is usually quite different. To some people communism implies a horrifying totalitarianism, and to other people it represents the salvation of the masses. In all translation work, one must be careful to check constantly the connotation as well as the denotation of words. This is especially true of borrowed words. For example, in many of the tribes of Latin America there are two borrowed words designating a 'priest.' One of these comes from the Spanish *cura* and the other from the Spanish *sacerdote*. Both of these words are employed to mean a 'priest,' but in many instances the first word, derived from *cura*, has all the connotations of ecclesiastical tyranny, while the word derived from *sacerdote* is lacking in this bad connotation.

In some instances it will be found that the native people have been taught some foreign words such as *justification, sanctification,* and *predestination,* and so they assume that these words have some special religious value, even though they may not understand them. They may even insist on using them in a translation, rather than some native word which they understand. There is a great deal of so-called magic in words, particularly if they concern non-material objects. The translator must resist all efforts of the people to use words as fetishes and to cling to the connotation even when they do not understand the denotation. It is not uncommon for Indians of Latin America to pray in public in Spanish, even though they may conduct the rest of any religious service in their own native language. In such a case, the Spanish words have a connotation of appropriateness for some special religious act. The frequent tendency is to use such partially understood phrases, with the connotation of religious flavor, rather than to employ words which have full meaning to the native. In such problems of denotation and connotation the translator must always emphasize the full value of the native language. On the other hand, he must not lean over backwards in trying to 'purify' the language by eliminating legitimate borrowings that have both a full denotation and a full connotation.

Special attention must be paid to peripheral and central meanings when two possible words are suggested for some context. This is particularly important when one is dealing with borrowed words, for the borrowed word may not have the same central meaning in the native language that it has in the trade language. In fact, it seldom has such a meaning. For example, the word *santo* in Spanish has a central meaning of 'holy' for most educated people. This is rarely the case with the average Indian of Latin America. To him, the word *santo* is the name of an image in the church. This meaning of image is usually the central meaning, and often the only meaning which he knows. This word *santo* cannot be borrowed in such cases to mean 'holy' or 'pure.' It is true that such an Indian will probably know the words *Espíritu Santo,* 'Holy Spirit.' But the *Santo* part of the name either has no meaning at all by itself or designates the image of the Spirit.

Consider another instance of this same type of problem. The word *tabernáculo* in Spanish has a central meaning with approximately the same significance as English *tabernacle.* However, in the ritual of the Catholic church the *tabernáculo* is the high place on the altar where the Host is placed. To most devotees among the Indians of Latin America, if this word *tabernáculo* is known at all, it is usually with the specialized peripheral meaning. Accordingly, it cannot be used to translate the AV "tabernacle."

These problems of (1) denotative vs. connotative and (2) peripheral vs. central meanings are of utmost importance in considering the types of alternate choices to be considered in the next section, covering certain linguistic and cultural factors in alternate choices.

8.1.2   LINGUISTIC STATUS OF WORDS

The linguistic status of a word is important in determining the alternate choices in translating. Whether a word is (a) a native word, (b) a borrowed one, (c) a newly constructed word, or (d) archaic, is of considerable importance in determining the connotation of the word and its acceptability. A native word and a borrowed word may have the same denotation, but the connotation is almost always different. We may call the same flower a 'sunflower' or 'Helianthus annuus.' But the selection of one or the other of these names makes a great deal of difference. In a technical book on flowers we expect Helianthus annuus, but if someone in a crowd voices his admiration for a common sunflower by saying, "What a beautiful Helianthus annuus!" we immediately put such a person down as an obnoxious pedant.

The linguistic status of words in a language may be conveniently treated under (1) an outline of alternate choices and (2) problems of partial meaning.

8.1.2.1 AN OUTLINE OF ALTERNATE CHOICES

There is no way of formulating a set of rules which will cover all situations in which there are alternate choices depending upon the linguistic status of a word. Each circumstance will be somewhat different from the preceding one. We can only lay down a series of alternate choices and indicate the basis for these, leaving it to the translator to make the appropriate choice on the basis of similar types of data.

The major divisions of the following outline on alternate choices are based upon usage, which must be the ultimate criterion for any correct judgments of linguistic status. The three major divisions are (1) words in common use, (2) words in restricted use, and (3) words not in use. If one will bear in mind that priority of choice must be determined on the basis of usage, one should not run into great difficulty.

There is one feature about the following outline of alternate choices which is technically incorrect. It is impossible for two words to represent the same relative adequacy of meaning, both denotative and connotative. There are no complete synonyms. However, this often appears to be the case, and hence we state, "approximately the same area of meaning." On the basis of a practical analysis of the situation, the following outline should be valuable for making decisions as to alternate possibilities of choice if the problem is fundamentally one of linguistic status.

A. WORDS IN COMMON USE.

If the alternate words under consideration have approximately the same area of meaning the choice should be made as follows:
1 First choice: a native word.
2 Second choice: a borrowed word.

B. WORDS IN RESTRICTED USE.

If the alternate words under consideration have approximately the same area of meaning the choice should be made as follows:
1 First choice: a borrowed word.
2 Second choice: a native word.

C. Words Not in Use.

If the alternate words are not in actual use, the choice should
be made as follows:
1 Newly constructed words formed from native word-elements.
2 Borrowed words.
3 Archaic native words.

Several items must be explained in the above outline.

1 If the words are in common use, there is actually no difference
between a native and a borrowed word. In fact, most speakers
will not know that many words are borrowed. There are not
many people who recognize that *garage* comes from French,
spaghetti from Italian, *thug* from Hindustani, and *chocolate* originally from Aztec. Actually the distinction between native and
borrowed words, if they are both commonly used, is not fundamentally a problem of the linguistic status of the words. It is
a problem of the adequacy of the words as far as their denotative and connotative significance is concerned. Let us assume,
however, that there is an almost exact equivalence in the usage
and denotation of a native and a borrowed word. One usually
finds that the connotative significance of the native word is better, for the native word is probably more firmly and deeply rooted
in the consciousness of the people than the borrowed word.

2 Most translators operate under a double sort of pressure. The
one is to bring in borrowed words because they conform to the
usage of the trade language, which the translator and some of
the natives know. This seems to be a step in the direction of
progress and of acquainting the native with the trade language. On the other hand, most missionaries, after they have
gone to the trouble to learn an aboriginal language, have a
great respect for it. They consider that they are doing the
aboriginal language a service by preserving it from any con-
tamination by borrowed words. Both of these tendencies must
be resisted. The only criterion must be usage.

3 When words are in restricted use, it means that the borrowed
word is probably just being introduced. It has not had enough
time to make its way completely into the speech of the people.
On the other hand, a native word which is in restricted use is

probably an obsolescent word. Of course, there is the possibility that the native word is a new formation which is only beginning to gain wide acceptance. However, the influence of the trade language upon most native languages is such that usually a native word in restricted use (this must not be mistaken for restricted meaning) is in the process of dying out.

If one must choose between a borrowed word which is coming into the language and a native word which is going out (other things being equal), one should make the choice on the basis of the direction of the language development. Those who have attempted to resurrect dying words in a language have in most instances ultimately had to bury either the words or the translation. The native church usually grows in the direction of the usage of the trade language in many features of religious vocabulary. This is largely because of the fact that the training of native leadership is in the trade language and much available and desirable printed matter exists in that language. When the problem involves restricted usage of words, the newly borrowed words should have first choice.

4 When the words are not in use, the missionary may do any one of three things: (1) he may invent a new word, using native elements to form such a word, (2) he may adopt a borrowed word which has no meaning whatsoever to the natives, or (3) he may employ some archaic native word.

If the translator attempts to invent a new word (these are usually compounds), the form of the word must represent the native way of building words. For example, in English if we wanted to make up a compound verb having the meaning of 'worshiping animals,' we could construct the verb *to animal-worship*. We would not say *to worship-animal*. In English the order of the elements is important and the change of order from the syntactic phrase pattern to the word-formation pattern is significant. In an aboriginal language the translator must understand the methods of forming new words, and all new words must be formed in this way. They should, moreover, be almost immediately apparent. The native may hesitate a moment, for the form will be new, but he should have an almost immediate reaction as to the meaning of the word.

The missionary should not attempt to substitute a native

word which is not immediately apparent for a borrowed word which is in common use and is understood. This is a common error made by translators. For example, in one translation a newly constructed compound 'iron-house' was suggested in place of the borrowed form of the Spanish *carcel* 'prison.' The meaning of the compound was not immediately apparent, for the word 'iron-house' might denote several things to the native. It most surely would not be immediately understood as 'prison,' when the natives have another word in common use, namely a borrowed form of the Spanish *carcel*. Again, it must be reiterated that the basis for any choice of alternative words must be actual usage first and foremost.

It is often necessary to adopt a foreign word with absolutely no meaning in the native language. This is almost always the case with proper names. But proper names do not ultimately cause much difficulty. They are accepted by the natives as perfectly understandable, in that almost everyone they meet from the outside world has a strange name. Words which are not proper names and have a zero meaning are much more of a problem. The translator should introduce such words only in the case of extreme necessity.

The only words which have less priority of choice than borrowed words with zero meaning are native archaic words. An archaic word is an old word in the language which is no longer used by the people. It is seldom possible in an aboriginal language even to come across such words. The only possible means is by written records. (In a few instances a word in a related language may show by its form that it was originally borrowed from the language in question, but the use of such a term as this comes under the heading of borrowing.) Some translators have been very anxious to dig up old words of a language and attempt to resuscitate them. In some few instances such attempts have been successful. But a truly archaic word is a completely empty word, and the translator must give it all of its content by context and by teaching. The word borrowed from the trade language does have the advantage of some cultural force, and since the direction of the language development is usually toward the assimilation of more and more words from the dominant trade language, one should in almost all cases prefer the borrowed word to the archaic word. No purpose is served in resisting cultural synthesis by adherence to archaisms.

8.1.2.2 PROBLEMS OF PARTIAL MEANING

As has been implied many times, the equivalence of terms is in some instances comparatively inadequate. Such problems of partial meaning are often quite acute. When areas of meaning do not correspond, the translator does the best he can to rectify this situation by two means: (1) he attempts to use certain words in restricted types of contexts, and (2) he must rely upon teaching, oral and written, to assist the natives to understand the meaning of the Bible.

There are three principal types of problems of partial meaning: (1) those in which the native word has too restricted an area of meaning, (2) those in which the native word has too large an area of meaning, (3) those in which there is a wrong center of meaning.

It is seldom possible to find a native word which will correspond to the wide area of meaning of the English word *glory*, Greek *doksa*. The translator will have to use several native words, but even these may not be sufficient in all contexts. The "glory of God" implies a great number of attributes and concepts which only a knowledge of the Bible itself and personal experience of spiritual realities can possibly reveal. By using words consistently within certain types of contexts, and by teaching, the translator can extend the area of meaning of many words. We are all familiar with this situation in our own experience. Many words are at first only empty forms which must be filled with the meaning by the context. The same must be expected in the native language. The translator must, however, be sure that the word that has been chosen can acquire the full significance of the original.

The native words are often too extensive in area of meaning. It is often quite difficult in a native language to find a series of words to correspond to the Greek words for 'love.' In many instances, the native word for 'love' will be even more extensive in area of meaning than the English word *love*. The native word may include the ideas of 'want,' 'enjoy,' and 'love.' It may not be possible to find other words. In such cases, it is best to take the one large-area word and by teaching and by means of context in which the word occurs to indicate the proper significance. This is generally preferable to introducing some foreign word which has practically zero meaning. If the word has life—namely, represents actual usage of the people—the context is sufficient in most cases to convey the appropriate meaning. It is better to have to restrict the meaning of a native word by context and teaching than to endeavor to give meaning to a meaningless foreign word.

When corresponding words do not have the same center of meaning, many difficulties arise. For example, the central meaning of *spirit* in English may perhaps be stated for most people as a 'bodiless personality.' A personality may be defined as an entity which is able to initiate action, in other words, one which thinks and is able to carry out thoughts, even though this may be done by means of some other medium or mediator.

In most aboriginal languages the closest approximation to this meaning of *spirit* is usually 'a disembodied, evil personality.' Obviously, the native word and the English word cannot be made to correspond throughout all contexts. One cannot say 'Holy Spirit' and employ this native word for spirit which designates an evil personality. The combination would not make sense, for it would be a contradiction in terms. It would not be any more intelligible to the native than the phrase 'a rectangular circle.' Such expressions, we declare, are impossible, for they are senseless.

The translator must avoid meaningless combinations of words, and he can best do this by being sure that the centers of meaning-areas of words correspond. If they do not, he must be sure that the context is sufficient to make this meaning perfectly obvious. One cannot tack the word 'holy' onto the name of something which is thought to be essentially evil and expect the resultant phrase to have the proper meaning. The context can only bring together two words which overlap in at least some parts of their meaning, and if possible this should not be too far from the central significance.

8.2   A CLASSIFICATION OF LEXICAL PROBLEMS

A detailed examination of lexical problems covers all the range of human experience. Since language and all that language speaks about are essentially features of (1) the people themselves, (2) the natural environment, or (3) the cultural environment, the problems of meaning may be treated most adequately in terms of these three types of factors. Before considering the various problems individually, it is well to understand the entire range of these features and the relationship of these to each other.

The lexical problems of the Bible cover almost every aspect of existence. It will be impossible in the following six chapters to take up every word in the Bible and discuss the lexical problems. Moreover, though it might be possible to discuss any one word as it has been treated in some one, two, or three translations, it would be impossible to cover all the types of languages or the types of culture. One cannot expect to find in the following analysis the specific answers to all problems. The only thing which can be done is to illustrate the principles which have already been discussed. In doing this we are not attempting to group such illustrations under the various principles (this has already been done to some extent), but to analyze these illustrations in terms of the particular type of phenomena.

The following chapters cannot be an encyclopedia of translation equivalents, for more than a thousand languages, representing many very different cultures, have never been reduced to writing. Such data is not available, even if one did want to classify it. But actually, it is not necessary to treat every instance of equivalence in every type of translation. The basic objective and purpose is to point out the underlying principles and their application in various phases of human existence. The translator must determine the specific use in a new language, not upon the basis of some one suggestion given here but upon the general principles which are illustrated.

The various phases of human life may be classified first under (1) man and (2) his environment. Man himself may be studied as to his (a) physical form (anatomy), (b) his psychology, and (c) his diseases (pathology). The environment of man may be treated under (a) the natural environment and (b) the cultural environment. The natural environment of man includes (1) physical features of the universe, (2) the seasons, (3) fauna (animal life), and (4) flora (plant life). The cultural environment includes (1) material, (2) social, (3) religious, and (4) linguistic features.

The material culture of a people includes those objects manufactured or used by people in their adjustment to the physical environment, e.g., buildings, clothing, food, artifacts, and measurements. The social culture of a people includes those features which represent an adjustment of the people one to another, e.g., political systems, property, laws, war, family, class distinctions, and occupations. The religious culture includes those features which represent an adjustment to 'supernatural' phenomena, e.g., gods, spirits, divine sanctions, revelation, and rites. The linguistic culture includes all the features of the language, e.g., the sounds (the phonology), the words (the morphology), the arrangements of words (the syntax), and the meanings of parts of words, words, and combinations of words (the lexicon).

This outline includes all the features of culture except one, namely, the esthetic forms, e.g. artistic motifs, designs, music, and the dance. There is some mention made in the Bible of such esthetic factors in the culture, but these are not discussed nearly so fully as the other phases of culture. For the most part they may be omitted except for a consideration of the parallel forms and functions of the dance in native cultures and the culture of the Old Testament. This is a special problem which each translator must note.

Each aspect or area of culture will be considered in the order just suggested, but for convenience this material is divided under six chapters: (1) Terms for Man's Form, (2) Terms for Features of Natural Environment, (3) Terms for Features of Material Culture, (4) Terms for Features of Social Culture, (5) Terms for Features of Religious Culture, and (6) Problems of Linguistic Equivalence.

Under the principal subdivisions of each chapter are discussed certain words and expressions which have been found by translators to present special difficulty. Those terms which are illustrative of the general problems involved are treated first. The discussion of additional terms is printed in smaller type. In these latter sections the translator will find many helpful suggestions for the solution of certain detailed problems.

Chapter 9

TERMS FOR FEATURES OF MAN'S FORM

Terms for features of man's form may be conveniently treated under (1) anatomy, (2) psychology, and (3) pathology.

9.1 ANATOMY

Illustrative words: SIDE, CHEEK, BODY, BEARD, HAND.

SIDE

CHEEK

BODY

BEARD

Even in the words for the parts of the body there is by no means complete agreement among languages. The Eastern Aztecs, for example, do not have a word for "side." They only distinguish between the thorax and the abdomen. The translator must decide, therefore, whether Jesus was pierced in the side below the ribs or between the ribs. There is no positive way of knowing. The Eastern Aztecs likewise do not have a word for "cheek." The translator must employ the word for 'face.'

It is found in many languages that it is quite impossible to find a word for "body," in the sense of the English word. The only expressions which some languages have are 'corpse' (a dead body), 'my meat and bones,' and 'my self.' If the "body" in the text refers to the physical body, it will be translated 'corpse' or 'my meat and bones,' depending on the context; and if the "body" refers to the personality (the human entity), then the translation reads 'my self.'

Some peoples of the earth have no beards. It is necessary to describe this as 'hair on the face' or 'hair on the lower part of the face,' if in the language a distinction is made between the face in general and the lower part of it. It should be noted that we lack in English a single term to include just those places on a man's face where a beard grows. We would have to describe such a place by listing cheeks, jaw, upper lip, lower lip, and front and top portion of the neck. Other languages have terms which denote much more concisely this region of beard-growing.

HAND   In some languages the word for 'hand' and 'arm' is the same. In all such situations of nonconformity of the native language to the text language, one should use the word that designates the part of the anatomy which at least includes the special area denoted by the text language. The restriction of the area may be accomplished by the context.

9.2   PSYCHOLOGY

Illustrative words: BELLY, BOWELS, LIFE, SOUL, SPIRIT, FLESH, BODY, HEART, REINS, GALL, MIND.

People consider themselves as being more than physical form. They see in the movement and coordination of physical forms something which they interpret as being of a different order of reality. In most instances 'thinking' and 'feeling' have been distinguished from purely material features, but the centers of these psychological factors have been variously distributed by different peoples. To the people of Bible times the

BELLY   "belly" and the "bowels" represented the center of deep
BOWELS   emotions of the most intense type. In modern English these words are often translated 'inmost being.' "Bowels of mercy" no longer has any real significance for us, for the bowels are not considered as having anything to do with mercy or any other emotion. Moreover, the connotation of the words *belly* and *bowels* is not good. We consider them vulgar. Hence, a translation which is acceptable to most people will employ words which are understood and which will not offend the hearers' sense of propriety. In one language the closest equivalent for "belly" and "bowels" is literally 'the inside of you,' for this term designates the inmost emotion center of the personality. In another language, the closest equivalent is 'one's self.' The 'man himself'[1] is considered

---

[1] See page 196 concerning inadequacy of these literal translations.

as the center of his deepest emotions. In other languages this emotional center is the 'liver' or 'spleen.'

We are so used to speaking of the "heart" as the center of emotions (especially pleasant ones involving affection) that it is inconceivable to us that other people do not use the same term. For the Popolucas 'loving with the heart' is completely meaningless. They love with their 'livers.' In such a case the translator must take this into consideration, just as modern translators of the Bible into English are taking into consideration the psychological significance of "belly" and "bowels." In the Totonac language one may love with the heart, but any disaster in emotions is the result of the condition of the spleen. So one says 'spleen-broken' instead of 'heart-broken.'

LIFE   The English word "life" is a term which often includes many different words in an aboriginal language. The Eastern Aztec language differentiates between (1) the inner, or heart life, which is the life which animates every part of man's intellectual and emotional existence, and (2) the physical existence, which is the type of life which any animal has. Such a basic difference is common in many languages. "Eternal life" should be translated as more than 'unending existence,' this second term for life. There should be some qualitative distinction involving the first meaning.

The Greeks employed three words which are translated "life" in English. One of these, the *psuchē*, represented the central core of the personal life of the thinking, feeling creature. In some instances this word is translated "soul." The *zōē* was the life of moving, acting creatures, but not so essentially personal. The *bios* represented the most basic essentials of existence and the means for carrying on such existence. Hence it is sometimes translated "substance" or "property." One will never find another language in which the range of meaning of any three words is parallel to this division in Greek. The essential thing to do is (1) to understand exactly the meaning that is intended in the Biblical text in question and (2) to attempt to find the closest correspondence to this in the aboriginal language.

SOUL
SPIRIT
FLESH
BODY

It is impossible to discuss the various factors of human psychology without including those words which have very special religious significance, e.g. 'soul,' 'spirit,' 'flesh,' 'body.' We are so accustomed to the trilogy of 'body, soul, and spirit,' that we assume that these terms must represent certain basic features of an individual which are recognized by all peoples. This is by no means the case. In many instances, aboriginal languages only differentiate between (1) the thinking without emotion (the 'mind,' 'thoughts,' etc.), (2) the

HEART

thinking with emotion (the 'heart,' 'liver,' 'spleen,' 'bowels,' etc.), and (3) the personality which leaves the body at death (the 'breath,' 'phantom,' 'ghost,' 'spirit,' etc.) The body is either 'my meat and bones' or 'a corpse,' depending upon whether it is alive or dead.

Those who hold to the trichotomist view of human personality, namely, the threefold division into body, soul, and spirit, are often involved in considerable difficulty because of the apparent overlapping of the terms "soul" and "spirit." It should be pointed out that, because there are two words, namely, "soul" and "spirit," it must not be implied that there are necessarily two separate entities. In fact, the dichotomists, who include equally devout students of the Bible, would contend that instead of three entities, the body, soul, and spirit, there are actually only two. The words are interpreted as representing three areas of meaning which cover only two essentially distinct entities in the human personality. However, be that as it may, the important thing to note is that all languages do not divide up the so-called spiritual nature of man as the Greek or English does. In some languages it will be impossible to separate these. In the Mazatec, the 'heart' and 'soul' are identical. When both of these words occur in the same text as in Acts 4:32, the translation has been literally 'heart and thoughts.' In other languages, the "heart" and the "spirit" are identical.

In order to meet the difficulty in overlapping of terms

for man's psychological features some translators have attempted to introduce entirely foreign terms. The difficulty with this usage has been that the only way of explaining the meaning of such a term is to describe what it means in terms of another word which to the native completely covers this area of meaning. It is possible to introduce a new term for something entirely foreign to a people's culture, but to introduce a new term for something which is covered by a word which they already know is an almost hopeless situation. The new term is thought of only as a synonym for the better known term and has the disadvantage of being a rather helpless sort of word. It does not have enough strength to stand on its own. Often the entire passage collapses because of dependence upon such a weak member.

In many cases the translator must distinguish between the soul of a live person and the soul of a dead person. This distinction may seem quite awkward at times, but failure to note the distinction may result in a passage being quite incomprehensible.

FLESH   The term "flesh" designates a part of the human personality, but the specialization of meaning in this word is extreme, since in many contexts the ethical significance is of primary importance. Only very rarely can it be literally translated into another language. 'My meat' or 'my muscle' does not make sense in most languages. In some instances, the "flesh" has to be identified with the 'body.' In one language, it was possible to use 'self' as an equivalent for "flesh." Some translators have used an expression such as 'in a human way' for "after the flesh," John 8:15. This last type of usage seems to be one of the most valuable.

The following questions may be helpful for the translator in attempting to arrive at some analysis of the divisions of human personality as indicated in the language usage. Note that these questions are by no means exhaustive. They are given only as suggestions of what may prove to be valuable leads in arriving at some type of adequate solution to the problems.

1 What are the basic divisions of human personality?
2 What functions do these divisions have in the life of the individual?
3 What lives on after the body dies?
4 Does such a part of a person always abide with one till death?
5 How is this part which lives on after death related to the person while he is alive?
6 Is it related to the breath? Blood? Excretions?
7 Does it leave one during dreams? Trances? Sickness?
8 Do animals possess a similar non-physical quality?
9 If man's 'spirit' or 'soul' is different from an animal's, how is it different?
10 Is the spirit or soul centered in any part of the body? Any organ?
11 With what organ or part of the personality does one think?
12 Is thinking related to desiring?
13 Is desiring centered in any part of the body: Heart? Liver? Spleen? Intestines?
14 What is the center of affection: Heart? Liver? Spleen? Intestines?
15 Is any part of man good and another part bad?
16 Is there anything like a higher (human) and lower (animal) nature in man?
17 How is the spirit or soul related to these ethical elements?
18 What part of man convicts him of having done wrong? Transgressed taboo?
19 What is the focus center of the personality?
20 Can the spirit and soul be distinguished?
21 Are these distinguishable from the mind?
22 Does every person have just one spirit and one soul?
23 Are there too many spirits or souls in the universe so that they compete for bodies in which to dwell?
24 Do spirits or souls return to take up abode on the earth in different bodies?
25 Does the tribe or family group have a common soul or spirit?
26 Are the souls and spirits of men related to those of animals? How?
27 Can souls and spirits of men be exchanged? Can men exchange souls and spirits with animals?

REINS   The word "reins," which literally means 'kidneys,' constitutes a similar problem to "belly" and "bowels." The difference is that we no longer use the word "reins" with the
meaning of 'kidneys.' Those who do not know the former
meaning of reins give it some meaning from the context, since
to them it is an empty word. But this is a rather unsatisfactory way to have to translate. Words with zero meaning
should be used as rarely as possible. A similar change in
"reins" may be made as has been done with "belly" and
"bowels."

Certain excretions of the body have been considered as
having psychological functions. The gall bladder and gall
have been associated with meanness, bitterness, and jealousy.
GALL   The expression in Acts 8:23 speaking of the "gall of bitterness" is quite meaningless to a Mazatec Indian. It would
be the same as for us to say "the duodenum of misery."
A better translation in Mazatec reads literally 'intense
jealousy.'

MIND   For us the mind is a unity. In many languages there is no
such corresponding word. For the speakers of such languages,
there is no 'mind,' only 'thoughts.' The only way of translating the word "mind" is to say literally 'the thoughts,'
or in some instances a verbal noun may be made, meaning
'the thinking.'

9.3   PATHOLOGY

Illustrative words: PALSY, FOUNTAIN OF BLOOD, SICKNESS, DIS-
EASE, LUNACY, LEPROSY, PLAGUE, SCALES.

PALSY   The Greek word translated "palsy" in the AV denotes
all types of lack of nervous control. "Palsy" is at present restricted to mean that type of paralysis which is
accompanied by shaking and jerking. The Greek word,
however, denotes all types of paralysis.

Languages often do not have a word for paralysis.
They simply describe the infirmity by saying 'a person
who cannot move himself.' In some languages the same
expression is used to denote paralysis as describes rigidity of the body because the joints have become calcified.
If the translator has difficulty finding the exact word
for paralysis, he only needs to describe the symptoms
and obtain from the informant the native way of

describing such a state. One form or another of paralysis is common among all people, so there will always be some term, though the term may be so restricted that it describes only one type of paralysis, e.g. "palsy," or it may be so extensive in meaning that it includes other infirmities as well.

FOUNTAIN OF BLOOD   This expression refers to the menstrual flow. The literal translation of this phrase is in some languages completely ambiguous and confusing. In one instance, the translator used the literal phrase 'spring of blood.' The natives received the impression that the woman possessed a spring some place which gave forth blood instead of water. In some cases one may translate 'flow of blood' or 'bleeding.' If the language permits a plain statement, without becoming vulgar, it is well to state the situation frankly. The AV expression "dried up," used in the same passage, does not make sense in many languages. It is often necessary to translate 'the blood which flowed ceased.'

SICKNESS DISEASE   There are several words in the Greek New Testament which are translated "sickness" or "disease." They cover a wide area of meaning. The meanings for the various contexts may be determined from commentaries, lexicons, and concordances.

In many aboriginal languages there is an abundance of words for various types of ailments, but in some cases there is no general term for 'sickness' or 'disease.' In such instances one must usually employ the words for the most general types of sickness or disease, whether such terms are completely generic or not.

In some languages ailments are classified as to their supposed origin, namely, whether they are brought on by spirits or are the result of some accident. In other instances, ailments are classified as to (1) obvious ones, e.g. a protruding tumor or withered hand, and (2) non-obvious ones, e.g. stomach ulcers. Whatever the classification in the native language, the translator must understand the area of meaning covered by the words and choose the most appropriate one for the context.

LUNACY   Words for mental aberration are likely to be quite varied in different languages. The phenomenon is rarely understood even by so-called civilized people. The native word may mean literally 'out of one's head,' 'one's mind has taken a trip,' or 'one's mind has been captured by a whirlwind.' These expressions are no more strange than the Greek word and the Latin equivalent, which literally mean to be 'affected by the moon.' In translating "lunacy" one should avoid a form of expression which means 'demon-possessed,' for this latter expression is used in other contexts.

LEPROSY   In many parts of the world there is a special term for the form of leprosy which is found in that particular region. This pathological form of leprosy may differ considerably from that occurring in Bible times, but the general appearance and pathology are probably sufficiently similar to justify the use of the native word. In some places there is no form of leprosy. One must describe it. This may usually be done by a phrase such as 'diseased skin.' Such a phrase may also describe certain skin ulcers, but the term is usually sufficiently adequate so that the native reader will understand something of the specialized meaning from the context. To introduce a borrowed form of the word "leprosy," when the word is completely unknown to the people, is generally unwise.

PLAGUE   The Greek word *mastiks*, literally 'a scourge' or 'a whip,' is translated "plagues" in the AV. It denotes certain types of diseases and sicknesses but from the viewpoint of their origin. Plagues were considered as types of diseases which were sent upon people as a form of punishment for nonconformance to certain aspects of a divinely enforced moral code. Many languages have a close parallel to this word. In other instances, there is no way of indicating the supernatural origin of such a disease without stating this by some paraphrase. However, such an explanation tends to add more emphasis to the supernatural origin of the ailment than may always be implied in the Greek.

SCALES   The scales which Paul had over his eyes, Acts 9:18, were not some disease, but they closely approximate some types of pathological forms and so are discussed here. Some translators have found it valuable to employ a descriptive expression such as 'coverings like skin.'

Chapter 10

TERMS FOR FEATURES
OF THE NATURAL ENVIRONMENT

M AN's natural environment may be analyzed as composed of four types of features: (1) the physical features of the earth and sky, (2) the seasons, (3) the animal life, and (4) the plant life. There are hundreds of words in the Bible which deal with various aspects of this natural environment. We can consider only a few. These will be merely illustrative of the many problems which are encountered.

10.1 PHYSICAL FEATURES OF THE EARTH AND SKY

Illustrative words: EARTH, WORLD, WIND, SNOW, MOUNTAIN, RIVER, HEAVENS, SKY.

EARTH In a considerable number of languages there is no word for "earth" in the sense of the entire globe. This is also true for "world." In the Totonac language the only expression which conveys the meaning of "earth" is literally 'an extension of cornfields.' To the Totonacs, this is the earth. The cornfield is the soil, and the extension may be almost unlimited. As localized as this expression may seem, it does express the concept in the Totonac language. It should be remembered that the Greek word *gē*, which has been translated "earth," could include anything from a small plot to the entire earth. The Greek word *gē* is used principally to contrast the surface of ground from (1) the heavens and (2) the surface of bodies of water.

Some geographical limits are quite hard to translate. In the Tarascan it is confusing to say 'ends of the earth.' This seems impossible for the natives to understand, and in terms of a globe it is even more difficult to explain. The closest equivalent to this is 'beyond the

158

horizon.' Since this may be considered as an ever-re-treating demarcation, it is quite adaptable in the Tarascan as a translation of the phrase "ends of the earth."

WORLD   "World" has been used as a translation of two Greek words *kosmos* and *aiōn*. The first word denotes in such contexts the order and system of the creation. The second denotes the periods of time in which the world exists. The word *kosmos* may denote either the system of the physical creation or the system of man's organization in the creation, that is to say, his patterns of behavior, his customs, and his manner of life. The word *aiōn* may in some instances be almost equivalent to the culture pattern which the anthropologist speaks of. These two Greek words approach each other quite closely in meaning. Both may denote the systems of human culture and behavior, but one of them implies the formal arrangement and design and the other the period of time during which such situations exist. Note, however, that the word *aiōn* in certain contexts and derived forms designates an unlimited period of time, namely, eternity.

WIND   In some languages no one word will be found for "wind." There may be several types of winds, e.g. 'zephyrs,' 'tornadoes,' 'hot winds off the desert,' or 'freezing winds,' but there may be no general word for 'wind.' The translator must also be careful about his context. When the "four winds" are used for the four directions in Revelation 7:1, there are considerable difficulties for some peoples. In some regions there may be only two or three kinds of winds, and they may all blow from the same direction. This is true of some Aztec regions of Mexico. The translator may in such cases substitute 'directions' in place of 'winds,' for 'winds' would not make sense.

SNOW   No topic attracts so much popular interest as the translations of the word "snow," for almost everyone knows that in many parts of the world there is no such thing as snow. In some cases, there may be snow at a considerable distance from an aboriginal people, and though they do not know it by personal observation, they may have heard about it. If such is the case, one may use the native expression, though the people may know only that it is cold and white. In some localities, people may have frost which is quite white, and they may be able to see snow on distant mountains. In the Mixteco Indian country of southern Mexico this is the case, and the people have given "snow" the name of 'volcano frost.' To the Mixteco, then, the angel's raiment becomes 'as white as volcano frost,' Matthew 28:3.

Where there is absolutely no snow nor any knowledge of a similar phenomenon, some translators have attempted to introduce other parallels, e.g. 'white as egret feathers.' This is not a very wise practice, though it does have the advantage of having some very concrete meaning. It would usually seem preferable in such a situation to say 'exceedingly white.' Then, as the occasion for explanation arose, one could explain the degree of whiteness in terms of egret feathers. As a basic policy it should be understood that when there is absolutely no material parallel and when it is not obligatory to introduce another substance, a general term which conveys the meaning of the Biblical phrase is to be preferred to the introduction of entirely new elements into the text.

MOUNTAIN   This problem has already been discussed on p. 135. If the people have no feature in the natural environment which corresponds to a mountain in Palestine, one must adopt whatever word the native language may have for an elevation of land, even though it may be very low. If the terrain is extremely level, not rising more than a dozen feet above the level of the sea, as is the case in some of the Pacific Islands, one must employ some type of descriptive phrase, such as 'ground in a big heap,' or 'a very high mound of earth.' Even these descriptive terms may not mean much, but they will be better than importing a word which does not mean anything to the native reader. Regardless of the borrowed word, the native will understand it only in terms of his actual experience.

RIVER   There are some features of the physical environment which are completely lacking in some localities. The word "moun-

tain," just cited, is illustrative. "Rivers" do not exist in some
parts of the world, either because of lack of rainfall, or because the soil is so porous that it absorbs all the rainfall before it has a chance to run off. In one language a "river"
was translated 'running water.' This is probably not too
satisfactory, for though we may speak of 'running water' in
English, there is no evidence that this may be done in other
languages. We also speak of 'puddles of water standing in
the road.' It would seem quite inconceivable that any other
language would employ the same word, namely, 'standing,'
to describe the position of (1) a water puddle and (2) a man
in an upright position. We cannot take for granted any of
our familiar figures of speech.

HEAVENS   There is rarely any difference in a language between the
SKY   word for the 'sky' and the word which is adopted for 'heaven'
or 'heavens.' In some languages the word for 'sky' is nothing
more than the phrase 'that which is above.' The word for
'heaven' in the sense of celestial abode of the righteous dead
will be discussed later, p. 231.

10.2   SEASONS

The rendering of seasons is very difficult in many translations.
This is because so many translations are made for people in tropical countries, and the Bible represents a semitropical climate. For
most people in the tropics there are only two important seasons,
the rainy season and the dry season. In some cases this distinction
is not even very significant. In a few regions of the tropics there
is something of a difference in temperature between summer and
winter, but this is usually not very important.

One very difficult passage to translate is Matthew 24:32, dealing with the leafing of the fig tree. In the first place, fig trees do
not grow in many tropical countries, but even if they did, this
would not be of much help, for in some regions the trees do not
lose their leaves seasonally. In the Maya country, however, the
trees do lose their leaves during the dry season, which lasts from
about November until May or June. Usually just before the beginning of the wet season, most of the trees have lost their leaves,
or at least have lost a greater part of them. Then, within about
a week after the rainy season begins, all the trees come out in leaf.
One cannot employ a term which designates the calendrical summer, for the beginning of the rainy season varies considerably. To

add to this complication is the fact that the Spanish *verano* is the only word which the Mayas know and which might apply to the calendrical summer, but this word is used by them to designate the hot season from February to June. The only solution to the problem is to translate, 'When the fig tree puts forth its leaves, you know that the rainy season is near'; but actually this is somewhat wrong, for the rainy season has to precede the putting forth of the leaves. This is, however, the closest adjustment which can be made in this instance. Even the best is not always entirely satisfactory.

Seasons of the year may be designated in the native language by reference to such factors as (a) temperature, (b) rainfall, (c) prevailing winds, (d) growth or flowering of plants (in Eastern Aztec, summer is designated by 'when corn is in tassel'), and (2) position of heavenly bodies. The translator should adopt the normal idiomatic expression for the indication of the seasons.

10.3   ANIMAL LIFE (FAUNA)

Illustrative words: WOLF, CAMEL, FISH, ASP, WASP, BEES, OX, WORM.

The differences to be found in fauna of different parts of the earth are considerable. For example, the horse, cow, and sheep were not known to the inhabitants of the Western hemisphere at the time when the European conquerors came. At the present time these animals are still unknown in some parts of the world.

The varying distribution of animal life presents many problems in translation. There are five principal types of solutions: (1) one may employ the name of another, somewhat related animal; (2) one may employ the name of another, entirely different animal, but one which has the same function in the culture; (3) one may qualify the name of the indigenous animal by some such expression as 'like'; (4) one may describe the animal briefly; and (5) one may employ an entirely foreign name, usually with a footnote.

a. Solution, type (1).

In many instances one may substitute the name of a very similar animal for the name of the Biblical animal. This similarity should be based upon the form of the animal and its functional significance as far as man is concerned. In some regions, e.g. parts of Africa, there

 OLF   are no wolves, but the hyena is the formal and functional equivalent. Both the wolf and the hyena belong to the dog family and both live by depredation. In other regions 'coyote' or 'fox' is used in place of the non-existent wolf. In places where there are no wolves nor foxes, it has sometimes been possible to use 'wild dog.'

b. Solution, type (2).

It is possible in some cases to use the name of an entirely different animal, but one which has the same function in the society. For example, among some peoples there may be no wolves nor any predatory animal which would attack a sheep except a tiger. There may not even be any wild dogs which might substitute. In some instances tigers have been substituted for wolves. Hence instead of "wolves in sheep's clothing" the translation reads 'tigers in sheep's clothing.' It may be preferable, however, in such instances to retain a borrowed word which has no meaning and explain in a footnote that such an animal 'resembles a large dog and hunts like a tiger.'

c. Solution, type (3).

CAMEL   If there is no closely corresponding animal, it is often possible to use some qualifying term. For example, camels are generally unknown in Latin America, but they are quite closely related to the llamas, which are well known in the Andean region. Moreover, the function of the camels of Bible times and of the llamas of present Andean culture is quite parallel. It would be possible to translate camel as 'a large llama-like animal.' Or one might prefer to use the borrowed word *camel*, preferably the Spanish *camello*, and in a footnote explain that this animal is 'a large llama-like animal.'

d. Solution, type (4).

FISH   It is possible that a brief descriptive name of an animal is all that is necessary. There may be no word for fish, for people may not have seen such creatures. It is sometimes possible to use a phrase such as 'things which live in the water' to describe fish. This is after all about the only part of a description in a note which would be intelligible to any natives who had not actually seen fish.

ASP

There may not be in the locality the exact species that is mentioned in the Bible. For example, there may be snakes but no asps. In such a case, one can translate "asps" as 'dangerous snakes' or 'poisonous snakes.'

WASPS
BEES

In almost all localities there are some kinds of flying insects. These may not be wasps, but one can use a descriptive term for wasps, namely, 'flying insects which sting.' "Bees" may be called 'flying insects which collect sweet liquid.'

e. Solution, type (5).

When none of the other suggested solutions are possible, one may employ a borrowed word and then in a footnote explain something about the animal. Such a description should attempt to state something about (1) the form of the animal (general size and shape), usually in terms of some other animal that may be known in the culture, and (2) the function of the animal in the society; whether, for example, it is wild and destructive or domesticated and helpful to man. All this should be brief, not a resumé of an article in the encyclopedia.

Ox

For example, an "ox" may be defined for some Pacific Island culture as follows: 'An ox is an animal about ten times the size of a pig. It is taken care of by men and is used to pull heavy loads.' Such a definition describes the size of the animal in terms of an animal which is already known, namely, the pig. The fact that the ox is domesticated, that is to say, is taken care of by men, is very important. This fact explains man's relationship to the animal. The fact that the ox does certain work for man defines the animal's relationship to man. It would probably be impossible to say 'the ox works for man,' for the word 'work' would probably imply some human type of activity. It is true that pulling heavy loads is not all that oxen did in Bible times, but it is one of the very important jobs. It would be unwise to try to list all the tasks, since many of them would be outside the understanding of the people. The one job is sufficient to explain the general cultural significance of the animal.

Instead of having difficulty finding words to correspond, it may be that the native language makes finer distinctions of meaning than are made in the English WORM or Greek. For example, the English word "worm" covers quite an area of meaning, for it includes several types of worms; e.g. ground worms, intestinal worms, and maggots. In describing Gehenna, Mark 9: 48, it is important to use the name for a worm which designates that class of worms which feeds upon refuse and carrion, for this is the picture of the valley of Gehenna, which was the dumping ground for the refuse of Jerusalem.

10.4 PLANT LIFE (FLORA)

Illustrative words: VINE, CORN (WHEAT), HERB, CEDAR, SYCAMORE, OLIVE.

The distinctions in plant life are as numerous as those in animal life. Similarly, the use which is made of plants is quite different, and this factor must not be overlooked. For example, among the Eastern Aztecs VINES there are vines, but these are not grapevines. They bear bitter-tasting berries and are not cultivated. The vine of the New Testament means the grapevine, which is quite rare in tropical countries. In one instance, the translator used a word for vine which designated one of the vines of the jungle which was used for tying together rafters of the house but which produced no fruit and was never cultivated. The translation of John 15 did not make sense. Since there was no fruit on such a vine, the exhortation to fruitfulness was lost. Moreover, the vine was only valuable when the branches were cut away and used in house construction. They were never cut off because they failed to bear fruit. In fact, the only resemblance between the grapevine and the vine in this translation was the manner of growth. Such a resemblance is not sufficient, for the whole functional significance of the comparison is lost. When there are no fruit-producing vines in any region, the translator is frequently obliged to translate, 'I am the plant, you are the branches. ' This is the closest equivalent which can be intelligible to the native, and the translation must be intelligible, otherwise it is useless to translate.

CORN
(WHEAT)
The confusion of "corn" and "wheat" has become quite difficult for American readers of the AV. One must remember that the corn of the Bible was wheat. Indian corn, also called maize, was not known in Europe before the discovery of America. It was developed by the Indians of the Western Hemisphere. In many parts of the Western Hemisphere there is still no other type of grain. Hence, it is impossible to use the word for "wheat" in such a passage as John 12:24. There is, of course, a certain amount of confusion, even as there is for some American readers of the AV, but it is better to use a word that has some meaning than to use a word which the natives do not know. One will often find it impossible to say 'corn-like grain,' for to some Indians there is actually no grain except corn. In fact, the word 'seed' in many languages of the Americas has as its central meaning 'the grain of corn.' The entire agricultural economy centers about this one plant. However, where people have knowledge of wheat or other small grains, the translator should not make the mistake of following an uninformed interpretation of the AV.

Special expressions are often associated with certain plants. For example, the Bible speaks of "white unto harvest." In some parts of the world this type of statement is not intelligible. To such people the fields may be 'red unto harvest.' The Greek word *leukos* designates the color of light, but this may be all the way from white to yellow. The expression 'red unto harvest' is in some ways as good a description as "white unto harvest," and it is not too far from the Greek idiom.

The classification of plants according to size and general habits of growth may be expected to be different in different languages. In English we distinguish generally between such classes as grass, flowers, weeds, bushes, and trees. These are not well defined and exclusive classes, but they are more or less the general

terms for different types of plants. Herbs constitute
another special class of plants, which are used in medi-
cines and cooking. It is difficult, however, to establish
fixed divisions in our popular terminology. We may
often be at a loss to define when a plant ceases to belong
to one of these classes and becomes a member of another
class. For example, when does a plant cease to be a
bush and become a tree? Also, for some of us one plant
is a weed, but for others it is a flower. This indefinite-
ness of distinction is characteristic of our own language,
and we must expect it in other languages as well.

Some languages make a major distinction between
plants which live year after year and those which are
only seasonal. Others distinguish between plants which
are good for firewood and those which are not. Another
division may be based upon the value of the plant to
man, e.g. flowers vs. weeds.

The translator must determine the exact meaning of
the word used in the text and then find that equivalent
HERBS   term in the native culture. For example, Greek *lachanon*,
Mark 4: 32, translated "herbs" in AV, designates plants
which grow in dug-up soil. They are principally the
seasonal vegetables.

It is often difficult to find trees in the vicinity of any
CEDAR   culture which correspond to such trees as "cedar,"
SYCAMORE   "sycamore," and "olive." It is often necessary to bor-
OLIVE   row the meaningless names for these trees. If this is
done, it is wise to use a classifying name as well, e.g.
'cedar tree,' 'sycamore tree,' and 'olive tree.' This same
principle may apply to all empty words, including
proper names, e.g. 'river Jordan,' 'mountain Lebanon,'
and 'country Egypt.' All peoples are accustomed to
foreign names employed by foreign peoples. If a classifying word is employed, so that the otherwise empty
word is known to be a foreign name for some type of
recognizable object, the zero significance of the name itself is not such a problem. In such a situation it is supported by the classifying word, which does have some
meaning. This process may be applied to many types
of features, e.g. animals, plants, people, and events.

Chapter 11

TERMS FOR FEATURES OF MATERIAL CULTURE

THE features of the material culture include material objects which a people make or use. They may be divided for our purposes into (1) food, (2) clothing, (3) constructions, (4) manufactures, and (5) measurements.

11.1   FOOD

Illustrative words: LOAVES, WINE, LEAVEN, LOCUSTS.

Articles of diet are by no means similar in various cultures. Moreover, the manner in which food is prepared also differs considerably. If it is possible, one should make the closest approximation possible to both the form of the food and the functional significance of LOAVES   this food in the society. For example, the loaves of bread in ancient Palestine were more like our large buns than like our loaves. Many a child in Sunday school has been amazed at the boy who presented to the disciples his lunch containing five loaves. He is likely to exclaim, as some have, "What a lunch!" For the Indians of many parts of Latin America the *tortilla*, although made of corn rather than of wheat or barley, is the closest equivalent to the barley loaves of the New Testament.

WINE   One of the very difficult words in the Bible is "wine." In some societies there are no grapes and, accordingly, no locally made wine. Some tribes know what wine is because they import it. Some translators object to the use of the word 'wine' on the basis that, according to their contentions, Jesus never drank anything but unfermented grape juice or the juice from raisins. A close examination of the arguments employed by certain advocates of such a position reveals some lack of understanding of the historical and cultural factors involved. However, if translators object to the use of wine for the reason that the functional significance of the drinking of wine is quite different now in some Christian communities than it was in the time of Christ, there is no objection as far as the Bible Society is concerned. If the translator insists on translating "wine" as 'the juice of the grape,' and by such not stating whether it is fermented or not, this is all right. If, on the other hand, the translator prefers to use the word 'wine,' meaning 'fermented grape juice,' and depends upon teaching to explain the different cultural significance of wine, this likewise is perfectly satisfactory. In situations where there are no grapes and no wine, translators have employed 'the juice of a fruit.'

LEAVEN

Most people employ some type of fermentation to change the form of certain foods. Whether this is made of fruit juices, soured dough, or soured milk, the general function is the same. A word which denotes the 'starter' of the process is usually sufficient to be used for yeast. "Unleavened bread" is bread without this fermentation agent and "leavened bread" is bread with this fermentation.

LOCUSTS

It is not always necessary to take into consideration whether a particular group of people eat a certain type of food mentioned in the Bible. In certain aboriginal societies fish are not eaten, but all peoples are more or less accustomed to the fact that other people eat different things from what they themselves eat. English readers are almost always amused and sometimes amazed at the eating of locusts in the Bible. Nevertheless, the translation should represent accurately the text of the Bible. Only in such a matter as the comparison noted on p. 131 must one consider the advisability of some adaptations.

11.2   CLOTHING

Illustrative words: SHOES, SANDALS, COAT, CLOAK, EARRINGS, BRACELETS, GRAVECLOTHES, LINEN, SILK, WOOL.

The differences in clothing worn by different peoples and the differences in social meaning of such clothing are sometimes amazing. Even in our own culture, we have the expression that "the clothes made the man." We all state that we do not believe this, but we immediately classify people by the clothes which they wear. Moreover, we recognize that certain occasions call for certain types of dress. A man does not want to appear on the beach in a formal dinner coat nor in the Waldorf Astoria dining room in a bathing suit. Aboriginal people are equally conscious of the relationship between clothing and social propriety. For example, one informant insisted that the translator change from 'sandals' to 'shoes' in Luke 15:22, for he insisted that the owner of a great estate would never give his returning son a pair of sandals. In most parts of the world, the 'sandal' is the closest formal and functional parallel to "shoes" used in Bible times. The sandals are the customary footgear for most aboriginal peoples. If the translator gives all the people of Bible times 'shoes,' they may be immediately classed as detestable government officials.

SHOES

SANDALS

The Biblical culture contained many more types of garments than one is likely to find among some aboriginal peoples, especially those who live in the tropics. About the only distinction which can be made is between (1) the inner garment, which may be worn constantly, and (2) the outer garment, which may be put on (a) for certain special occasions, (b) during certain seasons of the year, or (c) at certain times of the day.

It is important to note the relative difference in garments in a passage such as Matthew 5:40. The garment which is requested is the smaller, less expensive tunic, but the additional garment which is offered is the outer, more expensive cloak. Descriptions of the various garments may be found in lexicons, Bible dictionaries, and commentaries. The translator must choose the form of native dress or a short descriptive name for the Biblical equivalent. For many Indians of Latin America the tunic, Greek *chitōn*, is equivalent to the (1) pants and shirt, (2) dress, or (3) breech-cloth (if the natives wear nothing else). The cloak, Greek *himation*, is equivalent to the blanket which they may throw about them in cold weather. Where natives wear nothing except a breech-cloth, the best thing to do is to get them to give names for various parts of the translator's clothing. Some equivalent terms may then be worked out, even though they may be new to native speakers.

Figures of speech which are dependent upon the wearing of certain types of clothes may be difficult for some people to understand. Girding the body for action is quite meaningless if translated literally in some languages. The belt or girdle is only used to keep the clothes from falling off, not as a means of keeping them close to the body so they may not interfere with one's actions. If "gird thyself" in Luke 17:8 is translated just to mean 'put on your belt,' the meaning of the passage may be lost. The real meaning is to put the clothes on or to adjust them so that one can work efficiently. The expression "gird up the loins of your mind," I Peter 1:13, is completely hopeless in most languages if translated literally. The literal meaning in some languages is equivalent to 'put a belt around the hips of your thoughts.' The expression should usually be changed to 'make your mind ready.'

EARRINGS
BRACE-
LETS

Earrings and bracelets may often be described briefly as 'rings worn in the ears' or 'rings worn on the arm.' These types of decorations may seem very strange to natives. The San Blas people, for example, cannot understand why a woman would hang a gold ring in her ear, when it is much more conspicuous, and to them more beautiful, if it is worn in the nose.

GRAVE-
CLOTHES

There may be no term for "graveclothes" in the native language. People are usually buried without clothes or with the clothes which they wear every day. The "graveclothes" of the Bible must usually be translated by a phrase such as 'cloth that people are buried in.'

LINEN
SILK
WOOL

Some types of cloth are unknown in some localities. It is necessary therefore to borrow the name from the trade language. In such cases, it is often convenient, as with proper names and other unknown objects, to employ a classifier, e.g. 'linen cloth,' 'wool cloth,' and 'silk cloth.'

11.3   Constructions

Illustrative words: HOUSE, HOME, TEMPLE, GATES, DOORS, TAB-
ERNACLE, TOWER, UPPER ROOM, JUDGMENT HALL, PRETORIUM,
WINEFAT, TOMB, SEPULCHRE.

The variety of constructions in various parts of the world is
extreme. The houses of some aboriginals bear practically no formal resemblance to those in Palestine, and yet both of them have
a similar function. The translation must make use of these functional parallels. Sometimes this is quite difficult. For some of the
people of Africa, a man who desired to proclaim something from
a housetop could only be considered a lunatic. For others, the
idea of building an upper room would seem unutterably silly. As
one native remarked after having seen a picture of a skyscraper
in New York, "You people in the United States must be very
foolish. You go to all the trouble to build many houses on top of
one another, and then you have to go to all the effort of climbing
up in order to get into them." Formal correspondences are often
at a minimum, but functional ones are usually quite obvious.

A few hunting and gathering peoples use only caves
and brush shelters, but almost all cultures have two or
three types of permanent buildings. One of these serves
HOUSE   for living purposes. These are the equivalent of "house"
HOME   and "home," whether the building is occupied by one
family unit or whether it is a communal lodge. The
functional significance is the essential matter. Most
peoples also have some large buildings, perhaps for
public meeting halls. If these halls or large constructions
TEMPLE   have some general name, then the expression 'hall for
worship' may serve for the "temple." Many cultures,
however, make nothing larger than a house, and so one
must employ this word 'house' with various adjectives
to denote various classes of buildings. The expression
'the house of prayer' or the 'house of worship' may be
used for the temple in Jerusalem. One may want to
SYNA-   distinguish between the temple in Jerusalem and the
GOGUES   synagogues by indicating a difference in size. A distinction in size may also serve to indicate a difference
in importance. The "temple" may be 'the big house of

worship' and the "synagogue" may be 'the small house
of worship.'

GATES   "Gates" and "doors" may also be unknown to people.
DOORS   There are comparatively few tribes which have gates
for their cities. When an aboriginal people have no
gates at all, it is sometimes possible to translate the
"gates of the city" as the 'edge of the city,' if only the
boundary is indicated, e.g. Luke 7:12. In other instances the "gates of the city" are used to indicate the
means of entrance and exit to the city. In Acts 9:24,
one may translate 'the exits from the city.' In other
instances, the emphasis is on the way by which one
passes to a certain point. In such cases one may use
'way,' e.g. Matthew 7:13. In still other cases, the gates
are actual objects, as in Acts 12:10. They may be
translated 'large iron doors.' The difficulty with using
'doors' throughout is that so often a 'door' is thought
of only in terms of a house. The entire account is confusing to the native, because he cannot understand the
setting.

TABER-   The word "tabernacle" must often be translated by two
NACLE   different words. The tabernacle of Moses may sometimes be
translated as 'a large house of cloth.' The expression 'a
small house of cloth' may be used to translate "tent." At the
Feast of the Tabernacles the people set up little booths covered with branches. Such constructions parallel the temporary lean-to or brush shelter which many people use for
a temporary shelter either in their cornfields or along the
trail.

TOWER   A "tower" is a strange thing to many peoples. It may be
translated in some languages as 'a high house' or 'a high
house one looks out from.'

UPPER   An "upper room" must often be translated 'a high room.'
ROOM   A "judgment hall" may be translated in many languages
JUDGMENT 'a house where people are judged.' But if there is some special
HALL   public hall in the local village, it may have the function of
such a judgment hall and the name of it can be used. Such a
PRETO-   hall may also serve as the "pretorium," John 18:28 (ARV).
RIUM   In Latin America, however, a great many Indians are ac-
quainted with the *palacio del gobernador*, 'the palace of the
governor.' Both the phrase and the associated meaning are

very imposing and foreign, but so was the Roman Pretorium to the Jews of Jerusalem.

WINEFAT   Some types of constructions are unknown to aboriginal peoples. The "winefat" of Mark 12: 1 may have no parallel. The only thing which may be done in the Eastern Aztec is to translate with a descriptive phrase such as 'a pit where people squeeze out juice.' One cannot use a passive construction, e.g. 'a pit where juice is squeezed out,' for the language has no passive forms. There is also no word for 'grape,' for the people do not have grapes. As in every case, one must say something, and this something must make some sense, even though it may not constitute an exact equivalent.

TOMB
SEPUL-
CHRE   The words "tomb" and "sepulchre" often give considerable difficulty. Most cultures have nothing that corresponds to tombs hewed out of the hillsides or built up into small mausoleums. In many instances one must translate 'place where they bury the dead.' The description of the construction must be left for explanation. In some cases, 'small cave' is the closest equivalent for the term used to denote the type of tombs in which Lazarus and Jesus were buried.

11.4   MANUFACTURES

Illustrative words: THRONE, SEAT, TABLE, VESSEL, BED, CANDLE, STONE WATER JARS, CHARGER, CANDLESTICK, CHAINS, FETTERS, CROWN, MILLSTONE, OINTMENT, VEIL.

It is frequently inconceivable to us that certain peoples do not have some of the manufactures that we find so indispensable to any type of adequate living. For us a chair is essential, but for some people it is considered a terribly hard, awkward thing on which to sit. They may much prefer to sit on a pillow on the floor, which may be much more comfortable. However, in translating the Bible we usually need to employ not only one word for an object people sit on, but two words. One must be used to designate a seat which ordinary people sit on, the other a seat on which only rulers sit.

THRONE   This latter will be somewhat equivalent to a "throne." The cultures of many African tribes provide a 'stool' for the first word and 'a king's stool' for the second. In

SEAT   some cultures one must translate 'a small stool' for the ordinary seat and 'a large stool' for the "throne."

TABLE Where a table does not occur in the culture, one may translate in certain contexts 'where they eat,' if the process of eating is involved, or in other contexts 'where they place things,' if tables with this other function are denoted. In every instance the translator must visualize the situation thoroughly. By visualizing we do not mean imagining, but rather getting a complete comprehension of the details from adequate sources of information as to Biblical life. On the basis of such an accurate picture, one can then substitute names for objects in the aboriginal culture or employ descriptive terms which will convey to the native at least the essential features of the setting.

VESSEL One must be careful not to let the meaning of a word in English or some other European language distort the meaning of the word in the aboriginal language. For example, the Greek *skeuos* 'vessel,' or in fact almost any kind of an implement, is translated in the de Valera Spanish Version by *vaso*, which is known most generally in Latin America as 'drinking glass.' If one translates literally the meaning of *vaso* in its present central meaning, the resultant phrase in Acts 10: 11 is 'a drinking glass like a sheet,' which of course is as ridiculous as 'a flower like a kitchen stove.' One may not use *vaso* in its present central meaning but must translate it as 'vessel' or 'container.' Translators should be constantly warned against translating words always in their present central meaning. These words may have been perfectly legitimate when they were first used, e.g. AV "prevent," I Thessalonians 4: 15, and "let," Romans 1: 13; but one should check all such verses with modern commentaries and translations.

The critic is likely to be aghast at the natives' incomplete understanding of the setting of the Bible. When a native preacher describes certain things in the Bible, the translator may have to struggle to keep from laughing at a description of such an event as Jesus in the boat with his disciples during a storm. The native preacher may never have been in a boat nor have seen one. His description may be quite distorted, for it must be given in terms of the only experiences which he and his audience have had. If they are not seafaring people, their understanding is likely to be strange, to say the least. Such failure to perceive the exact meaning of the passage is not much different, however, from the statements of some preachers who describe a scene in Palestine with about as much accuracy as the painters of the Italian Renaissance painted it. We must not expect aboriginal peoples to understand all the features of cultural correspondence immediately. Some of them may never understand. The important thing is to bring the truths of the Bible to these people in a form which is intelligible to them. The cultural features will be understood in terms of the local parallels, despite what the preacher may say.

Descriptive terms are especially useful in translating certain manufactured items which do not occur in the native culture. A "bed" is 'what one lies down on.' A "candle" is 'a small torch' or 'a small light.' "Stone water jars" are 'vessels made of stone which hold water.' A "charger," Matthew 14: 8, is 'something one holds things on.' A "candlestick" is 'a place where a small light is placed.' "Chains and fetters" are 'metal bands on one's hands and feet.' Most people know of some types of metal though they may not be acquainted with iron. A "crown" may be 'something around the head.' These descriptive translations are only to be used if the culture does not possess special names for such objects. If there is something like a millstone, even though it may not resemble the Biblical one any more than the three-legged *metate* in Mexico does, the native word should be used. The name for the *metate* may be used for the millstone of ancient times, since its use is practically the same, and the effect of it, when tied about one's neck, would be identical. The superficial differences in form are not sufficient to make it necessary to borrow another word for "millstone" or to employ a descriptive phrase. Likewise, though the natives may not have anything corresponding to the "charger" upon which John the Baptist's head was placed, they undoubtedly have some type of large platter-like dish. Such a word may be employed, for the function is the same even though the form may be somewhat different. Descriptive terms should not be used if there are some comparatively close cultural parallels.

Margin terms: BED CANDLE STONE WATER JARS CHARGER CANDLESTICK CHAINS AND FETTERS CROWN MILLSTONE

OINTMENT   Some societies have no such things as ointments. Ashes may be the only substance which they rub on their bodies. For such people it is quite difficult to describe an ointment. In some languages, however, this has been done by translating 'sweet-smelling water' or 'sweet-smelling oil.' These are probably the only expressions which would make sense.

VEIL   The use of a word in a restricted meaning may also produce difficulty. For example, the "veil of the temple," Mark 15:38, has been translated literally into some languages in Latin America by a word which designates the central meaning of *veil*, namely, 'a veil worn over the head.' Such a word designates either a wedding veil or one worn in grieving or on certain church occasions. Such a word cannot be used for the veil in the temple. The phrases 'the wedding veil of the temple' or 'the mourning veil of the temple' would be senseless. Actually, one must use a word which corresponds more closely to 'curtain.'

11.5 MEASUREMENTS

The problems involved in rendering Biblical terms of weights and measures are very adequately and scientifically treated in Supplement No. 1 to the *Guide for Translators, Revisers, and Editors*, prepared by James Oscar Boyd and published by the American Bible Society. This supplement is reproduced in the Appendix to this volume.

Chapter 12

TERMS FOR FEATURES OF SOCIAL CULTURE

THE social culture includes those features which define the ways in which people adjust themselves to each other. They may be conveniently divided into two types: (1) the social units, from the individual personality to humanity itself, and (2) the social mechanisms, namely, controls and institutions by which people regulate their relationships to each other.

12.1   THE SOCIAL ENTITIES

The social entities are those units in any society which are recognized as significant functional elements. For every society they differ more or less. In general, however, we may conveniently class them under (1) the individual personality, (2) the family, (3) classes, and (4) ethnic groups.

12.1.1   THE INDIVIDUAL PERSONALITY

NAME

The Biblical attitudes toward human personality are of great theological importance. There is, however, only one word which produces any considerable difficulty in other languages. This is the word "name." The great difference attached to the significance of the name of a person in the Bible times in contrast with our own culture is very important. Note such phrases as "whatsoever ye shall ask in my name," John 14:13, "believed in the name of the only begotten Son of God," John 3:18, and "life through his name," John 20:31. These expressions are generally difficult for us to understand, for the word "name" does not mean the same to us as it meant to those of Bible times. To them the name was the symbolization of the authority and personality of the individual who possessed the name. To us a name is far less important. It may be changed whenever one can convince a judge that another name

178

(Name)   might be more economically advantageous. The name is also a legal method of giving one's written assent to certain business transactions, but to us it is not the symbol of the personality. To the Eskimo, who thinks that each person possesses a body, spirit, and name, and that together these form the important trinity of each personality, the word 'name' has a meaning somewhat equivalent to that of Bible times. For some tribes of aboriginals in which each person possesses several names, one by which one is known to outsiders, one by which one is known to one's own tribesmen, another to one's family, and still another by which one is known to the spirits, the problem is still more confusing.

It may be necessary in most instances to employ the native word for 'name' for each instance of occurrence of the word in the Biblical text. One must then depend upon oral explanations or footnotes to explain the meaning.

In some instances the use of 'name' may be so meaningless that it is legitimate to change the rendering in the native language. For example, in Aztec the expression "I have come in my Father's name," John 5:43, is meaningless. One cannot 'come in the name of anyone.' One can translate, however, 'I have come on my Father's authority.' This makes sense to the Aztec and actually represents the meaning of the text. "Life through his name," John 20:31, is likewise meaningless in many languages. In fact, in some instances the impression is that the name of Jesus is to be used as some magic word in religious incantations. It would probably be much better in some languages to translate 'life through him' if the word 'name' is meaningless and confusing. Or this alternate reading may be given in a footnote, to avoid changing the text.

There is considerable importance in building up to some extent the Biblical significance of the name, for it is so deeply associated with much of the Biblical culture. But one should likewise beware of usages which will make the name a 'fetish' rather than a symbol of the personality.

The name actually plays a double role. On the one hand it is a symbol for a psychological entity, the person. It is also a symbol for this entity in the social group, for the name symbolizes the relationship of the one person to others. In such a case it represents the authority of the person concerned. Accordingly, the word "name" may be treated under psychological forms or social culture. It is, however, in most contexts associated with the social culture.

12.1.2   THE FAMILY

Illustrative words: FATHER, SON, MOTHER, BROTHER, SISTER, PARENTS, ORPHAN.

It is taken for granted by some people that all societies have approximately the same type of family life. This is quite wrong. For example, in the system of communal marriage practiced by the people of the Ponape Islands before the coming of missionaries, there was no parallel for the word "father" (see page 136). Similarly, there was no word for "son." It was impossible to translate "Son of God" by any word-for-word parallel. The only possible way to translate such an expression was by 'one belonging to God.' In translating the word "son" when it was used alone, the translators had to employ the words for 'male' or 'man.' This was the closest parallel in the language.

FATHER
SON

Many tribes have very elaborate systems for identifying family relationships. The son may speak of his father with one term, but the daughter must use another. The same situation may exist for the word

MOTHER

'mother.' Also, the father may use certain terms in speaking to his son or daughter, but the mother may use entirely different ones. To the translator the differences of terms employed in designating the members of both the immediate and the extended family may be most confusing, but he must work out the system if he is going to translate successfully.

In many languages a difference is made as to the relative age of the brothers and sisters. For example,

BROTHER
SISTER

in the Maya language an older brother is called one thing and a younger brother is called another. A similar difference exists in the words for 'sister.' We are not always told the relative age of brothers and sisters in the Bible, but in order to translate into the Maya it is necessary to decide upon the relative age in all instances. One must use one term or the other, and the usage must be kept consistent. In the Bible the older brother is usually mentioned before the younger. For example, it is always "James and his brother John." In our own culture we often give the name of the more important brother first, but the Biblical order is generally according to age. In the case of Mary, Martha, and Lazarus, we do not have such definite information. In John 11: 1 the phrase "Mary and her sister Martha" gives us the clue that Mary was probably older than Martha, but there is no statement as to the relative age of Lazarus. However, in some languages one must make the distinction. One may judge that, since he is a mature man, it is probably better to use a word for older brother so that people may not receive the impression that he is a small boy. In John 2: 12 one must be sure that the word for designating Jesus' brothers means his 'younger brothers,' if the language makes such a distinction. Any other translation would seriously affect the teaching of the virgin birth.

PARENTS

It is quite impossible in some languages to say 'parents' in one word. One must often say 'father and mother.' On the other hand in the Maya there is just one word for 'brothers and sisters.' Both classes are combined into one term which may be translated into English by the rather rare word *sibling*.

ORPHAN

In some languages there is no word for an orphan. Such a person is either 'without a mother' or 'without a father' or 'without a father and a mother.'

The designation for the family unit as a whole is often called in the Bible "a house," e.g. "thou and all thy house," Acts 11:14. The word for 'house' or 'household' in the aboriginal language may not be a term for the immediate or extended family unit.

In such a case one must translate 'you and all your family.'

12.1.3   Classes

Illustrative words: SIR, LORD, COMMON PEOPLE, SERVANT, SLAVE, HIGH CAPTAINS, CHIEF ESTATES, HONORABLE COUNSELOR, ELDER, EUNUCH, GENERATION.

The classes in any society may be based upon such factors as hereditary privileges, wealth, education, military prowess, and political leadership. The classes existing in certain cultures and the relative degrees of respect paid them differ greatly in various societies. In some of the societies of the Orient, e.g. Korea and Japan, one must use certain forms of words to designate the relative social position of the speaker, the one spoken to, and the one spoken of. Among the Aztecs in Mexico there is a similarly elaborate system for indicating respect. These features will be discussed on p. 262 ff.

SIR   The titles of respect equivalent to English "sir" and
LORD   "lord" are almost always difficult. One must be very
careful in following the text language, for the correspondences are never automatic. For example, the Spanish *señor* means either 'sir' or 'Lord.' It is capitalized in the second meaning, but when it occurs initially in a sentence or direct discourse, this distinction of capitalization is not apparent. In an attempt to make all words conform, one translator had been very meticulous and mechanical in his work. The result was that in John 4:19 the woman at the well said, 'Lord, I perceive you are a prophet.' It does not make sense to acknowledge Jesus as God and then turn about and say that he is a prophet. In such an instance one must use some form of polite address, translating something equivalent to *sir* or *mister*.

One must be very sure of the forms of address in any society. One translator had noticed that when the natives spoke of him, they employed a rather rare word but one which seemed to indicate great respect. In certain instances it was also used of some few rich and influential native men. This term, however, actually indicated a good deal of resentment which the people had against (1) those who came from the outside, hence were foreigners, or (2) those who acquired so much wealth that they classed themselves as superior to the rest of the people. When the translator found this situation to be the case, he immediately changed the salutation to that form which was used for any native man.

Salutations are usually very full of connotative significance. In one language it was found that the title of 'sir' which the translators had used of Jesus always meant a man who was married. Such a form should not be used in salutations addressed to Jesus. When the translator comes across any term of salutation, he must find out its full area of meaning; namely, where, when, by whom, and to whom it is used.

COMMON
PEOPLE

Words to designate common people are often more difficult to find than terms for leaders. The common people are often the less colorful and less easily distinguishable in any society. There may be no term which designates them in contrast with the leadership of the society. In Mark 12:37 the "common people" were the crowds of uneducated persons who were deprived of the opportunities of education and leadership. These constituted the proletariat of their day. It is quite difficult in some societies to find a word to describe these common people. They generally have many characteristics, e.g. they are poor, uneducated, backward, despised by the upper classes, and exploited; but one term to include all the underprivileged class is usually not easy to find. In the Maya language the translator found a very excellent means of designating this class. He noticed that one's social status in a Maya village could be classified very accurately on the basis of the distance one lived from the center of town. The rich and influential people lived on the central plaza or very near it. The less important people lived a little farther away. The "common people" were those who could be described as living in the back part of the village. Hence, the phrase 'those in the back of the town' was used to designate "the common people."

SERVANTS
SLAVES

It is quite important to distinguish between "servants," Greek *diakonoi*, and "slaves," Greek *douloi*. In the Pauline Epistles this contrast is very significant. However, in some societies there are no slaves. If this is the case, one should attempt to make a distinction between two different classes of servants. A "slave" may be 'a servant who is not paid wages.' Such a descriptive term may be employed to distinguish between one who hires out for pay and one who enjoys no such privilege. Sometimes a "slave" may be a 'have-to worker,' that is to say, a man under obligation to work. Such phrases are not entirely satisfactory, but they help to convey the different social status of the slave from that of the servant.

It is often difficult to obtain a sufficient number of native terms for the upper stratas of society. For example, the guests at Herod's birthday party, Mark 6: 21, are usually a

LORDS

source of trouble. The first group, AV "lords," were those rather closely associated with the king, the so-called courtiers. For a society in which there are no such parallels, one must often translate simply 'big rulers.' King Herod may often be translated as the 'biggest ruler,' where there is no regal sys-

HIGH
CAPTAINS

tem. The "high captains" were equivalent in status to modern generals. If a culture has no highly developed military system, one may translate this by 'big warriors.' The "chief

CHIEF
ESTATES

estates of Galilee" may be translated as the 'leading men of Galilee.' In each case the translator must attempt to compare the society of Bible times with the society existing within the primitive culture and to find parallels. If he cannot, then he must introduce some type of descriptive phrase which conveys to the native an idea of the relative importance and function of the person in the Biblical culture.

HONOR-
ABLE
COUN-
SELOR

The phrase "honorable counselor," AV, Mark 15: 43, sometimes produces difficulty. In the de Valera Spanish Version it is translated aptly as *senador noble*, but, for the average primitive society, there is usually no direct parallel. The term "counselor" must often be translated 'one of the men in the council' and "honorable" may be translated as 'important.' The area of meaning of the Greek word *euschēmōn* includes 'honorable,' 'of good standing,' 'influential,' 'wealthy,' and 'respectable.' The term 'important' may be the closest native equivalent to this area of meaning.

ELDER   A term for "elder" is usually not difficult to find. 'An old man' may often be used. In most societies, the old men have certain prestige, and function in an important advisory capacity. If they have any special title, this may be employed. If not, a word descriptive of their age is usually the best.

EUNUCH   The term "eunuch" is in some contexts synonymous with 'servant.' Such men were employed as servants for women's quarters. At times they held very important posts, e.g. the Ethiopian eunuch in Acts 8:27. The term "eunuch" denotes primarily an emasculated man, but it may also be used to designate one who is naturally incapacitated for marriage. "Eunuch" is also interpreted by some as designating one who abstains from marriage, e.g. Matthew 19:12c.

The translation of the word "eunuch" is not easy. A descriptive term based upon the man's physical state is often considered vulgar in the native speech. The term "eunuch" is frequently transliterated without explanation. In other instances it is translated 'official' or 'servant' as the context may supply the meaning. In any event, obscurity of meaning is better than vulgarity.

GENERA-   The term "generation" designates a class of people who are
TION   contemporaries. It may often be translated as 'these people' or 'the people living today.'

12.1.4   ETHNIC GROUPS

Illustrative words: GENTILES, TRIBE, NATION, WORLD.

GENTILES   Almost all peoples recognize two ethnic groups: (1) the in-group and (2) the out-group. The in-group constitutes those people who are looked upon as having practically the same customs as the central unit. The out-group includes all others. The in-group may be the tribe or some division of the tribe which recognizes itself as a special unit. The out-group includes all other tribes and foreigners in general. The Jews of Jesus' time considered almost all the descendants of Jacob as being in the in-group. The out-group were Gentiles.

There are many features which in any society help to define the in-group in contrast to the out-groups, e.g. descent from a common ancestor (real or fictional), identity of government, intermarriage, language, commerce, similarity of religion. Language is the most

(GEN-
TILES)
common criterion, for there is nothing quite so revealing as linguistic differences. But whatever the criteria may be, one should closely examine native bases for ethnic grouping. This is important in finding the proper equivalent.

The word "Gentile" seems to provide considerable trouble. In Latin America it is quite generally inadvisable to borrow the word in some Spanish form, for in most instances the word is already used with the meaning of 'unbelievers' or 'unbaptized persons.' The Catholic church employed a clear case of adaptation in the usage of the word "Gentiles." To the Jew a Gentile was outside the proper religious group. To the Catholic the unbaptized person was outside the proper religious fold. Since the word "Gentile" has already been borrowed with a highly specialized meaning, the translator must use some other term which will designate the out-group. Such a phrase as 'the other peoples' or 'the different people' may be adequate. It is usually unwise to specify the basis of the difference, for there are so many different factors. In some translations, the translators have attempted to employ some such expression for "Gentiles" as 'those who do not love God.' This is quite unwise, for there were some Gentiles in the Old Testament times who did love God. This was unquestionably true in New Testament times. One should not adopt a descriptive expression which cannot be used more or less consistently throughout.

The designations for the in-group and the out-group are very seldom rigidly defined. Each person usually belongs to a successive series of groups. He belongs to an immediate family; then he belongs to an extended family including all his blood relatives and those who have married into his family. He may also belong to a certain clan which claims an actual or mythical ancestor. He undoubtedly belongs to other groups on the basis of such factors as marriage restrictions, geographical location, religion, and language. He will belong to a tribe or a special division of a tribe. Beyond each of these groups of which he considers himself a member comes the out-group. Aboriginal people rarely consider themselves as members of the human family, even as civilized people rarely act as though they are members of it.

TRIBE   The translator must attempt to find the closest approximations between the Biblical society and the aboriginal. The "tribes of Israel" may parallel the 'clans' of another society. The "tribes of earth" may be equivalent to the 'different peoples of the earth.'

NATION   The word "nation" usually designates a political entity. This may be completely synonymous with 'tribe' or 'people' in some languages.

WORLD   The "world" often designates mankind. "The sin of the world," John 1:29, must often be translated 'the sin of the people on the earth.' It may be impossible to translate "world" by an expression which also means the 'globe' or the 'ground.' 'The sin of the ground' is not the meaning of the passage. In Matthew 24:14 it is often important that "the world" be translated by 'the people of the earth.' The Greek designates 'the inhabited earth' and the emphasis is upon the individuals in the earth, not the physical form of this planet.

As in all other phases of culture, the translator must make a careful study of the manner in which the native society classifies various entities. He may then find the closest approximation to the Biblical usage and employ it.

12.2   SOCIAL MECHANISMS

The individual and the various units of society are regulated in their interrelationships by certain mechanisms. These are almost unlimited in number and variety. Religious aspects of these social factors are especially important in most societies. This was especially true of the Biblical culture. In our society religion tends to be compartmentalized (set off to itself), whereas in aboriginal societies almost everything is under the control of magic or religion. Therefore, it is quite difficult to discuss social mechanisms apart from the religious culture. However, because in some cultures the social and religious factors tend to be separate, the social mechanisms will be discussed in so far as possible in terms of their purely social aspects. Those words which have very important religious significance will be discussed under Religious Culture.

Many different divisions of social mechanisms may be made. One which may be as helpful as any other for our purposes is the following: (1) socio-religious rites, (2) patterns of general social intercourse, (3) government, (4) laws, (5) property, (6) occupations, and (7) war.

12.2.1   SOCIO-RELIGIOUS RITES

The socio-religious rites are so called because they almost invariably combine social and religious factors. They include those rites which accompany what are considered in most cultures as being the four most important times in any person's life, namely, birth, puberty, marriage, and death. The importance which may be attached to these various phases of life differs greatly in various cultures. In our own culture, birth, marriage, and death are much more emphasized than puberty. In another culture, puberty rites may be very elaborate, but almost nothing may be done in the case of death. Great variety will also be found in the form of these social mechanisms. Accordingly, the translation problems which involve these features of culture are often quite complicated.

Illustrative words: BIRTH, WITH CHILD, KNOW A MAN, BETROTH, MARRIAGE, VIRGIN, CIRCUMCISION, BIRTHDAY, BEGET, CONCUBINE, DEATH, BURIAL.

BIRTH   The words of socio-religious rites and events are often highly specialized in connotative values. Such words describe relationships which are quite intimate and highly interpretative in most cultures. Very special care must be exercised in every phase. The word for 'birth' may be highly specialized in meaning, depending upon whether an animal is being born, or a human, or whether the birth is single or multiple. Some terms for birth may be perfectly proper terms, but other terms may have highly vulgar connotations. Expressions

WITH CHILD   which denote pregnancy are not so likely to be evasive as in English, but one should check all terms with both men and women informants in order to obtain an accurate knowledge of the connotations of such words.

KNOW A MAN   An expression such as "knew her not," Matthew 1: 25, may scarcely ever be translated literally into another language and still make sense. Moreover, the translator does not want to be either ambiguous or vulgar in this passage. It is possible in almost any language to use some term for the avoidance of sexual intercourse which is clear and at the same time not vulgar. Such expressions should be checked with several informants.

BETROTH   Some societies have no form of betrothal. If such is the case, they will not have a word to denote this type of relationship. People just do not have words for things of which they have had no experience. We do not have a special word for a three-headed monster with onyx eyes and a blue beard, wearing a graduate's cap and gown, unless this is our special vision of the dean of men at the old alma mater. We usually do not have a name for such an object, for we have never seen such a thing. In a culture where there is no such thing as betrothal, there will be no special word for it. The translator may look a long time, but he is doomed to disappointment. However, as in so many cases, he can describe the situation in Matthew 1:18 by saying, 'when Joseph had asked Mary to marry him' or 'when Mary had been promised to Joseph in marriage.'

MARRIAGE   Marriage may be quite an elaborate rite, as it is in Western culture, or it may be nothing more than a man and a woman coming to live in the same house. The obligations under this second form of marriage may be just as binding as when an elaborate ceremony is performed. However, in most places in the world the patterns of Western civilization have been laid down by the dominant political powers and so a marriage, in order to be legal, must involve some sort of ritual, whether civil or religious. Despite these changes in customs, the people may retain the older terminology.

"Marriage" may be translated by 'a man coming to live with a woman' or 'a woman coming to live with a man,' depending upon whether the woman or the man changes the place of residence.

In almost all societies marriages are both made and broken. In fact many societies, in addition to Hollywood, live in a state of brittle monogamy. In some instances, divorce is as easily accomplished as marriage. The man or the woman may leave without ceremony. In discussing divorce in Matthew 19:7 it is quite important to employ some type of expression which conveys in so far as possible the legal factor in divorce.

VIRGIN   It is extremely important that the translator use all care and caution in the use of the word for "virgin." The use of a word which designates both a virgin and one who participates in certain puberty rites is often quite dangerous, unless the translator is fully aware of all the practices in such puberty rites. The word for 'young girl' is often not sufficient, for in many societies a considerable amount of pre-marital and pre-puberty sex experience is taken for granted. In the use of a word for virgin one should be specific but not vulgar. The translator must have the usage checked by informants of both sexes. A descriptive term based upon the physical condition of the girl or upon her lack of sex experience may in some cases be used. The careful assistance of trustworthy informants is of utmost importance in obtaining the proper word for "virgin." The expression used should be readily understood but perfectly proper in polite discourse.

CIRCUM-CISION   A word which is very difficult in many languages is "circumcision." If this is practiced among the natives, there is usually no difficulty in finding some non-vulgar word to describe the operation or the state. However, if it is not practiced, it is usually necessary to employ quite a long descriptive expression. Such an expression might be difficult to construct without including some words with vulgar connotations. Moreover, a long, unwieldy phrase is difficult to use in the Epistles, where those of the circumcision are contrasted rather frequently with those of the uncircumcision. Several translators have transliterated the word "circumcision." In some instances they have attempted to define the meaning of the word in a footnote. In other cases, the word has been left without explanation.

BIRTHDAY   The word for "birthday" is quite hard to find when people make no practice of remembering such special days. In some languages of Latin America it has been translated simply by the equivalent for Spanish *fiesta*. In the Navaho language a phrase may be used which means literally 'day on which he was born come around again.'

BEGET   The word "beget," denoting the relationship of the father to the son, is difficult to translate in many languages. One must often change "Abraham begat Isaac" to 'Abraham was the father of Isaac.' The expression "only-begotten Son" must in some languages be translated 'only Son.' The use of 'his' in 'his only Son' implies the necessity of such a relationship as is indicated in the word "begotten."

The function of the father in the birth of the child is quite differently interpreted in various cultures. In some, the father is considered as 'giving life to' the child. The mother is thought to give only the body to the child. Sometimes the mother is considered to give the body and the life, but the father to give the mind and the strength. It is for this reason that in some cultures the couvade is practiced. In such a case, almost immediately after the birth of the child, the father goes to bed and abstains from certain types of food and drink. It is thought in some societies that as long as the soft spot remains in the top of the child's head, the father is giving the child its personality. All these factors are important in the meaning and the usage of the words denoting 'to beget.'

CON-CUBINE   Concubinage is more frequently practiced in primitive societies, at least among some classes, than is commonly thought. However, even when such a system is not in existence, it is possible to translate a "concubine" as a 'lesser wife' or a 'wife of less importance.' It should be remembered that a concubine in the Biblical culture did have certain rights and the man had obligations to maintain her. She was not in the class of prostitutes. Hence, the translation of 'a lesser wife' is often a more satisfactory description of her status.

DEATH   Words for "death" and "burial" can give some trouble. The word for "death" may mean literally 'to pass out through one's big toe,' in accordance with the belief among some people. Usually, however, some other expression may also be found which will not involve quite so much of the native religious beliefs.

BURIAL   Words for "burial" may mean 'he was sent on his way' or 'he went down.' These phrases may have no more literal meaning than our expressions such as 'laid to rest' or 'committed to the earth.' The thing to do is to employ those expressions which are most idiomatic and which do not violate any subsequent teaching that the translator should give.

12.2.2   WORDS OF GENERAL SOCIAL INTERCOURSE

Illustrative words: LOVE, GLORY, MAJESTY, ADULTERY, FORNI-
CATION, FRIEND, ENEMY, DENY, GO IN PEACE, FAME.

Words which define the various aspects of social
intercourse are exceedingly numerous. These situations
are, however, more or less alike in most cultures, so that
such words do not present the difficulties which are
found in words denoting more specialized patterns of
behavior.

LOVE   An adequate word for "love" is quite rare in many
languages. The division of area of meaning is usually as
follows: (1) the relationship of a parent to a child or the
child to the parent, (2) sexual love, (3) general admiration, approval, or desire, like that which a person may
have for a material object or a person. Even though
this latter word may be rather broad in meaning and
often quite weak in significance, it is often necessary to
employ it rather than a word with a wrong center of
meaning. Teaching and the Bible text must be counted
upon to give this word its full meaning in the various
religious contexts.

GLORY   The English word "glory," Greek *doksa*, covers a
wide area of meaning. Moreover, its cultural setting is
in a highly elaborate society in which certain individuals
surround themselves with pomp and ceremony. Few
primitive cultures have such corresponding features in
their own rather drab and colorless circumstances. For
this reason, it is often hard to find a word for "glory"
which adequately expresses the implications of the
Biblical terms. Quite frequently one must make a
difference between the word used for divine glory and
that used for human glory. Without special care, it is
quite easy for the translator to get some word for 'boast-
ing' and 'haughtiness' if he takes the first word which
natives may give him when he describes the exalted
position of one who has or receives glory. On the other
hand, one may find, as one translator did, that the
word which he had used actually meant 'lightning,' and

not 'glory.' The translator's amazing description of the glories of heaven could not be interpreted by the native as anything else than an electrical display of considerable magnitude. In some instances, the native may think that the word which the translator wants is 'miracle'; for the description of the glory of God and of heaven can only be thought of in terms of a miracle.

MAJESTY   It is sometimes impossible to differentiate in the native language between majesty and glory. The first, however, can usually be described in some terms of 'greatness,' while the second can often be described in terms of 'radiance' and 'shining.' In other cases, the basic meaning in "glory" is 'beauty.' In one language the expression for "glory" is a combination of 'beauty' and 'prestige.' In another language, the translation is literally 'the quality of magnificent beauty.'

Some translators assume that once one has found a word for "glory," it can automatically be employed in translating "glorify" as 'to give glory to' or 'to make glorious.' If 'glory' in the aboriginal language denotes the personal grandeur of God, then it is quite awkward to translate 'to give personal grandeur to God.' Such a statement can only be true in a very restricted and specialized sense. "To glorify God" must frequently be translated 'to praise God.'

ADULTERY   Words for "adultery" and "fornication" are sometimes hard to find. It is important to distinguish between these two words and to make an accurate distinction. Adultery denotes unlawful sex relationships which involve the marriage bond. Fornication denotes all types of illicit sex relationships. Fornication is the more general term. In the Eastern Aztec there is no general word for "adultery." If a man commits adultery the word is literally 'he-woman-changes.' If a woman commits adultery, the word is 'she-man-changes.' A translation of the noun "adultery" must be given as 'he-woman-changes and she-man-changes.' There is no general word for 'mate' or 'spouse.'

FRIEND   One rarely has much difficulty in finding a word for "friend," and yet there are some specializations of meaning which should be closely noted. In one language the phrase "his friends," John 15: 13, was found to mean literally 'those who liked him.' The point of the passage is the love which a man has for his friends, not the love which they may have for him. The mutuality of friendship is something important to imply in all passages dealing with the words "friend" and "friendship."

ENEMY   The name for an enemy is almost always quite evident. People are usually more concerned with their enemies than their friends. An interesting word for "enemy" is found in Yipounou. It means literally a 'professional hater.'

DENY   The word "deny," in the sense of John 13: 38, may not have any very obvious parallels in the aboriginal language. One translator used the phrase to 'turn one's back on.' This may be the equivalent in some languages, but it may not be in others. In some instances it has been found better to translate "deny" as 'to say that one is not acquainted with.' 'To deny one's self,' as in Matthew 16: 24, is, however, quite different in some languages. The closest equivalent is often 'to say that one's self is nothing.'

GO IN PEACE   Salutations and greetings are often highly specialized in meaning. The expressions in the Bible such as "go in peace," Luke 7: 50, are very difficult to translate into other languages. The word for "peace" is sometimes related to 'quietness.' The phrase 'go in quietness' may mean literally 'go and say nothing.' This is the meaning of the expression in the Tarascan language. The equivalent expression in the Tarascan to "go in peace" is literally 'God go with you.' As in other instances, it may be valuable to use this greeting in the text or, as is perhaps preferable, to give the equivalent Tarascan expression in a footnote.

FAME   Words which denote the "fame," "honor," "praise," and "glory" of a person may appear to overlap in areas of meaning. "Fame" must be translated in some cases as 'everyone heard about him.' "Praise" may be 'people say great things about.' "Honor" may be expressed in some languages by 'people think great things about.' In some instances, it is impossible to distinguish between (1) the "glory" which a man may possess and (2) the "honor" or "praise" which men receive. The native language may class all these expressions as one, and thus make it completely impossible to distinguish the lexical areas as indicated in the English.

12.2.3   GOVERNMENT

Illustrative words: RULER, KING, EMPEROR, KINGDOM, QUEEN, PRINCE, GOVERNOR, VILLAGE, TOWN, CITY, COLONY, AUTHORITY, POWER.

The Biblical words for government are quite varied because of the highly elaborate and complex systems of government which are described in the Bible. Few primitive cultures have anything like this complexity of jurisdiction and of titles.

RULER   The tribe usually distinguishes a 'chief,' whom they may call simply a 'leader.' In most instances they also have terms for officials who represent outside governments. For these foreign officials, they may have only the term 'far-away chief' or 'white chief.' They usually distinguish some degrees of leadership within the tribe, but frequently such leadership is in direct proportion to age or military prowess. Hence, age or military classifications are the important ones. Some titles are highly idiomatic; e.g. the Aztec title for one of the leading male officials in the pre-Columbian culture was 'Snake-woman.'

In translating the various types of terms for government officials (this was briefly considered on page 184, dealing with classes), one is usually forced to use a term for 'ruler' or 'leader' and by certain attributives to attempt to qualify this basic word, so as to indicate the relative rank of the government officials. For example, KING   a "king" may be the 'big ruler.' The "emperor" then EMPEROR   becomes the 'biggest ruler.' We would normally assume that a governor would be less than a king, but in Palestine the Roman governor was a person of much more influence than such a person as King Herod. It is somewhat valuable to attempt to use a term in this case which represents a 'foreign ruler,' for to the Jews Pilate was just that. The words "deputy," "tetrarch," "governor," and "emperor" can frequently be graded as classes of foreign rulers.

When it is impossible to obtain a word which denotes a hereditary ruler such as "king," it will also be impos-

KINGDOM   sible to have a corresponding word for "kingdom." The "kingdom of God" must in some instances be translated by 'rule of God.' In some cultures there is no word for "rule" in the sense in which we know it. People are not forced to do anything by a compulsory edict of any one man. The closest equivalent which they have is a type of tribal 'leadership' or 'chieftainship.' Such a leader is able to maintain his position only as long as his followers are willing to follow. For such people, the only possible equivalent for "rule" or "kingdom" is the word 'leadership.' Hence, the translation reads 'leadership of God' for our "kingdom of God." However, it should be noted that to the native of such a culture his expression 'leadership' is not equivalent to 'leadership' in English. We have several different ways of designating mechanisms of governmental control. For the native of the society in question, his word 'leadership' includes every aspect of governmental jurisdiction.

At this point it should be noted that the literal translations which are given here for the different native words are not at all adequate to convey the meaning which the particular expression has for the native speakers. The literal translation is only a very inadequate means of giving the reader some idea of the cultural and lexical problems involved. The meaning of the phrase cannot be the same as its literal meaning in English, for the phrase gets its meaning from the local practical situations in which it is used. It would be, however, quite impossible to explain the full meaning of every phrase. This would necessitate an expansion of this material into many volumes. The reader is urged to think of the meaning of a native phrase in terms of the local situation and not in terms of the bare meaning of the words in English.

QUEEN   A "queen" may be translated as a 'woman ruler,' or 'wife of the ruler,' depending on the context. The first translation, e.g. in Acts 8: 27, may seem exceedingly strange to some people. On the other hand, a position of authority granted to older men in the tribe may seem just as inconsistent in a society which is matriarchal.

PRINCE
A "prince" is a 'chief' or a 'leader.' One should not translate "prince" as a 'son of a king' in an attempt to indicate one usage of this word in English. The "prince of the devils," Mark 3:22, is simply the 'chief of the demons.'

GOVERNOR
Borrowed terms for government are sometimes quite valuable, for the parallel is frequently close to the Biblical situation. The Spanish *gobernador* is thought of by many of the Indian peoples of Latin America in practically the same light as a Roman governor was considered by the Jews. Some names, however, have very specialized meanings. One who borrows the Spanish *rey* for 'king' may find difficulty, for this word is known among many tribes only as a title for Jesus Christ, e.g. *Cristo Rey*, 'Christ King.'

VILLAGE
TOWN
CITY
Words which designate government units are frequently without any parallels in primitive society. In some instances there are no 'cities,' 'towns,' and 'villages.' One must use some sort of word for a cluster of dwellings, e.g. Tarahumara *karírari*. One may then call a village 'a small *karírari*,' a town 'a large *karírari*,' and a city 'a very large *karírari*.'

COLONY
The word "colony" is especially difficult. However, "a (Roman) colony" can be translated 'a place where some people from Rome went to live.' The Spanish *colonia* usually cannot be borrowed, for in many places it means a suburb of a large city.

AUTHOR-
ITY
POWER
Expressions for "authority" and "power" are very confusing in some languages. Authority is basically the right or position to do or say something. Power designates the inherent force which makes a certain action possible. In many languages the distinction is made on the basis of whether the potentiality is within oneself or whether it is a derived quality. In some instances this differentiation parallels the difference between 'power' and 'authority,' but not always. In some cases, the word 'strength' must be used for "power." In other cases, "power" must be expressed by some verbal phrase which means 'to be able.'

12.2.4   LAW

Illustrative words: LAW, COMMANDMENT, JUDGE, JUDGMENT, LAW-FUL, WITNESS, TESTIMONY, ADVOCATE, WILL, COVENANT, TESTAMENT.

Legal procedures among some aboriginal peoples are very rudimentary. There are frequently no formal courts, judges, juries, nor witnesses. The only laws are the traditions of the tribe, and the only means of determining and administering these laws rests with the elders or the chief men. The distinction between a law, which implies a definite, traditional, binding form, and a command-ment, which denotes the specific order of a person with authority, may be the only basic distinction which is made in a language with regard to legal authority and sanction. In some cases, there are only customs on the one hand and commandments on the other. The customs which are accepted without dispute or serious ques-tioning and carry enforced penalties are essentially 'laws,' even though they may not happen to be written. One finds that most aboriginal peoples have given comparatively little thought to the factors of law and tradition. One might say they operate un-consciously, as compared to our more sophisticated attitudes toward social regulations. The natives' answer to a curious mis-sionary is simply, "We do it this way because we have always done it this way." Such traditionalism may be quite a hindrance to any type of change, but at the same time it tends toward per-sonal and social integration as opposed to maladjustment and disintegration. At any rate, the entire social structure must be thoroughly investigated in order to find those words which may have some correspondence to the legal terms of the Bible.

LAW
COMMAND-
MENT

To contrast the different sanctions resting behind "law" vs. "commandments," the Maya language uses 'ordered-word' for "law" and 'spoken-word' for "com-mandment." This may seem a considerable weakening of the Biblical meaning, but there are certain features of these words which are important. In the first place, the older legal system of the Mayas almost completely disappeared with the coming of the Spanish, who instituted their own legal system and thrust upon the people the Spanish terms for it. Many of these terms are well known, but in almost every case the connota-tions of these words are quite bad, for they stand for foreign domination. In the second place, the two words 'ordered-word' and 'spoken-word' are used idiomatically with almost the difference in meaning which we attach to "law" and "commandment." As has been noted before, it is quite difficult to determine the actual mean-ing of a word from the literal translation which is given in English.

JUDGE
JUDGMENT
The words "judge" or "judgment" are much more difficult to find in some languages than one might at first imagine. In many languages there are perfectly good words for 'to condemn' or 'to acquit.' But the process of judging impartially is frequently quite hard to describe. A phrase such as 'to choose the true' may be used in some cases, but only if the phrase has a rather specialized connotation. One must also be aware of the fact that the word "judgment" sometimes denotes the process, e.g. "the day of judgment," and sometimes the result, e.g. "eternal judgment." Several different Greek and Hebrew words have been translated "judgment" in the English Bible. These should be examined closely in the various contexts. In Latin America, where the Spanish and Portuguese legal systems have dominated the judicial features of the culture for several centuries, the Spanish and Portuguese words for "judge" and "judgment" are often known quite widely. Where the connotation permits, they may be used quite effectively. Special care should be taken to differentiate in all cases between "judge" and "condemn."

LAWFUL
It is valuable to relate the word "lawful" to the same stem which is used in the native language for 'law.' This cannot always be done, however. Sometimes it is necessary to translate 'what one is permitted to do' for "lawful."

WITNESS
TESTI-
MONY
Words for "witness" and "testimony" may be very troublesome in some languages where it is not a common practice for people to witness in trials. Some translators have used the expression 'to tell good things' for "witness." This is, of course, only half of the truth and as such may constitute a legal untruth. The important thing about witnessing is telling the truth or telling what one has actually seen. 'To say a true word' has been used by some translators for "witness" and "testimony." In other cases, a short phrase which means

FALSE
WITNESS
'to speak from experience' may be employed. To "bear false witness," Mark 10: 19, has been translated in Totonac as to 'say with lies that he is guilty.'

ADVOCATE
One who intercedes for another is called in some languages 'one who comes between.' In some languages this is the same word as that employed for an attorney. Anyone who repre-

sents one's interests in a legal proceeding is designated as 'one who comes between.'

WILL
COVENANT
TESTA-
MENT

Words for different types of contracts and agreements are often not so specialized in meaning as the Greek words. For example, the Greek *diathēkē*, translated "will," "testament," or "covenant," indicates primarily a type of contract which is made by one party to be fulfilled by others. In this it differs from *sunthēkē*, which is more properly a 'contract' in our meaning of the word. These specialized distinctions can rarely be indicated. In the aboriginal language one must usually employ some such term as 'agreement' or 'arrangement.' In Mark 14:24, "This is my blood of the new testament" must be translated in Eastern Aztec as 'This is my blood with which I make a new arrangement with you.' The word "testament" must be turned into a verb phrase. A literal rendering is impossible in Aztec because of the syntactic structure. In the Totonac language there is an excellent expression for "will" or "testament." It is literally 'the word which is left over,' that is to say, the word which is left over when the maker of the will dies.

12.2.5   PROPERTY

Illustrative words: POSSESSIONS, RICH, POOR, HEIR.

The entire concept of personal property is almost unknown in some societies. An individual may have the recognized right to use land which he has cleared, or a canoe which he has made. But personal ownership as we know it is utterly foreign to them. A term such as

POSSES-
SIONS

"possessions" can be translated 'what a man has,' but the meaning will be quite different in different societies. However, the very rapid infiltration of the concepts of Western culture is necessitating many adjustments in the local economies. Private ownership is coming more and more into force. As a result, a translation of 'those

RICH
POOR

who have many things' for "rich" and 'those who do not have much' for "poor" is coming to mean more in certain aboriginal societies.

HEIR

The term "heir" is comparatively rare in some societies. Even among the Aztecs, who now have generally adopted the Western system of private property arrangements, the language has no single word for 'heir.' In Mark 12:7 it is necessary to translate, 'This is the man who will receive the property.' To be "joint-heirs with Christ" we 'receive things together with Christ.'

12.2.6 OCCUPATIONS

Illustrative words: LAWYER, TEACHER, CARPENTER, BUTLER, SCRIBES.

LAWYER

Some translators are confused because they cannot find single words to correspond to the various occupational names. In most primitive societies specialization of labor is comparatively restricted. We must not expect to find separate designations for men who do not have special types of tasks. A descriptive term can usually be applied. A "lawyer" may be called 'a man who studies (or knows) the law,' in other words 'a man educated in the law.' Note that a "lawyer" of the Bible does not correspond to a present-day attorney. A

TEACHER
CARPENTER
BUTLER

"teacher" is 'one who teaches.' A "carpenter" is in the Navaho 'one who makes houses.' In another language it is 'one who saws.' A "butler" is 'one who serves food.' Similar descriptive names may be found for almost all occupational titles in the Bible.

SCRIBES

It might seem at first glance that to translate "scribes" as 'men who can write' would hardly be sufficiently descriptive of the class of men whose learning distinguished them. However, it should be remembered that, in an aboriginal society, those who can write are decidedly in a special class of educated people. They represent the native intelligentsia just as surely as the ancient scribes of Israel dominated their own society with their very impressive learning.

12.2.7 WAR

Illustrative words: HELMET, BREASTPLATE, SWORD, CHARIOT, CENTURION, CHIEF CAPTAIN, OFFICER.

All people know what war is. If they do not practice it much themselves, they are at least acquainted with war conducted by their more civilized neighbors. Many aboriginal people use a great number of the implements of war which were employed in Bible times. This is especially true of offensive weapons, but they seldom have anything like the elaborate types of defensive armor. The various parts of armor must usually be translated in terms of the function which they had for the warrior. For example, the "helmet" is 'a protection for the head' and the "breastplate" is 'a protection (covering) for the chest.'

HELMET
BREAST-
PLATE

Some slight adaptations of terms may make it possible to translate certain words. A "sword" may be translated as 'a large knife' or 'a large war-knife,' in order to convey something of both the size and the function of the instrument. In Latin America, the local name for a *machete* is usually sufficient as a translation for sword.

SWORD

A "chariot" may be called 'a wagon (or cart) for war (or fighting).' This will give the reader some idea of the type of ordnance.

CHARIOT

Even though an aboriginal people may have a rather highly developed army organization, there is little chance of its being organized as ancient armies were. One should try to find some type of corresponding terms for "band," "legion," and "army" and attempt to apply these consistently. Similar descriptive and equivalent terms should be used for officers of the army. A "centurion" may always be translated as a 'leader of a hundred warriors,' and a "chiliarch," AV "chief captain," may be translated as a 'leader of a thousand men.'

CENTU-
RION
CHIEF
CAPTAIN

An "officer," as in John 7: 32, may be equivalent to the 'police' in some native societies.

OFFICER

Chapter 13

TERMS FOR FEATURES OF RELIGIOUS CULTURE

THE religious culture of any people contains by far the most complicated lexical problems. Religious systems usually differ far more widely than any other part of culture. There is a somewhat limited number of basic types of material and social adjustments which people can make. There is no limit to the imagination of man and hence no limit to the differentiation of his ideas as to supernatural factors. Religious phenomena are, moreover, much more difficult for the translator to analyze. Ideas are very intangible things. There are many subtle turns to any religious system, many incongruous elements, and many different possible reactions on the part of the adherents. To add to the difficulties of analysis, people are naturally reticent in confiding information about their religious beliefs. This is particularly so of the native Christian, who often feels embarrassment about his former superstitions. Religion constitutes a very intimate sort of experience and is usually not to be publicized before the profane eyes of foreigners. Moreover, the native is probably not desirous of making converts to his system. There is usually no evangelistic enthusiasm about his religion that makes him wish to tell others about what he believes. Furthermore, much of that belief may be quite intangible to him. His religion has not been organized in terms of a systematic theology. In addition, many of his religious practices are so automatic that he is not conscious of them as religion, and certainly it would rarely occur to him to tell anyone about such a habitual pattern of behavior.

In many instances the translator has not been a very sympathetic listener to the native informant's explanations of his own religion. The translator may have laughed at his stories about the native gods or may have criticized the informant severely for even thinking that such stories could be true. Regardless of the religious system the translator will be able to find some truth in it. He should attempt to find this, in order that he may have some

203

common ground on which to speak with the people. It may be nothing more than an observation such as Paul made in Athens, but it provides a basis for common understanding. The translator must, however, push his research into the pagan religion just as far as possible. To do this he must exhibit a sympathetic interest. The translator must work like the psychiatrist who attempts to ferret out the underlying facts and circumstances of an individual's life. The psychiatrist finds that he must be genuinely interested in the patient, even though he may think him completely deluded. If translations fail to use the proper vocabulary in religious matters (unfortunately this is too frequently the case), it is largely because of the translator's lack of understanding of the pagan religious culture, not because of a failure to appreciate the Biblical truths. A translator may know the meanings of the Greek and Hebrew with amazing clarity and yet fail to translate accurately because he does not understand the pagan religious vocabulary. The translator should know the pagan religion thoroughly. This may seem strange at first, for so much emphasis has been placed upon Bible teaching in the mission field. This emphasis is correct, but the native words which must be used in teaching Biblical truth also have meanings in the pagan religious system. Many times the translator has completely missed the mark because the words that he has used have not meant what he thought. An examination of the lexical problems in the religious culture should make this fact quite evident.

For the sake of convenience the words dealing with religious culture will be treated under the following heads: (1) supernatural beings, (2) revelation, (3) features of religious culture involving moral and ethical criteria, (4) eschatology, (5) specialized religious activities, (6) religious personages, (7) religious constructions, (8) religious groups, (9) religious artifacts, and (10) religious events.

13.1   SUPERNATURAL BEINGS

Illustrative words: GOD, LORD, SPIRIT, HOLY SPIRIT, CHRIST, DEMON, DEVIL, SATAN, ANGEL.

GOD   The name for God in an aboriginal language is one of the keystones to the entire theological structure and Bible teaching. The problem is by no means as simple

(GOD)   as it may at first appear. Some translators, not finding in the pagan religious system, exactly the word which they think appropriate, have introduced a foreign name for God, e.g. Spanish *Dios* or English *God*. They have thought that such a word would have prestige because it comes from the language of a culturally dominant group. The fact that such a borrowed word seems to have no bad connotations appears to justify its use. It is assumed that the native people will automatically come to understand by the borrowed word for "God" exactly what we understand by the same term. The translator has counted upon taking a word with zero meaning and giving it the proper content. This is not so easily done as imagined. In almost every case the native will immediately try to equate this new name of God with one of the gods of his own religious system. Since all people attempt to understand the unknown in terms of the known, it will not be very long before the natives will have worked out what seems to them a perfectly consistent equivalent for the new term. In the Aztec culture in Mexico it turned out that *Dios* was equated with the sun and the Virgin Mary was considered to be the moon. Jesus was the offspring of the two. As exemplified in the crucifixion, he has come to be more or less a cultural hero related to the gods. It is possible to introduce a zero word for such an object as an airplane, for people have nothing to correspond to such an item in their own native culture, but for something as common and familiar as a god this is not the case. They will no doubt have several gods with whom they might quickly equate the new name. Before the translator realizes it, instead of being able to fill an empty word with the proper meaning, he has a name which has already been given a content from the pagan religion. The word will at the same time have the connotation of being a foreign name for a foreign equivalent of a native god.

On the other hand, the translator may attempt to use some native word for 'God' which seems applicable. A further investigation may reveal that there are many

(GOD) characteristics which are given to this god in native legend which are quite inconsistent with Biblical truth. The translator's examination must be thorough, for he does not want to run the risk of using a term which does not contain at least the central core of meaning which is essential.

The translator should not be fearful of using a native word for "God." He should remember that in terms of the native culture the Greek word *theos*, the Latin *deus*, and the Gothic *guþ* could hardly be termed exact equivalents to the concept of God as taught in the Bible. Nevertheless, these terms did possess the essential core of meaning. It is interesting to note that they are generic terms. In no case were they the names of one particular god. The use of names such as Zeus, Jupiter, or Woden would not have been wise, for these specific names included a great deal of legend as to the individual peculiarities, excesses, and immoral actions of the particular gods. In the generic terms, however, there existed enough of the fundamental core of religious significance that they have been used successfully. In Greek, *theos* designated any god. In the plural it could be used to include all the gods. In the Bible this generic term is used and made to apply specifically to only one God. The Christians took a term which designated any important supernatural entity and by context and teaching made it apply to only one such entity. Where this same situation exists in another culture, there is no reason for believing that this process could not be repeated, and with good results.

One should also note that, when the native generic word for 'God' is used, there is not the likelihood that the native speakers will immediately equate this God with one of their own specific deities. On the other hand, any foreign word impresses the native as being a proper name, for most such zero words are proper names. Since it is interpreted as a proper name, the object which this name stands for is immediately equated with one of the gods in the pagan theology. If a native generic term is employed, the tendency to find immediate

(GOD) equivalents in the two religious systems is avoided.

In some instances translators have been able to use the name of a specific god. Among the Guajira the native term *Maleiwa* fulfilled all the necessary qualifications of a beneficent, all-powerful Creator. The translators found that the Christian Guajira Indians had automatically made the correspondence between the Christian God and their own *Maleiwa*. They considered them identical. The insistence upon a foreign name would only have confused them.

In choosing the name for God it is important to consider the usage of the trade language. Very frequently the native church is assimilated into the church group speaking the trade language or the national language. The native church also draws much of its leadership from among those who speak the trade language. A similar name for God is valuable, but it is not absolutely essential.

In order to understand something of the meaning of the native words for 'God' and something of the problems of interpretation, one should attempt to find the answers to the following questions. This list is by no means complete, for the varieties of religious belief are almost unlimited. These questions should, however, give one a lead to some of the more important problems which will be encountered either in using some native word for 'God' or in predicting the types of equivalents which the native speaker will attempt to make if a foreign term is employed.

1 Are there many gods or one? (If many, then the following questions should be answered for each god. *He* will be used throughout these questions to designate any god, even though the deity may be a goddess.)

2 What is the exact meaning of his name? Is the word used in any other sense?

3 What are the characteristics of the god: Human? Animal? Sex? Perfect specimen? Deformed?

4 Is he a "big spirit"? A "great ancestor"? Both? Neither?

(GOD)

5 Does the god have a distinct personality or is he more of an influence or abstract power? Is he like a man?

6 Is he moral, immoral, amoral? In what terms of conduct?

7 If there are many gods, are they arranged in a hierarchy? May one god oppose the other?

8 Where does the god dwell? May he change habitation? Periodically? By invitation?

9 Does the god live everywhere but have a center of existence?

10 Is he a kind of culture hero?

11 Is he eternal or created? If created, by whom?

12 How did he obtain his position as god: Birth? Craftiness? War? Innate prerogative?

13 Did the god create the world? Men? Animals?

14 Does he now operate in nature?

15 Is he in touch with creation personally or through emissaries?

16 Is he concerned with man's welfare?

17 Does he act more or less as a policeman?

18 Is he beneficent? How? When?

19 What is the basis for his beneficence: Goodness of man? Observance of taboo? Prayer? Ritual? Ceremony? Performance of vows?

20 What types of gifts does he bestow: Food? Clothing? Protection? Success in war? Success in gambling?

21 Does the god mete out judgment to men while men are still alive?

22 What is the basis for punishment: Disobedience to taboo? Neglect of worship?

23 What types of punishment: Sickness? Death? Loss of property?

24 Are all his judgments based upon the moral issues involved?

25 How may he be appeased: Sacrifice? Ritual? Confession? Penitence? Penance?

26 Can man have communion with the god? How: By prayer? Ritual? Trance? Dream?

(GOD)   27 Are there restrictions as to when the name of the god can be uttered?

The above questions may seem to the translator as rather unnecessary. In fact, one translator said to the writer that it would take him months to learn the answers to such questions. That is undoubtedly true. Nevertheless, if one is going to bring to people the good news about God and His plan for mankind, he can hardly afford not to understand the meaning of the words which he must use in talking about these facts. The qualified and competent doctor does not depend upon one medicine to cure all ailments. He knows that he must examine the patient carefully in order to make the proper diagnosis and to apply the proper cure. The translator must make a most careful diagnosis of the spiritual ailments of his constituency before he will know how to administer the cure and have the certainty that what he is administering is the cure. If the doctor makes a mistake, he may bury his patient. If the translator makes a mistake, his error may be perpetuated for generations and hence darken the spiritual life of countless thousands of people.

It is hoped that the reader of this will not be as impatient as are some students, who complain that, after all the explanations of the problems, they still have not been told specifically what should be done in any particular circumstance. This is exactly what the writer cannot do. Every circumstance is different from every other. No rules can be formulated to cover all situations. The translator himself must decide which is the most valuable and accurate choice after having examined all the types of evidence and having noted the implications of all the possible problems suggested here. The Versions Secretaries of the Bible Societies will be glad to consult with translators on their specific problems and to make what suggestions they can on the basis of the data which the translator can supply. But no one can formulate rules to be followed willy-nilly. Translation is not a problem in arithmetic in which hypothetically constructed units are compared, but a problem in the evaluation of some of the most complex phenomena in human experience.

LORD   The distinction between "Lord" and "God" is sometimes perplexing. The Greek *kurios* covers a very wide area of meaning. The central core of meaning which has been generally employed in translating *kurios* is 'master,' as one who controls and directs others. The relationship is essentially one of ruler to subjects or owner to possessions. The 'Lord' in an aboriginal language should be one who has authority and power and to whom the other people are subject. In the Maya language the term *Yumtsil* has been used. This term designates the head of a village or of a municipality. Such an individual is usually of considerable wealth, so that he controls and directs the lives of many people. This word is also a title of respect.

In some languages the word for 'sir' is also applicable for "Lord," e.g. Spanish *señor*. Some people may object that such a title as is used in the Maya or the Spanish cannot be adequate. They forget the specialization of meaning which a word may have in certain contexts. Some are also likely to place too much emphasis upon the derivation of a word, thinking perhaps that the English *Lord* is some mysteriously remarkable term especially applicable to God. They do not realize that this English word *lord* comes originally from two stems which mean literally 'loaf-ward.' The ancient lord of the castle was the guardian of the loaves of bread. Many words are quite inadequate in their so-called etymological meanings. The important thing is how they are used.

SPIRIT   Translators usually have as much difficulty with the word for 'spirit' as with any other in the language. To a considerable extent this is due to the fact that the Greek *pneuma* and the English *spirit* have such very wide areas of meaning. The central meaning of the Greek word is 'a movement of air.' The 'breath' is also a basic meaning of this word. From this is derived the meaning of spirit in the sense of the vital principle by which the

(SPIRIT) body is animated. The spirit is also a non-material essence having the power of knowing, desiring, and acting. As such, it is applied to the human soul which has left the body, to angels, and to evil spirits. The word is also applied to God's Spirit, and as such defines God's essential character and agency of operation in the world. The Greek *pneuma* may also designate a disposition and quality of an individual personality as in I Peter 3:4, "a meek and quiet spirit." A careful study of the meaning of the Greek word *pneuma* should be made in some unabridged Greek lexicon or in some adequate treatment of Greek word studies. One will rarely find in an aboriginal language any word, or even two or three words, which will cover or correspond to the whole area of meaning included in the Greek or English words.

In most aboriginal animistic cultures one encounters a definite belief in 'spirits.' The spirits are almost unlimited as to variety. They are usually given the characteristics of personality, in that they may design and carry out actions, even though in some cases they need some medium through which to work. Such spirits are sometimes classified as to origin, e.g. whether they are eternally existing spirits or the disembodied spirits of animals or people. In other instances, spirits are classified as to their habitation, e. g. whether they live in trees, houses, animals, or people. In other religious systems, spirits are classified as to whether they are good or evil, helpful or hostile. In some cases, however, the spirits may only be mischievous, the incarnations of people's delight in practical jokes. Another classification distinguishes whether the spirit may be seen or not.

Before deciding upon the words to be used for 'spirit' in the aboriginal language, one should obtain the answers to the following questions. These questions are not all-inclusive. They are only suggestive of items for which to look. The translator should examine fully all suggestions received from the answers to such questions, for only in so doing can he be absolutely sure of the appropriateness of the words which he may

(SPIRIT)   have chosen to distinguish the various types of spirit
phenomena.

1 Are there many spirits or one? (If there are many
  spirits, the following questions should be answered
  for each spirit.)
2 What types of spirits are there?
3 Does the spirit have a distinct personality? Is it
  like a human? Animal?
4 Is the spirit impersonal and more like an 'influence'?
5 Does it have a special point of dwelling? If so,
  where: River? Mountain? Tree? People?
6 May the spirit move about freely?
7 May it enter various objects at will?
8 Must the spirit always be in or attached to some
  object?
9 Is each spirit classified by its relative power?
10 Is the spirit moral, immoral, or amoral? Good?
   Bad? Mischievous? Haunting?
11 Is the spirit controlled by any spirit force?
12 Does each spirit or type of spirit have a special
   name? What are these names?
13 To what is the spirit similar: Vapor? Smoke?
   Shadow? Ghost? Fire? Dream image?
14 Does each type of spirit have a special function?
15 Has the spirit always existed?
16 Where does the spirit come from?
17 Is the spirit the soul of a dead person or animal?
18 May the spirit do good or evil at will?
19 May it be controlled by men? What types of men?
20 How is it controlled: Magic words? Ritual? Ceremony? Sacrifice? Prayer?
21 Does the spirit favor good people? Does it dis-
   favor evil people?
22 If it attacks men, how? From within, by sickness
   and death? From without, by accident?
23 Does it enter into people? How: By the nose?
   Mouth? Toe?
24 How does the spirit leave a person? How can it
   be recalled or spoken to?

(SPIRIT)   25 If a spirit enters a person, how is this manifested:
By frenzy? Strange language? Prophetical sayings?
26 What causes the spirit to do harm to one? To do
good?
27 How is the spirit appeased?
28 May one obtain the help of a spirit to do evil?
29 Can a spirit be captured?
30 If a spirit dwells within one, where does it reside:
Whole body? Liver? Bowels? Spleen?
31 What is the relationship of this supernatural spirit
to a man's own spirit? His soul?
32 Are certain material objects venerated because they
are indwelt by a spirit?

An analysis of the above questions may reveal several distinct areas of meaning which must be indicated. In the first place, in a passage such as "he sighed deeply in his spirit," Mark 8: 12, one will often find it necessary to change the expression to read 'he sighed deeply in his heart.' If one employs the aboriginal word for spirit, the translation may imply that Jesus possessed a familiar spirit. Hence, Jesus would be considered a witch doctor who performed his miracles by association with the world of demons.

In a passage such as Matthew 26: 41, ". . . the spirit indeed is willing, but the flesh is weak," it may be necessary to use some such expression as, in Navaho, 'that which stands in me,' for "spirit." This is the regular idiom for the central core of the personality and is the closest equivalent to the English "spirit" in this context.

In many instances translators have had to use the same word for 'evil spirits' and 'demons.' It is often impossible to distinguish between them. On the other hand, the word for 'good spirit' is often quite different from the term 'evil spirit.' In fact, one should always be very careful about using the same stem for 'spirit' in the expressions 'Spirit' (meaning 'Holy Spirit') and 'evil spirit.' The use of the capital letter at the beginning of the word is often not sufficient for people to know that this is the Spirit of God, since the translation will probably be read to many more people than will themselves read it. The translation should not have to depend upon capitalization to change a word with a bad significance into a word with a good significance. Such a specialization of orthography is unreliable. Where "Spirit," e.g. I Timothy 4:1, is used alone to designate the Third Person of the Trinity, it is sometimes necessary to employ a qualifying word such as 'good' or 'holy' in order that there may be no misunderstanding.

One rather frequent error made by translators is to use a word for 'spirit' which in the native language has as a central meaning the disembodied spirit or soul of a man. The 'Spirit of God' then comes to imply that God died and that His 'spirit' is now active in the world. In such a case, one may all too easily repeat an error which has been made before, in which Christ is considered to have died, and that His disembodied spirit became the Holy Spirit, while God is equated with one of the pagan deities. Translators are sometimes unaware of the terrific confusion in the minds of the natives because of some of the words used.

HOLY
SPIRIT

The meaning of a borrowed term must be very closely investigated. In Latin America the Spanish *Espíritu Santo* is known quite widely as a name for God. Of course, in some places the name is nothing more than a designation for the replicas of doves which are hung on the walls or on a chain around the neck. However, the denotation and connotation of *espíritu* are usually good. Some translators have borrowed the term *Espíritu Santo* directly from the Spanish. In some instances they have also attempted to use *espíritu* wherever the English version employs the word "spirit." This, however, has often created great confusion. A 'bad *espíritu*' is completely incongruous to the natives, for they only know *espíritu* as a name for God or something good about God. When the term *espíritu* is borrowed, it is often necessary to restrict it to contexts which denote the Holy Spirit.

In many parts of Latin America it will be found possible to use 'wind' for "evil spirit." The belief that winds are spirit personalities, particularly to do evil to people, is quite widespread in the Western Hemisphere.

Certain types of spirits are often given rather highly specialized types of names. A "spirit of divination," Acts 16:16, may be translated into the Mazatec by saying 'a girl had two spirits which know things.' Everyone is considered to have one spirit, but a person who has two spirits is a person who can divine the future. The phrase 'which know things' indicates the characteristic of a spirit which may foretell the future. It is a highly specialized idiom. But this idiom is not any more specialized than the Greek word in Acts 16:16 which employs the name of a mythological monster who was supposed to have guarded the Oracle of Delphi, the most famous place in the ancient world for obtaining ambiguous statements about the future.

CHRIST

In some instances "Christ" has been translated as 'the Anointed.' There is usually considerable difficulty in such a translation. The native culture seldom employs the process of anointing in the sense of the ordaining or setting aside of a person for a special religious function. If there is no cultural significance in anointing, it is probably better to use the name of Christ as a proper name and explain the significance of the name by note or by teaching.

DEMON

An adequate term for 'demons' is by no means as difficult to find as one for 'spirit.' Almost all animistic societies have beliefs in many types of evil spirits. The difficulty is to find a generic term which will include them all. However, it is well to avoid any words which will denote that such demons are disembodied human spirits or souls.

DEVIL

It is very important to distinguish between 'demon' and the 'Devil.' At all events, one must be consistent in the usage of these terms. The AV is particularly delinquent in this matter. In some cases, one may translate the Greek *diabolos* 'Devil' as 'Slanderer.' This is, however, rarely satisfactory, for the aboriginal culture usually has some native term for the Devil. A name such as 'Slanderer' does not usually designate such a personality. It seems inconceivable to the native speakers that one would call the Devil a 'slanderer' when they already have what seems to them a perfectly satisfactory term. Where there is no special word for the Devil, one may sometimes use the name of 'Chief of the Demons.' In some instances, there are two grades of demons. The name for the worst of the two may be used for the Devil, provided it is plain in the context that he is the only one.

The Devil may have several names in the native language. For example, he may be called 'the Ugly-Faced One' and 'the Evil One.' Between these two terms one should choose the latter, for the emphasis is upon the moral factors involved rather than upon the appearance.

Translators should be careful not to employ some term which dilutes the personality of the Devil. In one language a translator employed the phrase 'the Evil Thing.' This expression was made up by the translator, for he had found that people were just a little embarrassed to hear the native word for 'devil.' It is true that people in the particular culture do not use the word 'devil,' any more than cultured people in America use certain words of profanity. But in its proper context the native word for 'devil' is perfectly acceptable, even as a word such as *damn* is acceptable in the pulpit in its proper context but objectionable in certain stratas of society when used colloquially. The translator's desire to avoid a vulgar word was wholly commendable. He had just not investigated the matter fully enough. Moreover, the substitute which he proposed almost completely destroyed any semblance of personality for the Devil.

SATAN   The term "Satan" should generally be treated as a proper name.

ANGEL   "Angels" are quite foreign to most animistic cultures. The belief in special emissaries of God is generally confined to rather highly complex religious systems. Accordingly, one translating into an aboriginal language will often find it difficult to discover an adequate word for 'angel.' It should be noted, however, that in the Greek New Testament the word *angelos* is simply the word 'messenger.' (Compare also the Hebrew.) The meanings of 'angel' and 'messenger' are only distinguished by the context. The same may often be accomplished in an aboriginal language. In some instances, however, it is considered important to make some type of distinction where the context is not evident. In such a case, one may add 'of heaven' or 'from heaven,' but this should be done with care. Translations such as 'inhabitants of heaven' and 'people of heaven' are not recommended. The native may receive the impression that we all become angels at death.

If the language possesses a word for 'angel,' one should be very careful to check its complete area of meaning. In some parts of Latin America the word employed for 'angel' actually means to the native 'a dead baby.'

13.2   TERMS OF REVELATION

Illustrative words: WORD, SCRIPTURES, SIGN, MIRACLE, PARABLE, GOSPEL, PORTENTS, VISION, DREAM, REVELATION, MYSTERY.

WORD
A term equivalent to English "word" may be almost impossible to find in an aboriginal language. Normally, aboriginal peoples have not studied their own language sufficiently to have discovered any linguistic unit which they call a 'word.' It should be noted, moreover, that the Greek *logos*, translated "Word" in John 1, does not necessarily mean 'a single word,' but rather 'a meaningful expression.' The nearest native equivalent to the *logos* of John 1:1 will probably be some word which covers an area of meaning included in the English words *phrase, sentence, speech, conversation, statement*, and *expression*.

SCRIPTURES
The "scriptures" may be translated the 'writings.' The context is usually sufficient to make it obvious that the writings of the Bible are meant.

SIGN
Translators have generally been rather inconsistent in their use of words for 'sign' and 'miracle.' Wherever the Greek employs *sēmeion*, one should use the native word 'sign,' even though the AV frequently employs "miracles." A single word for 'sign' may not occur in the native language, but a descriptive phrase such as 'that which points out' may usually be found. Some translators have used 'that which was revealed' for "sign." The emphasis should not be upon what is in the incident but upon what the particular incident reveals. "Signs" are not 'things which are shown' but 'things which show.'

MIRACLE
It is important to contrast "miracles" and "signs." The first may usually be described as 'wonderful events.' In some cases the native language used some such terms

as 'surprising things.' Taking the clue from the Greek *dunamis*, 'miracle' and 'power,' some translators have used expressions such as 'that which shows power' for "miracles." These usages have not seemed to be very successful. The Greek word has a very special range of meaning, which is quite difficult to duplicate in another language.

PARABLE   The word "parable" finds no parallel in many languages. The use of parables is by no means a universal culture trait. One translator called parables 'difficult words.' His memory of courses in exegesis and hermeneutics may have prompted this descriptive term. It is not, however, a very adequate or accurate translation. Some such translation as 'likeness statement' or 'comparison words' is more likely to convey the proper significance. In the Navaho the idiom for English "parables" is 'story by which people have understanding.'

GOSPEL   A descriptive term for "gospel" may be constructed in almost all languages. The gospel may be called 'the good news or 'the good message.' One should avoid using some borrowed word such as the Spanish *evangelio*. Such a word does not have much vital meaning for the native. Non-Christians may link it merely with *evangélicos*, the usual name for Protestants.

WONDERS   The "wonders," Greek *terata*, of such passages as Mark 13: 22, may be translated by a descriptive term such as 'things to be looked at.' Such portents in ancient times were often astronomical features which attracted much attention and which were used to divine the future.

VISION   It is sometimes quite difficult to separate "visions" and "dreams." The Mazatec Indians make a difference between 'dreams' and certain types of visions which are brought on by eating a special kind of mushroom. One would not, however, want to use this latter word to describe Peter's vision in Acts 11: 5. One descriptive translation, 'to see a story inside of oneself,' was found adequate to describe the area of meaning desired in "vision." Sometimes it is necessary to translate "vision" by 'a kind of dream.'

REVELA-   The word "revelation" may be translated into an expression denoting the process or the resultant state. This depends upon the context and the translator's interpretation. The process of revelation may be translated in some languages as 'the showing' or 'the making it known.' The resultant state may be translated as 'that which is shown' or 'that which is made known.' In most New Testament contexts the emphasis is upon the process, not the state.

MYSTERY The word "mystery" may be translated as 'secret' or 'hidden thing.'

13.3 FEATURES OF RELIGIOUS CULTURE
INVOLVING MORAL AND ETHICAL CRITERIA

Illustrative words: SIN, EVIL, GOOD, BAD, BLAME, SAVE, SAVIOR, GRACE, RIGHTEOUS, RIGHTEOUSNESS, JUSTIFY, JUSTIFICATION, HOLY, PURE, SANCTIFY, OFFEND (CAUSE TO STUMBLE), CURSE, SWEARING, BLASPHEME, DOUBT, TEMPT, REPENTANCE, CONVERSION, FAITH, TRUE, TRUTH, SAINT.

In the Biblical system all moral and ethical criteria are given in terms of supernatural sanctions. From the standpoint of the Bible, Christianity is entirely God-derived. Accordingly, every feature of man's existence which has any religious significance must also involve some moral and ethical criteria. On this basis, therefore, many more words should be included within this analysis. However, in treating the problems from a practical standpoint, we are including the following words because of the special difficulties which they exhibit in some languages.

SIN A word for 'sin' is not easy to find in many languages. This is not to say that the speakers of such languages do not commit sin, but rather that their terms for it are sometimes completely specific, not generic. They may have many words for particular types of non-conformity to tradition and to that part of the tradition to which is attached some degree of moral or of supernatural sanction. But no two tribes of people have the same moral and ethical standards of actions. Even within a culture there may be wide discrepancies. In our own society there are considerable differences of viewpoint as to what particular items of behavior are to be considered as sin. Nevertheless, the general principles of non-conformity to and transgression of the supernatural dictates reach a certain point of agreement in most cultures. The religious systems may proscribe different items as sin, for the general code of behavior is different; but no society has yet been found which did not have some concept of a violation of or lack of conformity to a supernaturally imposed code. This is essentially the significance of sin.

EVIL
GOOD
BAD

Before going further in the analysis of words for 'sin' and 'evil,' it is well to examine the following questions. They are designed to help the translator become acquainted with the problems of supernatural sanctions and relationship of these to such words as 'sin,' 'evil,' 'good,' and 'bad.'

1 What is meant by 'wrong' or 'bad' in the native religious system? Does it imply non-conformity to certain taboos? Violation of a moral code? Violation of tribal tradition which is non-moral in content?

2 What deeds are considered wrong?

3 Are right and wrong types of actions determined by supernatural sanctions?

4 For what types of deeds are people punished by the community? Is there any religious significance attached to these actions?

5 For what types of action are people punished during life by spirits or gods?

6 Are the gods or spirits concerned with moral guilt? Violation of taboo? Neglect of their worship?

7 Does the god or spirit respect righteousness (quality underlying moral conduct)?

8 For what types of action are men punished in the next world? By whom? How? For how long?

9 Is punishment graded according to types of violation? What is the scale of value?

10 What actions are praised by the people? What actions are honored?

11 Do the people distinguish between (1) 'sacred' and (2) 'secular' or 'profane'? Between 'sacred-good' and 'sacred-evil'?

12 Are members of society ever ostracized? For what reasons?

13 Which do the gods consider the worse transgression: (1) violation of moral code or (2) non-observance of taboos?

14 Do the people have a definite concept of life after death?

15 Where do souls go after death?

16 On what does the status of life after death depend: Personality? Morality? Observance of taboo? Manner of death? Social and economic status on earth?

17 What is the nature of the life after death?

18 What may men do to overcome judgment for 'wrong' actions?

19 Do the spirits or gods ever forgive wrong actions?

Having once found a word for 'sin' it will probably be quite difficult to find other words such as 'iniquity,' 'transgression,' and 'evil.' The chances are that at least some of these areas of meaning will be covered by the general word for 'sin.' In so many cultures the concepts of 'bad' and 'good' are the primary generic terms for all transgression and conformity. It is completely impossible in some cases to make further distinctions in accordance with the Hebrew, Greek, or English usage.

If at all possible, the attempt should be made to distinguish between evil as a sin and evil as misfortune or trouble, Luke 16:25.

BLAME   The words for 'sin' and 'blame' are often closely related and in some instances identical. In many languages there is no distinction made between the act and the resultant blame arising from such a transgression of the divine code. One must be careful, however, that the native does not understand the removal of guilt or blame to be identical with the removal of sin.

If the language has an adequate word for 'sin,' though the meaning may not be identical with the translator's concept of sin, it is better to use such a word and depend upon the teaching of the Bible to correct the slightly distorted impression than to depend upon some rather fanciful descriptive translation. One translator attempted to use 'lack before heaven' in place of the more common word for 'sin.' This is hardly justifiable. In some instances, translators have introduced rather specialized concepts of their own by such descriptive translations as 'one who has to pay something,' for "sinner." Such a translation may have some merits in teaching the meaning of redemption, but the justification for a shift of emphasis from the action to the punishment for such an action is highly questionable.

SAVE
SAVIOR

Stories have often been repeated about missionaries who waited many years before finally discovering the appropriate words for 'to save' and 'savior.' Such stories are often given on good authority and imply that the missionary has been delayed for years in translating because of the lack of this necessary word 'save.' If these stories are true, it is exceedingly unfortunate. No one ever should wait for years for a word 'to save.' The translator should take down many texts in the native language. In these he will almost inevitably come across a word which will be satisfactory. But if this is not the case, by telling a hypothetical story he can construct a situation in which a man is drowning or is in other great peril. He can then explain that someone came and extricated the victim from these terrifying circumstances. A discussion of this process of rescuing the victim will almost inevitably lead to a word which will serve for 'save' and 'savior.' In the Mazatec language the word 'to save' means literally 'to lift out on behalf of.' In the Eastern Aztec the word is literally 'to cause people to come out with the aid of the hand.' These are the regular idioms in the respective languages. In the Quechua language the expression 'to make to escape' has been used for "to save." There is nothing essentially difficult in finding a word meaning 'to save.' One should not permit his ministry to be crippled by rather aimlessly waiting to hear the exact word which may be acceptable.

One must be careful to distinguish two aspects of 'to save.' In the Maya language, there are two words which are given by informants to translate 'to save.'

The one means 'to rescue,' as from a well or a fire. The other has a much more involved meaning. In the case of certain diseases a black chicken is used by the shaman as a 'savior.' The disease is transferred to the chicken, which is then released into the jungle, supposedly carrying the disease with it. At first glance, the substitutionary features of this second word might seem to recommend its usage. However, the part played by the shaman and the very specialized significance of the word make its use inadvisable.

GRACE   The Greek word *charis*, usually translated by English "grace," is one of the desperations of translators. The area of meaning is exceptionally extensive. Note the following possible meanings for this word in various contexts of the New Testament: 'sweetness,' 'charm,' 'loveliness,' 'good will,' 'loving-kindness,' 'favor,' 'merciful kindness,' 'benefit,' 'gift,' 'benefaction,' 'bounty,' and 'thanks.' The theological definition of 'unmerited favor' (some translators have attempted to employ this throughout) is applicable to only certain contexts. Moreover, it is quite a task to find some native expression which will represent the meaning of 'unmerited favor.' In some languages it is impossible to differentiate between 'grace' and 'kindness.' In fact, the translation 'kindness' is in some cases quite applicable. In other languages, a translation of 'grace' is inseparable from 'goodness.' In the Mixtec language a very remarkable word has been used for 'grace.' It is made up of three elements. The first of these is a prefixial abstractor. The second is the stem for 'beauty.' The third is a suffix which indicates that the preceding elements are psychologically significant. The resultant word may be approximately defined as 'the abstract quality of beauty of personality.'

RIGHT-   Terms for 'righteousness' and 'righteous' are some-
EOUS   times closely related to the expressions for 'truth.' One
RIGHT-   should, however, attempt to include something of the
EOUSNESS   legal implications in the word for 'righteous,' if this is possible. Where this implication is not possible, one should introduce something of the principle of con-

formance to certain standards. In one language, "righteousness" is literally 'walking straight.'

In some cases it is almost impossible to differentiate 'righteous' and 'righteousness' from the area of meaning covered by the word for 'good.' Such a broad expression as 'good' is preferable to introducing the term for 'pure,' as has been done in some instances. This latter term is more applicable to 'holy' and 'sanctified.'

One should not attempt to read too much into a word for 'righteous.' One translator employed the phrase 'those who have no sin.' Except in the strictly forensic sense, such a translation is incorrect. This limited imputational significance of justification should probably not be made the exclusive or principal feature of terms for 'righteous' or 'righteousness.'

JUSTIFY
JUSTIFICA-
TION

In a surprising number of cases, translators have employed an expression such as 'to make good' for "justify," and 'to be good' for "justification." This is not a recommended usage if it can possibly be avoided. Such terms are too easily confused with "sanctify" and "sanctification." Moreover, the meaning of such an expression is rarely a satisfactory equivalent for the Greek *dikaioō*. The essential underlying significance of this term is 'to make something such as it ought to be' or 'to declare a thing such as it ought to be.' In every case something should imply a standard of action and judgment. In most of the contexts in which this word occurs one of the central meanings is 'to declare a thing guiltless.' In the Eastern Aztec the problem has been solved very neatly. "To justify" has been translated literally 'to heart-straighten.' 'Justification' is a derivative of the verb form and means the 'process-of-heart-straightening.' "Righteousness" has been translated as the 'result-of-heart-straightening.' The use of 'heart' gives the terms an essentially moral and personal quality, for the 'heart' is in the Aztec the central core of the personality. The use of the element 'straight' implies conformance to a definite moral code.

Note that in some contexts "to justify" must be translated 'to declare just' or 'to declare righteous.'

They "justified God," Luke 7: 29, must be translated they 'declared God just.' One must not say, as some translators have attempted to do, 'they made God just.'

HOLY
PURE
SANCTIFY
SAINT

The terms for 'holy,' 'pure,' 'saint,' 'sanctity,' 'sanctification' are crucial words in the translation. Together with the words for 'spirit' and the titles of Deity they are the most serious lexical problems in the entire translation of the Bible. This may not seem at first to be the case, but the relationship of these words to the entire problem of taboo greatly complicates the picture. We assume in so many instances that those things which are 'holy' are also 'good,' in terms of our own moral and ethical system. This is by no means universally or even occasionally the case. A religious system in which there is no essential relationship between morals and religion presents an entirely different picture from that to which we are accustomed. For example, in some religious systems promiscuous sex relationships are a central feature of intensely devout religious rites. Drunkenness and lasciviousness, if practiced at certain times and places, may be regarded as most 'holy' features of worship. In other words, in many religious systems the basic dichotomy is not between the 'good' and the 'bad' in terms of any system of morality, as we know it, but between the 'sacred' and the 'profane.' The 'sacred' things are those which involve objects and practices prescribed by the religious system. The 'profane' things are those in which there is no supernatural significance. The sacred objects and practices are generally the 'tabooed' objects and practices. These objects must not be touched or approached except in accordance with definite instructions which are a part of the religious system.

In most aboriginal cultures everything which concerns religion is considered as more or less filled with supernatural power or force. Even if these objects are not themselves filled with this power, they are at least watched over and guarded by supernatural power. Everything must be approached and carried out with a constant recognition of the supernatural significance

(HOLY,
ETC.)

of such matters. It does not make any difference whether such an object or practice is morally good or bad, destructive or beneficial to mankind, pure and holy or foul and loathsome. The entire perspective is different from ours. It is not morality but relationship to the supernatural that is important. The primary division of life is between that which involves the supernatural and that which does not. Moral distinctions, as we understand them, are completely secondary or tertiary. The missionary must get accustomed to this basically different way of looking at things. At first it may seem impossible. But he must do so, if he is to understand the moral ailments of his patients. The psychiatrist cannot help a patient until he understands the patient's standard of values. Neither can the translator be of assistance in presenting to men the truth of God's Word unless he understands their standard of values and the words which they employ to designate this standard.

Before going further into the problems of the sacred and profane, the translator should examine the following questions in the light of his own particular problems. These questions are by no means exhaustive. They only introduce the subject. But the answers to these questions will be significant in determining those words to use for 'holy,' 'sacred,' 'saint,' 'sanctity,' and 'sanctify.'

1 What objects are tabooed: Trees? Rivers? Lakes? Mountains? Ceremonial dress? Temples? Animals? Certain persons? Names? Numbers?
2 How are they tabooed: May not be touched? May not be looked upon? Mentioned by name?
3 What happens if taboos are violated? Who punishes for offense: Spirits? Gods? Power within the tabooed object?
4 What actions are tabooed?
5 Is there any relationship between the taboos and moral actions?
6 How do objects obtain their taboo?
   a. From mandate of a god?

(Holy,
etc.)

    b. Association with religious ceremony?

    c. Inhabited by a god, spirit, or spiritual force?

    d. Some miraculous occurrence at or in their vicinity?

    e. Special inherent power?

    f. Association with persons or objects having a strong taboo?

7 Do tabooed objects make other objects taboo by contact?

8 Is there any essential difference between 'holy' things that may not be touched and 'unclean' things which may not be touched?

9 Can sacredness be imparted to an object by prayer? Sprinkling? Washing? Dusting?

10 Who possesses the power to make things sacred?

11 Is sacredness permanent or temporary?

12 If it is temporary, at what time: Specific seasons? Critical circumstances?

13 Does any strange object or event have a certain amount of taboo or sacredness?

14 Are objects sacred to the gods normally clean and pure?

15 Are concepts of cleanness and goodness related?

16 Does morality induce respect and reverence?

The Greek word *hagios* 'holy' is the basic word in Greek for the various derivatives such as "saint," "holiness," "sanctify," and "sanctification." The Greek word includes two basic meanings: (1) separation and (2) moral purity. The meaning of separation is closely associated with the taboo complex, which is common to all religious systems. The meaning of moral purity is intelligible in the Christian system, but in other religious systems it is not necessarily an accompaniment of the meaning of 'separation.' This much is certain: one will probably never find such a word as Greek *hagios* or English "holy" in an animistic religious culture. As has been stated above, in many religious systems the sacred which involves separateness is not related to morality. Some translators have attempted to use a word meaning 'separateness' as an underlying form for the words indicating 'holiness' and 'sanctity.' In some cases there is distinct value in such usage. However, there is more danger of such terms being misunderstood, for they are too easily confused with the pagan system of taboo. Other translators have used words which denote 'cleanness' and 'goodness.' Such words emphasize the moral purity value of the Greek *hagios*. In most instances it would seem that this usage is to be preferred. It is usually easier to teach the meaning of separateness by using a term for moral purity than to reverse the process and teach moral purity by means of a term for separateness. The meaning of separateness may be completely obscured by the indigenous views of taboo.

One should refrain from assuming that a metaphor which may be used in English is perfectly understandable in another language. In one language the expression 'to make clean' may have no moral significance. It may mean nothing more than 'taking a bath.' One must be sure that the expression has the possibilities for some moral and religious significance.

OFFEND   The word "offend" as a translation of the Greek *skandalizō* seems to cause all sorts of trouble for translators. The difficulty is that the meaning of this word covers such a wide area. The basic meaning of the Greek is 'to cause to stumble by putting some impediment in the way.' The present central meaning of English "offend" is often quite different. In some languages there is no metaphorical value in a translation 'to cause someone to stumble.' If the language permits no such metaphor, the translator should not attempt to force it. In the Totonac language, the metaphor 'to show the wrong road to' is used in a manner almost exactly parallel to the Greek idiom. In most languages there will be some expression or set of expressions which will correspond to this Greek metaphor. But one should beware of a literal forcing of the passages. A literal translation of 'if your hand causes you to stumble' may not make sense in some languages.

CURSING   "Cursing" and "swearing" may not have any immediate
SWEARING   parallels in an aboriginal culture. Cursing involves a process of asking the supernatural powers to fulfill or assist one in his promises of woe for the person who is the object of the curs-

ing. Swearing involves a process of calling upon the deity to confirm and strengthen a promise or a statement. Sometimes the best translation of cursing which may be found is 'to say great evil against.' "To swear" may in some instances be translated 'to say strong words,' but every attempt should be made to find the local parallel if it exists. "To swear" and "to promise" must be translated the same in some languages, because of the absence of the oath complex in the culture. In Maya they are both translated as 'big-word.' "Adjure thee by God," Mark 5: 7, must be translated in some languages as 'say strongly to you before God.'

BLAS-
PHEME

"To blaspheme" presents somewhat similar problems to those encountered in "to swear" and "to curse." Blasphemy in the specialized sense of making oneself equal with God is not likely to be encountered in an aboriginal culture. But a translation such as 'to speak evil of' or 'to speak bad things about' may be employed in most contexts in which the word occurs.

DOUBT

There is usually no difficulty in finding a word for 'doubt.' One should be cautioned, however, to avoid a word for 'indifference' in the place of 'doubt.' Often the word for 'doubt' includes some concept of division of thinking. Note the Maya word for 'doubt,' which is literally 'two-things-soul.' In the Yipounou language of the Gabon one who has doubt is 'with two hearts.'

TEMPT

In translating the word "tempt," one must be sure that a careful distinction is drawn between the meaning of 'to test' and the meaning of 'to incite to evil.' A good commentary is the best proof against making mistakes in certain contexts.

REPENT-
ANCE

The translations of the words "repentance" and "to repent" are quite varied in different languages. If possible, the basic meaning should be 'to change the mind.' This follows closely the Greek *metanoeō*. In some instances translators have attempted to use such expressions as 'to ask forgiveness' or 'to stop sinning.' Such expressions only describe certain accompanying experiences, not repentance itself. A person may repent without asking forgiveness. He may even repent without stopping his sinning. The translator should not attempt to include in the meaning of repentance more than is implied and denoted in the Biblical words. One must be careful not to confuse 'repent' and 'renounce,' as has been done in some instances. Likewise, it is very important to make a clear dis-

CONVER-
SION

tinction between 'repentance' and 'conversion.' In the Mazatec this distinction is very neatly brought out. "Repentance" is translated literally as 'to think again' and "conversion" is translated literally as 'to turn oneself about.'

FAITH   In many instances the native expression for 'faith' is related to a term designating 'believe.' In the Mazatec language no noun such as "faith" can be employed. In every instance one must translate such a noun by a verb expression, e.g. in Acts 6: 7 one must translate "faith" by 'what people believed.' Care should be given to the problems of the active process of believing and the passive state of the thing believed. In the Totonac language this distinction must be made in all instances. For a word for "faith" some translators have attempted to find some term for transcendental insight or supernatural conviction. They are surely doomed to disappointment. If a choice must be made, they should simply use a term which means 'to believe.' The philosophical and theological aspects of the word may be intensified through the reader's experience. It is the Bible that must give meaning to the words, just as surely as the words give meaning to the Bible. That is to say, the totality of contexts is of utmost importance in defining the meaning of a word in the Bible.

TRUE   The words for 'truth' and 'true' are not always the most
TRUTH   readily discovered in aboriginal languages. In some instances the only expression which corresponds to "true" is something like 'it happened.' A falsehood is something that 'did not happen.' In a good many languages the meaning of 'truth' is expressed by the words signifying 'straight' and 'direct.' Untruth is accordingly 'crookedness.' An abstract noun such as English "truth" is quite difficult to find in some instances. Only an expression such as 'true statement' or 'true word' will be found to correspond to English "truth."

SAINTS   It is very advisable to relate the word for 'saints' to the other words indicating purity or holiness. Such a translation as 'men with God' is scarcely usable. 'Heavenly people' is even less desirable. In the Eastern Aztec, the 'heart-cleansed-ones' serves very adequately for "saints."

13.4   ESCHATOLOGY

Illustrative words: RESURRECTION, ETERNAL, HEAVEN, PARADISE, HADES, HELL, GEHENNA, PIT.

RESURREC-   In finding a word for "resurrection" translators have
TION   used two principal types of expressions: (1) words de-

noting 'lifting up' and 'arising' and (2) words denoting 'to live again.' In some instances translators have translated 'to arise from the dead.' It is sometimes necessary to add such a qualifying phrase as 'from the dead,' for the word 'to arise' may mean only 'to awaken' or 'to arise from a prostrate position.'

In some languages a considerable distinction is made as to various aspects of arising. One language distinguishes between arising from beneath the surface of the earth to the surface. Another word designates arising from a horizontal position to a standing position. Another word designates arising from the surface of the earth to a position above the surface of the earth. The translator must be sure that he has used the appropriate term for the particular language. In most instances, the most general term is to be preferred.

The usage of 'second-life' for "resurrection" has proven quite acceptable in some languages. One should investigate, however, to be sure that no belief in transmigration of the soul is implied. The Bible teaches resurrection but not reincarnation.

ETERNAL A term for "eternal" must usually be translated negatively by some such expression as 'not ending' or 'without an ending.'

HEAVEN The correspondence between 'heaven' and 'sky' is rather frequent. However, the abode of the righteous dead, or of the dead in general, is in some cultures considered to be down in the earth. Some translators have undertaken to use the native word for 'heaven' even though its location is considered below the surface of the earth. This has apparently never been successful. There are too many passages in the Bible about "ascending into heaven" to make it possible to change the Biblical description of the location of heaven. Such a usage would strike the informant as being as incongruous as a phrase 'up into hell' seems inconceivable to us.

PARADISE The word "paradise" may be transliterated as a proper name for an abode of the dead. It may also be translated as 'the beautiful place' or 'the good place.' Its basic meaning in the Greek is 'a park,' which renders Hebrew 'garden.'

HADES Special care must be taken to differentiate between "Hades," "Gehenna," and "the pit." The AV is not a satisfac-

HELL

GEHENNA

PIT

tory guide, for both Hades and Gehenna are translated "hell." Hades is best translated by 'the place of the dead.' In the Bible Hades is used as the name of the abode of both the righteous and the unrighteous dead. The name for Hades should not specify the character of the inhabitants, except to note that they are the dead. Gehenna may be treated as a proper name, which it actually is. It has been translated as 'place of lostness,' 'place of punishment,' and 'place of suffering.' These translations are legitimate. However, such a translation as 'place where evil spirits are in charge' is unwarranted. There is no evidence for such a descriptive expression. "The pit" may be translated as 'the deep chasm' or 'the deep hole.' It should not be equated with Hades or Gehenna.

13.5 SPECIALIZED RELIGIOUS ACTIVITIES

Illustrative words: BAPTISM, PRAYER, BLESS, SACRIFICE, OFFERING, HOLOCAUST, PROPITIATION, PROPHESY, PROPHET, HYMN.

BAPTISM

The great difference of opinion and practice with regard to baptism makes the choice of a word to designate this ritual a very important one. It has been the policy of the Bible Societies not to print a translation in which the word chosen for 'baptism' excludes the mode of baptism practiced by any mission working with the language group in question. Some translators have reacted rather violently against any such restriction. This is regrettable. It is felt, however, that the insertion of a particular phrase or word for 'baptism' should not be a means of stirring up religious controversy or of proselyting. Men equally devout and scholarly have been ranged on the various sides of the baptism question.

The solution to the problem is not altogether easy. Of course, the easiest, and in some instances the most satisfactory, method is to transliterate the word "baptism" in accordance with the form which it has in the trade language of the area. Some translators have used the expression 'wash with water.' This expression has very little specialization of meaning and is ambiguous as to the amount of water which is used. In some instances, a translation such as 'to set aside (ceremonial-ly) with water' has been employed. This type of translation has much to recommend it. The word 'to set aside' is used in a special religious sense of 'to hallow.' The use of 'water' indicates the medium. Difficulties arise in those passages speaking of the "baptism of the Holy Spirit." In such a case, the usage of 'to set aside (ceremonially) by the Holy Spirit' has been employed with apparent success. This terminology should not be confused, however, with 'sanctification.' At all events, one should avoid the use of a term which means 'to give a name to.' This is a common usage in many of the Catholicized tribes of Latin America.

PRAYER   Terms for "prayer" are not so easily found as may be at first supposed. One not infrequently finds in Roman Catholic areas a word for "prayer" which actually means 'to recite' or 'to speak doctrine.' Both such ritualistic types of expressions should be avoided. At the same time one should attempt to avoid the meaning of 'begging,' which has been used in several instances. A compound such as 'talk to God' has been found very satisfactory in some languages. There are essentially two factors in prayer which are usually clearly distinguished in most languages: (1) request and (2) worshipful communion. Usually, the translator must choose one or the other of these basic word areas and, by teaching, attempt to introduce the significance of the other.

BLESS   The Greek *eulogeō*, literally 'speak well of' and usually translated 'to bless,' covers a very wide area of meaning. It means (1) 'to praise,' (2) 'to invoke blessings upon someone,' (3) 'to consecrate something,' and (4) 'to bestow blessings upon someone.' No one aboriginal word can possibly cover all of these specialized meanings. The translator should consult a comprehensive lexicon to determine the meanings in the particular passages. In a great many instances, it will be found that an expression involving the word 'praise' will be of help. For example, in Eastern Aztec "Son of the Blessed," Mark 14:61, becomes 'Son of the One men praise'; and "blessed be the kingdom," Mark 11:10, becomes 'let people praise the kingdom.'

One will quite frequently find that the word which designates the act of blessing as performed by God may not be used to designate the act of blessing as performed by men toward God. That is to say, God's blessing us and our blessing God will frequently have to be expressed by an entirely different word. 'God's blessing us' denotes meaning number (4), listed above, while 'our blessing God' denotes meaning number (1).

SACRI-FICES OFFERINGS The terms "sacrifices" and "offerings" have few parallels in some languages, for not all peoples offer such gifts to the supernatural. One should beware of attempting to use too extensive a descriptive phrase. One translator employed 'an animal killed to pay for sin' as a translation for "sacrifice." This type of descriptive expression excludes many types of sacrifices and is quite interpretive. It would be better to translate "sacrifice" by an expression such as 'a killed gift.' It is seldom necessary to designate that such a gift is for God.

HOLO-CAUST The context usually makes this sufficiently clear. A "holocaust" is a 'gift which is completely burned up.' A "burnt offering" may be translated as a 'burnt gift.' An "offering" must often be translated by the word 'gift.' A careful study of these words in a Bible dictionary will be of help to the translator in finding expressions which will correspond adequately to the formal and functional significance of the Biblical features.

PROPITIA-TION "Propitiation" involves a specialized substitutionary aspect of religion which may not always be found in a pagan culture. A translation such as 'covering' in I John 2:2 is probably not very satisfactory, unless the native religious culture uses this term in a specialized sense. It may be translated 'that which appeases,' but a word for 'appease' may be equally hard to find. The best that can be done in some languages is to use 'gift,' e.g. I John 2:2, 'He is the gift in payment for our sins.'

PROPHESY PROPHET The tendency in many translations is to use 'to foretell the future' for "prophesy," and 'one who foretells the future' for "prophet." This is not always a recommended usage, particularly if such expressions denote certain special native practices of spirit contact and control. It is true, of course, that prophets of the Bible did foretell the future, but this

was not always their principal function. One essential significance of the Greek word *prophētēs* is 'one who speaks
forth,' principally, of course, as a forth-teller of the Divine
will. A translation such as 'spokesman for God' may often
be employed profitably. The term "prophecy" in the New
Testament may be translated in some instances as 'inspired
preaching.'

HYMN   A specialized word for "hymn" is not likely to occur where
singing is not directly associated with religious performances.
In some instances, a 'holy song' or 'sacred song' is used.
When, however, people do employ singing in their own religion, one must be careful not to use a name for a Christian
hymn which, because of pagan association, may be prejudi-
cial to its real significance.

13.6   RELIGIOUS PERSONAGES

Illustrative words: PRIEST, DISCIPLE, APOSTLE, MINISTER, DEA-
CON, BISHOP, PRESBYTER.

PRIEST   A priest is one whose specialized occupation concerns
religious matters. Many aboriginal cultures have no
priests. They do, however, possess shamans, or witch
doctors, as they are also called. These men may make
a living in the same way as any of the rest of the people,
but on the side they practice various types of healing
and exorcism. The priesthood is usually found only in
highly organized societies, where there is a considerable
specialization of activity. The priests are set aside from
all types of secular occupations so that they may devote
their time exclusively to sacred duties. Such specialization is generally considered by the natives as making
it possible for the priests to intercede more appropriately with the supernatural. Finding an adequate
word for the "priest" of the Bible is not easy. A name
which specifies activity in a pagan cult is usually not
satisfactory, for it would imply to the native reader that
the priest of the Bible indulged in the practices of the
pagan cult in question.

One must attempt to avoid a name for 'priests' which
is distinctly derogatory, for the patterns of priesthood
of the Bible are to be respected. Translators seem to

be too easily deceived into thinking that they can discredit the local priesthood by indicating how the 'priests' (using the derogatory native term) took such an active part in the death of Jesus. The implications of such usage are too great. Christ himself is called a high priest in Hebrews 9:11.

If there is no good term for "priest" in the language, it is quite difficult to find an adequate descriptive expression. One translator used 'one who offers sacrifices.' This is an extremely limited term, for the priests did much more than offer sacrifices. A translation such as 'one concerned with holy things' represents quite well the meaning of the Greek *hiereus*. A highly theological translation such as 'a man who represents men before God' is a rather unwieldly phrase and should surely be replaced by a less awkward and less specialized term. Certainly it would be undesirable to employ such a name for the priests of Baal.

DISCIPLE APOSTLE

It is surprising how many translations have inadequate expressions for "disciple" and "apostle." In some instances the translators have borrowed the words from some trade language. This is usually entirely unnecessary. In some translations no distinction is made between disciples and apostles. This is equally unfortunate. "Apostles" has been translated 'his chosen persons' and "disciples" as 'his people.' These are certainly incorrect, even though Jesus did choose his apostles and though his disciples were very closely associated with him. In almost all languages one can translate "apostles" as 'the sent ones,' and "disciples" as 'learners' or 'those who learn.'

MINISTER

In one language the Greek *diakonos*, meaning 'servant' and sometimes translated 'minister,' was translated as a 'preacher of the gospel.' This should not be done. A "minister" of the AV is only 'one who serves.' If he happens to be a minister of the gospel, well and good. The essential meaning is the fact that he serves, not that he serves in some special way. Note that the Greek *diakonos* is the word from which English "deacon" is derived. The "deacon" of the New Testament was only a special servant of the congregation.

DEACON

BISHOP

PRESBY-
TER

His authority was in terms of his service only. The "bishop" was only the 'overseer,' not the 'boss of the church,' as some translators have thought to translate it. The "presbyter" was an 'elder.'

13.7 RELIGIOUS CONSTRUCTIONS

Illustrative words: TEMPLE, SYNAGOGUE, TABERNACLE.

TEMPLE

There are two Greek words which are translated "temple" in the AV. The word *hieron* means 'a sacred place' and is used to designate the entire sacred enclosure, including the various courts, porticoes, and balconies. The word *naos* designates the sanctuary itself. In the temple of Jerusalem this included the holy place where only the priests went and also the holy of holies where only the high priest went on the Day of Atonement. The translator is usually fortunate if he can find one word for 'temple,' but he should be on the lookout for possibilities of expressing such a very important difference. In some instances, one may translate the Greek *hieron* as 'the holy building' or 'the holy place' and Greek *naos* as 'the sacred room.' The translation 'God's house' for "temple" has not proven satisfactory in many instances.

SYNA-
GOGUE

The term "synagogue" designates (1) those who constitute an assembly or (2) the building in which such assemblies were held. The primary function of such a building was for religious instruction. It did, however, also serve as a type of town hall. The translation 'building for gathering' is quite satisfactory in most instances. The translation 'house of God' is rather unsatisfactory. It will probably be confused with the 'temple' and the term for 'church.' The translation 'schoolroom' is descriptive of only one use of the synagogue, and the religious function is much more important. In order to differentiate between the temple and the synagogue, some translators have used 'large sacred building' for "temple" and 'small sacred building' for "synagogue."

TABER-
NACLE

"Tabernacle" has been discussed on p. 173.

13.8　　　　　　　RELIGIOUS GROUPS

Illustrative words: SECT, HERESY, CHURCH.

SECT
HERESY
　　　　　The words "sect" and "heresy" are translations of the same Greek word *hairesis*. This word designates the 'act of choosing' or a 'party.' One may usually translate this word as 'group' or 'forming a group.'

CHURCH
　　　　　The New Testament term "church" designates primarily a group of people, not a building. In most languages it may be translated as 'an assembly' or 'a gathering.' This is exactly the meaning of the Greek *ekklēsia*.

13.9　　　　　　　RELIGIOUS ARTIFACTS

Illustrative words: ALTAR, IMAGE, IDOL, SHOWBREAD.

　　　　　Many words which designate artifacts used in religious services are also used to designate very common features of the material culture, e.g. laver, veil, vessel, candlestick, and robe. Certain words, however, have specialized religious usage. In some cultures there are
ALTAR
no parallels to the "altar" of the Bible. In such instances, a descriptive term such as 'the thing on which sacred offerings are placed' is often the most satisfactory definitive translation, but it is rather long and cumbersome. In some instances, "altar" has been translated simply 'a place of sacrifice.' This is the etymological meaning of the Greek *thusiastērion*.

IMAGE
　　　　　It is important to differentiate clearly between an image and an idol. The image is only the likeness of something or someone. It possesses no inherent supernatural power. An idol, however, is the representation of a supernatural being and the earthly embodiment of his personality. The idol is considered to possess inherent supernatural power and is worshiped for its own sake. The "image" may generally be translated as 'likeness.' Most cultures have some types of idols, but if they do not, the word may be translated by 'a likeness which is worshiped.'

SHOW-   "Showbread" may be translated as 'bread which is
BREAD   shown' or 'bread which is put out to be seen.'

13.10   RELIGIOUS EVENTS

Illustrative words: PASSOVER, FEAST OF THE TABERNACLES, FEAST OF THE DEDICATION, SABBATH.

PASSOVER   It is advisable to translate "Passover" as 'a passing over' with the implication of sparing, if this latter denotation may be incorporated satisfactorily. In Latin America several translators have used the Spanish *Pascua*. The difficulty with this word is that it is used in many places to designate several different Catholic holy days and consequently should be checked carefully. In some regions it is used almost exclusively for 'Christmas.'

FEAST OF   The "Feast of the Tabernacles" may be translated as
TABER-   the 'Feast of the Brush Shelters.' In much of Latin
NACLES   America the Spanish term *fiesta* is in very common use and is usually very satisfactorily borrowed for English "feast." There are some places, however, where the specialization of meaning in the word *fiesta* does not make its use advisable.

FEAST OF   The "Feast of the Dedication" is somewhat more
DEDICA-   difficult to translate than the "Feast of the Tabernacles."
TION   The cultural feature of dedication, as we know it, is not very well developed in many societies. The word "dedication" may be translated 'renewing' or 'consecration.'

SABBATH   The word "Sabbath" has been translated in many different ways, e.g. 'God's day,' 'the seventh day,' 'the last day of the week,' 'the holy day,' 'Saturday,' and 'the day of rest.' The cultural feature of the week is so common to us that we assume that all other peoples in the world must be acquainted with our way of reckoning days. This is by no means the case. Accordingly, a descriptive translation of this word in terms of the week or the number of days in the week is often quite inadequate.

In translating "Sabbath" into various aboriginal languages of Latin America, a considerable number of translators have used the Spanish *sábado*, 'Saturday,' because it is derived from the Hebrew *sabbath* and seems to correspond to the English usage as well. The difficulty is that the word *sábado* means only 'Saturday' to most people. There is no religious significance about this word as there is with "Sabbath" in English. Accordingly, the natives cannot understand the significance of the persecution of Jesus because he worked on 'Saturday.' It has been found quite advantageous to use the translation 'day of rest,' for this accurately translates the Hebrew meaning of the term and resolves the problem in connection with the prohibitions placed upon some types of activities.

Chapter 14

PROBLEMS OF LINGUISTIC EQUIVALENCE

LANGUAGE is a part of culture. The various formal features of a language create just as many problems of equivalence as do the features of material, social, and religious culture in the aboriginal society. In fact, in many instances the differences in the linguistic structures present more problems to the translator than the differences of cultural structures. Furthermore, these formal differences of language are significant in all phases of the translation process and involve all phases of language. The problems presented by the differences of linguistic culture will be considered under (1) the phonology (the sounds), (2) the morphology (the words), (3) the syntax (the grammatical structure), and (4) the lexicon (the meaning of words).

Before, however, considering the detailed analysis of various linguistic factors which dictate the form of a translation, it is valuable to compare some different types of translations into English. Each of the following may be considered a translation, though in a technical sense the one by Harwood is rather a' paraphrase; and the word-for-word, literal translation might be termed a *tour de force*, though it is surprising how many translations into aboriginal languages are of almost the same character. Nevertheless, these widely divergent forms will be illustrative of the various methods of treating the linguistic factors in translation techniques.

ILLUSTRATIVE TRANSLATIONS OF COLOSSIANS 1: 27–29

Literal, Word-for-Word Translation

27 to-whom was-pleased the God to-make-known what the riches [of] the glory [of] the mystery this among the Gentiles, which is Christ in you, the hope of the glory,

28 whom announced-we, admonishing every man and teaching every man in all wisdom, that present-may-we every man perfect in Christ,

29 to which also toil-I striving according-to the in-working his the-[one] in-working in me in power.

American Revised Version, 1901

27 to whom God was pleased to make known what is the riches of the glory of this mystery among the Gentiles, which is Christ in you, the hope of glory:

28 whom we proclaim, admonishing every man and teaching every man in all wisdom, that we may present every man perfect in Christ;

29 whereunto I labor also, striving according to his working, which worketh in me mightily.

Translation by Edwin Harwood, 1768

27 to whom the Deity was desirous to discover the glorious transcendent excellency of this divine revelation, newly published among the Heathens, namely, that the Messiah is become to you Gentiles the author of the glorious hope of immortality.

28 These evangelical doctrines we proclaim to the world, solemnly admonishing every person, without distinction, carefully initiating every person into all this divine science, in order that, by the Christian religion, we may advance every person to the highest possible summit of perfection:

29 To accomplish which, I exert all my endeavours, sedulously labouring to effect this great end by those miraculous operations, he powerfully enables me to perform.

Revised Standard Version, 1946

27 To them God chose to make known how great among the Gentiles are the riches of the glory of this mystery, which is Christ in you, the hope of glory.

28 Him we proclaim, warning every man and teaching every man in all wisdom, that we may present every man mature in Christ.

29 For this I toil, striving with all the energy which he mightily inspires within me.

Certain features concerning the linguistic forms of the above translations should be noted, for they will help one to understand the basic principles involved in translation procedure:

1 It is impossible to make a literal word-for-word translation of the Greek text and still make sense in English. This is even more true when one is translating from English or Greek into some aboriginal language, of which the linguistic structure differs widely from the Indo-European type.

2 There are some phrases in the literal translation which have meaning, and some of the relationships can be followed and somewhat guessed at; but such a literal translation is completely unworthy of the translator's time and efforts.

3 In many formal linguistic details the ARV quite distinctly follows the word-for-word order of the original text. All principal items in these verses occur in the same relative order as the Greek, except the subject and verb sequences. This is even more evident in other contexts.

4 Harwood's translation preserves the same general order of items, but elaborates words in a very highly ornate style. Many of the words are obvious additions and highly interpretive, but no more so than some translations cited in this volume. Note that the syntactic structure is highly complex and involved.

5 The RSV rendering differs principally from the ARV in the simplicity of linguistic structure and the altered order of some of the constituent items. Note that while in Greek and the ARV these three verses constitute only one sentence, they are three separate sentences in the RSV. This is more in accordance with the average length of sentences in English.

6 The translator into any language should aim at a translation which is simple in its linguistic structure but at the same time idiomatic and faithful to the meaning of the original text. He must avoid (1) the excesses of literalness in the word-for-word rendering and (2) the interpretive extravagance of the type illustrated by Harwood's translation.

14.1   PHONOLOGY

The transliteration of proper names involves the equivalence of phonological features of the text language and the native language. No two languages ever have the same phonemic structure. Hence, it is impossible to transfer names from one language to another without some modifications. After a term has been transferred from one language to another, it is often almost completely disguised. The Shilluk transliteration of *Jesus* is *Jidhath*. In the Ponape the English word *governor* becomes *kopina*.

There are two ways of making transfers of words from one language to another. One of these methods is transcription and the other is transliteration. In transcription certain letters of one language are automatically transcribed into certain letters of the second language. For example, the Greek words which have been cited in this book are transcriptions. In New Testament times at least five different vowel symbols or combinations of symbols represented the same phoneme. Moreover, the English vowel symbols which we have employed to transcribe the Greek have very little correspondence to the more predominant values of these symbols in modern English. Nevertheless, we transcribe Greek by giving a letter-for-letter correspondence with very little regard to the pronunciation of the word in New Testament times, nor to the value of these vowel symbols in modern English. Transliteration, however, is based primarily upon pronunciation, not upon spelling. For example, there are five letters in the word *judge*, but there are only three phonemes. In transliterating this word into another language, we would consider only the three phonemes and pay no attention to the conventional ways of spelling the word. In transliterating from one language to another the purpose is to find the closest correspondence of phonemes, while in transcribing words from one language into another the purpose is to find the closest correspondence of letters.

Native speakers almost always make completely satisfactory adjustments in borrowing any foreign word. They seldom attempt to pronounce any sound or combination of sounds completely foreign to their own linguistic system. Rather, they mould the word to meet the form of their own phonemic system. When the Tarahumaras borrow a Spanish word they often change it considerably. For example, Spanish *presidente* becomes *bisirenti*. This Tarahumara equivalent is the closest correspondent, phoneme for phoneme, which may be made to the Spanish.

In most instances, the native speakers will automatically make the adjustments for which most missionaries have considerable difficulty in figuring out the system of correspondence. The difficulty is usually that the translator will not accept as valid the modifications which the native informant makes. For example, if the native insists on putting *i* on the end of the name of *Paul*, because in the native language no word ends in a consonant, the translator sometimes thinks that the native speaker is stubborn or simply ignorant. If the native speaker insists on word-final vowels and vowels between certain consonants when they occur in a cluster, e.g. saying *Kirisiti* for *Christ*, the translator usually gives up in dismay. He should, however, transcribe proper names exactly as the monolingual native would pronounce them if they were a regular part of his vocabulary. That is to say, borrowed words should be completely adapted to the phonological structure of the native language. Certainly most aboriginal languages have not changed proper names any more than we have in English. For example, the modern pronunciation of *Jesus* does not correspond in any sound to the Aramaic pronunciation of New Testament times, and there is only one sound in common with the Greek pronunciation. The problem is not one of how altered the word appears but how consistently one has used the closest corresponding sounds, in accordance with the native language structure.

In some instances translators have wanted to transliterate some words but not others. This is especially true when some proper names from the trade language are used very frequently among the native population with the spelling of the trade language. For example, translators in French territory in Africa have often considered it obligatory to use *Jean* (English 'John') instead of the native form, which might be written *Jan* or *Jã*. It is true that there are often great prejudices to overcome if one insists upon using the native transliteration throughout. Nevertheless, it is inadvisable to put in the way of the new reader any more stumbling-blocks than necessary, for each proper name written in an orthography which does not correspond to the native usage is bound to give more or less difficulty for the monolingual. If the native reads the Bible text in the trade language, he can see the familiar names spelled in the form which they have in the trade language, but he should be encouraged to appreciate the form of his own language and the fact that even his own name can be written in it. It has been necessary in some instances to preserve the artificial forms of the trade language, but this is not recommended.

One must not, however, make a fetish of the way words are written. In one translation the English word *God* was borrowed. The English spelling of the word was not changed. The translators continued to teach the pronunciation of this word with the *a* vowel, though they continued to write it with the *o* vowel. To introduce confusion into an orthography because of fetishism for spelling is completely unjustified.

In making transliterations the translator must be careful that they do not turn out to be homophonous to some native word. For example, in the Mixteco the correct transliteration of Spanish *Tiro* 'Tyre' is *tiro*, but this word also means a 'firecracker bomb.' In order to avoid confusion, the transliteration was changed to *tiru*. In one language in Africa the correct transliteration of *rabbi* was homophonous with a vulgar word. Because the context would not eliminate the possibility of the vulgar significance, one vowel in the transliteration was changed.

In transliterating, one should make complete adaptations of the sounds in terms of the native system. The sounds are what count, not the spelling.

14.2   MORPHOLOGY

No two languages correspond exactly in any set of features. It is obvious to even the most inexperienced person that languages differ greatly in the system of formation of words, the numbers of classes of words, and the categories which are expressed by certain classes of words. For the translator, the differences in morphology constitute two principal problems: (1) differences of word classes and (2) differences of categories.

14.2.1   DIFFERENCES OF WORD CLASSES

Some people take for granted that all languages have such parts of speech (word classes) as nouns, verbs, adjectives, prepositions, conjunctions, and participles. It is rather a shock for the translator to find that he cannot have a noun for "savior." The language may not have such a noun. In that case, the translator must use a verb expression, e.g. 'one who saves.' Someone may insist that it is always possible to form agent nouns from verbs, e.g. *dancer* from *dance* and *carrier* from *carry*, but a glance at English will soon convince him that this cannot always be done. We do not use, except perhaps in a facetious manner, such derivations as *be-er*[1] 'one who is,' *seemer* 'one who seems,' or *becomer* 'one who becomes.' Anyone who is to translate something into English

---

[1]The symbol * indicates a hypothetical form.

must use the words which we normally use, provided, of course, he wants us to read what he has translated. Otherwise it seems so strange and unintelligible that we tend to put it aside. The same thing is true of a translation into some aboriginal language. If the translation uses the words that the native knows, he will be able to understand and hence read it; but, if the forms are strange and unnaturally put together, the native is likely to put it aside because it is difficult or because his feeling for correctness in his own language has been offended. The native's reaction to style may be less trained than ours but no less emphatic.

The translator will find that his principal problem will be, changing the noun expressions of the Greek or English into verb expressions in the aboriginal language. The English language, as well as most of the other Indo-European languages, seems to be exceptional among the languages of the world in that so much meaning may be carried by the nouns. In fact, the developers of Basic English have reduced the number of verbs to eighteen. This is, of course, very artificial, but it is indicative of the heavy load of the vocabulary that may be carried by the nouns and the adjectives. Such a situation is practically never found in other languages. In a great many languages only the more tangible objects in the environment, e.g. *house, man, dog, tree, sun, water,* and *knife,* are classed together as noun-like words. All the processes, states of being, and actions are classed as verbs. In the Tarahumara language practically all the words which we consider as adjectives, e.g. *tall, short, sick, red,* and *bad,* are basically verbs. In some few cases even those objects which we would be absolutely convinced must be nouns actually turn up as verbs. For example, in the Eastern Aztec the expression "there was much grass," John 6: 10, is translated by a single verb.

To understand the manner in which adaptations of translation have to be made because of differences in word classes, one may examine some of the translations which have been made in various languages. Note that these changes have been made because there is no noun in the aboriginal language which corresponds to the noun of the English. In the Mazatec language the AV "for this is the love of God," I John 5: 3, becomes 'this shows that we love God.' There is no noun 'love' in the language. All such expressions must be changed into verb expressions with a subject. The 'we' subject is taken from the next clause, which reads "that we keep his commandments." There is also no copulative verb 'to be,' such as exists in English. In the Mazatec one must indicate more than just the existence of a situation; one must define precisely the manner in which this situation manifests itself. In this instance the "is" of the English must be translated 'shows' in Mazatec.

In I John 4:10 the English AV "herein is love" must be translated in Mazatec as 'in this we know how someone loves.' This may seem quite a wide departure from the English or the Greek, but every change is necessitated by the grammatical and lexical structure of the Mazatec. There is no shorter way of saying this. There is no adverb equivalent to "herein." The only way this may be translated in Mazatec is by 'in this.' Since there is no copulative verb equivalent to the English "is," one must indicate the manner in which a situation is known. In this context the most natural equivalent in the Mazatec is 'we know.' The English noun "love" must be translated by a corresponding verb expression and the verb must have a subject. Since the English noun in this instance indicates a process, the closest parallel in Mazatec is a clause 'how someone loves.'

"The lust of the flesh," I John 2:16, becomes in Mazatec 'what the self desires.' The English noun "lust" must be translated by a verb. The closest equivalent to the "flesh" is in Mazatec the 'self,' which is synonymous with the human nature.

In some instances two different classes of words must be changed in the same expression. In "his love is perfected in us," I John 4:12, the Mazatec translation reads 'we really love as he loves.' The word "love" must be made a verb, but it is impossible to have two verb expressions ('to love' and 'to be perfected') in the same phrase. Moreover, there is no adequate passive expression equivalent to the "is perfected." The English verb expression must be shifted to an adverbial expression 'really,' which is the closest equivalent of the "is perfected." Note also the change in the subject element 'we.' This is dictated by the fact that there is no prepositional phrase construction with 'in' which approximates the meaning of the English or the Greek. It is seldom that one has to revamp an expression so completely as this one, but in translating one must make sense; and had the translator employed a word-for-word rendering of the English or the Greek, the translation would have been quite unintelligible. Our objective in translating is to stay as close to the text as possible, but there is no purpose in putting words together which the native reader cannot understand.

Note the following verbal expressions for English noun expressions: 'what I teach' for "my doctrine," 'people murder' for "murders," and 'what I give' for "my gift."

In some instances it is possible to translate by using rather artificially constructed nouns, but these are frequently very difficult for people to understand if it is more natural for the speakers to employ a verb expression. For example, in one language the translators conformed very closely in such passages as "God commendeth his love toward us" and "have come short of the glory of God." It would have been preferable in the particular language if they had translated 'God shows that he loves us' and 'have failed to shine as God shines.' The translations which were used were somewhat understandable, but they were not natural. If the speakers of a language use verb expressions, even though we use noun expressions, we should attempt to conform in so far as possible to the native language. The translation should speak the language of the native, not indicate the classes of words in the English or the Greek.

Perhaps the most acute trouble encountered in the problem of equivalence of word classes occurs in the lack of prepositions in the aboriginal language. Greek and English are well supplied with prepositions. This is rarely the case in aboriginal languages, and seldom will the areas of meaning correspond with any degree of accuracy. In the Mazatec one preposition-like word *k'ao* means 'and,' 'with,' 'through,' and 'by means of,' but in several instances the context does not clear up the difficulty. For this reason the entire expression must frequently be changed. For example, in I John 4:9 the expression "live through him" (Greek *dia* 'through') is completely ambiguous if translated in Mazatec by the usual conjunction *k'ao*, for the most readily understood interpretation is 'live with him.' In order to convey somewhat the meaning of the original text it is necessary to translate 'live by what he did.'

The translator must constantly remind himself that anything in one language may be translated into another language, provided that he looks long enough to discover the modes of expression and is willing to shift into these new linguistic structures. As long as the translator has the idea that English, Greek, and Hebrew constitute the most perfect frameworks of human thought and that all languages should be conformed more or less to them, he will be hopelessly lost as a translator. Every language has potentialities of literary beauty. It is not a matter of the medium of expression but of the skill of the artisan. The ignorance of the translator, not the supposed poverty of the language, is responsible for poor translating.

14.2.2   Differences of Categories

The parts of speech of various languages often classify certain types of phenomena by the means of special forms of the words. For example, in English the nouns indicate singularity or plurality. We can usually determine from hearing the form of a word whether this word is singular or plural. If the word occurs without a plural suffix, we say that it is singular. There are some verb forms which to some extent express a difference between singularity and plurality. Certain adjectives and pronouns also indicate number. There is, however, no essential reason why a language should indicate the number of items in such an arbitrary way as we do in English. Why should a single object have one form and any number of such objects, all the way from two to infinity, be included in another form? We would be quite justified in considering this 'illogical,' but it seems so natural that we may not be able to understand how a language can get along without such a basic division of forms. Nevertheless, the speakers of the Tarahumara language manage quite well without this basic division or category. The word *towíki* means 'boy' or 'boys.' If it is not important to the context to make a distinction, the form is the same. Of course, if one wants to say 'many boys' or 'few boys' or 'some boys' or 'ten boys,' then the appropriate attributive may be added. However, the nouns themselves make no distinction between singular and plural. There is no point in evaluating a language system according to whether it does or does not indicate such differences. Both systems have their adherents. The purpose of the translator is to employ the native system with the same degree of perfection with which the native speakers use it. If he does that, he will find the system altogether adequate to say anything that he wants to say.

The category of number is only one of the many categories which are indicated in languages by special forms of words. It is quite impossible for us to deal with all types of categories here. We shall, however, mention a few and consider some of the translation problems which are involved. The following categories have been found to be significant in the problems of Bible translation: (1) number,

(2) aspect, (3) tense, (4) person, (5) voice, (6) mode, (7) possession, (8) comparison, and (9) respect.

14.2.2.1   NUMBER

The failure of a language to indicate number may seem to the translator as an inexcusable oversight. If he finds, as in the Mazatec, that the same expression may mean 'they hit him,' 'they hit them,' 'he hit them,' and 'he hit him,' he may decide that such a language is a hopeless set of barbarisms and that no precise type of translating may be done. On the other hand, where English may not be precise, the Mazatec language is. Of course, the Mazatec people may indicate a plural if they must; that is to say, if the context does not otherwise make it plain. In Acts 14:11 "the gods" will have to be translated in Mazatec as 'the two gods' in order to make it plain that both Paul and Barnabas were considered gods. In Acts 7:40 the translation will read 'many gods,' for in this passage it is important to indicate the plural. In Acts 4:26 "the kings" becomes 'all the kings.' In most contexts, however, plurality or singularity of a form is not indicated. In any one discourse the Mazatec speaker must indicate only once that something is composed of one specimen or several. He does not need to repeat the fact of singularity or plurality with each occurrence of a particular noun. As English speakers, we are chained by the very form of the language to go on repeating without end the facts of number about everything that we mention. From the Mazatec viewpoint, English is indeed a very clumsy and highly artificial type of language.

Some languages may have separate forms for the singular and the plural but use these forms differently. For example, in the Isthmus Zapotec the singular form of the noun is always used with numbers, literally therefore, 'ten man.' The pedantic scholar might tear his hair over such an apparent "linguistic monstrosity"; but one may argue that if the numeral indicates the number, why repeat in the noun that the items named are plural? (Note this pattern in Hebrew.) The Zapotec speaker would be convinced that the English system is repetitious.

Some words may not occur as plural in a language, even though most words do. That is true of almost all languages which indicate number. For example, we do not say in English *informations*, even though we do say (1) *notices*, a word with a somewhat similar meaning, and (2) *formations*, a word with similar linguistic form.

In the Eastern Aztec, number is indicated with most words, but it does not occur with 'sin.' There is no plural 'sins.' The one form does for both singular and plural. There is no more necessity of constructing an artificial plural for 'sin' in Aztec than there is for insisting on a plural *informations* in English.

In the expression of categories, as well as any other feature of the language, one must employ the form of the native language.

14.2.2.2   ASPECT

Verb expressions in English are classified primarily on the basis of the tense; that is to say, when the actions occur. We designate actions in the past by past tense forms, e.g. *ran, walked, has worked, had gone*. We have other forms which indicate present types of action, e.g. *runs, is walking*. Future actions are expressed by other forms, e.g. *will walk, shall go*. Because our grammar-school training in English has been based almost exclusively on the grammatical system of Latin, we immediately think of present, past, and future when discussing various forms of verbs. These indications of tense are, however, only a part of the system of verb expressions in English. We also indicate kinds of action. For example, we say *he walked* and *he was walking*. The first indicates an action in the past time but says nothing about the duration of it. *He* may have walked two steps or several miles, but from the standpoint of the linguistic form, the entire process is indicated as a single action. The second expression, *he was walking*, indicates that the action was progressing over a period of time. It is still past but is progressive. We also make distinctions of this kind in the so-called present and perfect tenses, e.g. *he walks* vs. *he is walking* and *he has walked* vs. *he has been walking*. The differences in time, namely present, past, future, perfect, we may call tense. The differences in the kind of action, whether it is progressive or non-progressive, we may call aspect.

In some languages, the aspect of the action is the fundamental feature. The tense may be only of secondary importance. Instead of the action being classified as present, past, or future, the action may be classified as progressive, completive, repetitive, anticipatory, inchoative, frequentative, momentaneous, or durative. Perhaps these aspectual terms do not mean much at first, but they are very important in the treatment of many language problems. For example, in English, as we noted above, we contrast progressive action with non-progressive. Other languages make other contrasts. They may indicate that an action has been completed (completive aspect). This completive aspect may not be associated with tense. In the Tarahumara language, the same completive form of the verb may be used whether the time is past, present, or future. The Tarahumara speaker may employ a temporal element such as 'yesterday,' 'today,' or 'tomorrow' without changing the verb. The important thing is whether the action is completed or not. The temporal matter is quite secondary.

Similarly, languages may indicate whether a particular action is performed only once or whether it is repeated (repetitive aspect). The action may be progressing or may be anticipated, with a meaning which may be translated as 'I am going to' (anticipatory aspect). If the action is only being begun, regardless of the temporal features, it may be defined as indicating an inchoative aspect. If the action is repeated frequently, this may be called a frequentative aspect. An action which happens as a single rapid movement may be defined as a momentaneous aspect. Any action which occurs over a period of time may be classed as a durative or continuative.

These aspects in various languages may be indicated in all sorts of ways. Each aspect may have a special affix, something added to the underlying stem; or the differences may be expressed in some change of the vowel, consonant, tone, or stress of the form. It makes no difference which word-forming devices are used or whether they occur as elements bound together with another word or as separate words or particles. The important thing to note is that many languages do express fine shades of distinction in the type of action.

Some missionaries have complained of the bewildering number of tenses that a language is said to have. They frequently claim that some languages have from fifteen to twenty tense forms. A close examination of such problems almost always reveals that the basic problem is not so much one of the tenses as of the aspect. Many an intricate and puzzling verb system has been made completely intelligible, once the translator attempted to handle the difficult elements on the basis of the type of action rather than the time of the action.

The complications in translation which are produced by aspectual problems are sometimes exceedingly difficult to handle.

The expression "the daughter of the said Herodias came in and danced" would seem easy enough to translate into any language. In the Mixtec language, however, it is not so immediately evident. The two actions of 'coming in' and 'dancing' are not just past tense actions. The 'coming in' is a complete action. Hence it occurs in the completive aspect. The 'dancing' must be handled somewhat differently. The daughter of Herodias continued to dance and was still dancing at the time when Herod and the guests were pleased with her performance. Accordingly, the 'dancing' must be placed in the continuous non-completive aspect. This does not mean that the daughter never stopped dancing but that she had not stopped before the next important happening, namely, the expression of pleasure voiced by the guests at her performance.

In translating "wheresoever he shall go in," Mark 14:14, one would assume that some type of future or potential form would be employed. In the Mixtec language, one may not use such a potential form, even though it does exist, for this form would indicate that the man carrying the pitcher of water may never have entered such a place before. Rather, one must use a type of perfective aspect which indicates that the action was customary, and that the water carrier was accustomed to entering into the place. This item may not seem to be very important, and yet to the Mixtec Indian the proper handling of such details is important.

14.2.2.3   Tense

The handling of the tenses of another language is not so complicated as the aspects, for we are accustomed to tenses. Nevertheless, we must be constantly warned that no two languages in the world use the same tenses in every corresponding situation. One cannot automatically translate tense for tense throughout any passage. For example, the present tense in French does not always correspond to a present tense in English. The French say *Depuis quand travaillez-vous?* 'Since when (how long) have you been working?' The French verb is in the present tense form. Literally then, the translation is 'Since when are you working?'—but this does not make sense in English. One must not expect languages to show automatic agreement. Each language is a law unto itself.

Note that all languages have their own special idioms. In English we say *I will hit him when I see him.* The *when* clause is surely in the future time, but the form is the present. This is not logical, but it is linguistic. There is no essential correlation between logic and linguistics. Resemblances are more or less accidental, even as all customs of people are accidental. The wearing of hats may have some useful function, just as tense indications in verbs have some usefulness; but the particular tenses which are to be used to describe certain types of events are almost as unpredictable as the style of women's hats one year in advance.

We must expect to find many irregularities in aboriginal languages, even as we find them in English or any other European language. The fact that we do not find the same types of irregularities is what exasperates us so often. Consider the problem in translating John 8:58 into Eastern Aztec. There is no present form of the verb 'to be.' Accordingly, one cannot translate literally, "Before Abraham was, I am." The expression "I am" is completely impossible. The closest parallel is 'Before Abraham was alive, I already was.'

14.2.2.4 PERSON

By indications of persons a language distinguishes principall y between (1) the speaker and those associated with him, called the first person, (2) the person or persons spoken to, the second person, and (3) the person or persons spoken of, the third person. There is no essential significance to the names first, second, and third. This is only the terminology that comes to us from the classical grammars of Greek and Latin.

Some languages distinguish a fourth person. This fourth person is the next third person introduced into the context. For example, in *I saw my father hit him*, the words *my father* constitute the first third person, and the *him* constitutes the second third person, or the so-called fourth person. This distinction can be very important. The sentence *My father said he saw him* may mean three different things. It may denote that (1) someone else saw my father, (2) my father saw someone else or (3) someone else saw still another person. In some of the Algonkian languages this type of ambiguity would be impossible, for the proper indication of the fourth persons would remove the ambiguity.

Several languages make distinctions between third persons on the basis of location and recognition. For example, distinctions are made between third persons which are near the speaker, near the hearer, or away from both of them. Some languages make distinctions as to whether the object is seen or unseen, whether it is present, recently present, or has been absent for a long time. If a language makes many of these distinctions, the translator may be hard put to it to reconstruct the exact situations in all contexts.

The most common problem which the missionary faces in dealing with problems involving the persons is the distinction made in the first person plural. The usage in English is ambiguous. *We* means either 'I and those associated with me, but not you' or 'I and you.' For example, the expression *we did it* may mean that 'I and my wife did it and I am telling you about it,' or it may mean 'you and I did it.' The first of these forms of the first person is generally called the exclusive first person because the audience is excluded. The second of these forms of the first person is called the inclusive first person because the audience is included in the statement. In translating the Bible it is not always easy to tell whether the "we" is the inclusive or the exclusive type. In Mark 9:5, "It is good for us to be here: and let us make three tabernacles," it is probably necessary to make a distinction between two types of first person plural pronouns. In the first clause Peter is quite obviously indicating the value which all of them experienced while being there on the mountain. He would probably have employed the first person inclusive form. But when he was asking for the privilege of building the tabernacles, he probably would not have suggested that all those there participate in the job of building the tabernacles. He may have intended that he and James and John could build the tabernacles for Jesus and the heavenly personages. For one thing, Peter made a distinction between the disciples on the one hand and Jesus and the heavenly visitors on the other, for he suggested only three tabernacles, and these were to be for Jesus, Moses, and Elias.

In Acts 16:10 the "we" in "we endeavored to go into Macedonia" must be in the exclusive form, for though it includes all those present, it does not include the one to whom the book was written, namely, Theophilus.

Paul frequently employs a so-called "epistolary we," e.g. I Cor. 9:5, "Have we no right to lead about a wife that is a believer...?" In some languages this "we" must be changed to a first person singular. In some contexts the "we" may be interpreted as strictly "I" or it may possibly have a somewhat wider meaning, e.g. I Cor. 9:11, "If we sowed unto you spiritual things, is it a great matter if we shall reap your carnal things?" If one employs the first person plural, it must be in the exclusive form in this verse. In I Cor. 9:25, "Now they do it to receive a corruptible crown; but we an incorruptible," the "we" may be interpreted as inclusive or exclusive; but in general Paul attempted as he wrote to include his audience as undergoing the same types of spiritual experience which he himself had. Hence the inclusive first person plural is probably preferable. Note, however, that the use of the inclusive or exclusive form is dependent upon the application of the designation to the individuals to whom the letter was addressed, not its inclusion of us as modern readers. Our inclusion is hermeneutical and not linguistic.

In John 8:33, "We be Abraham's seed," the chances are that the Jews would employ the exclusive first person plural, for they had no inclination to identify themselves with this person Jesus whom many of them considered an impostor. Later in the same chapter, verse 48, it is recorded that they considered him a Samaritan and one who had a devil.

14.2.2.5 VOICE

Voice defines the relationships between the subject and the type of action, state, or process, as expressed in the verb. We normally speak of an active voice when the actor is performing the action, e.g., *John is hitting*. If the subject is the recipient of the action, e.g., *John was hit*, then we call this the passive voice. If the subject is both the actor and the recipient, e.g., *John hit himself*, then it is the reflexive voice. If several people engage in reciprocal activity, e.g., *they hit each other*, we generally term this a reciprocal voice. In Greek the so-called middle voice defines an action done to or for one's self. These are in general the major types of voice found in various languages. But as usual we cannot expect any two languages to agree entirely.

The principal difficulties involving voice are usually problems of active vs. passive forms. Some languages simply do not have passive constructions. No amount of persistence by the missionary would ever be sufficient to convince the Eastern Aztecs that they needed a passive voice, any more than one can convince the average American that he should wear two hats instead of one. "And (she) had suffered many things of many physicians," Mark 5:26, must be translated as 'many physicians had caused her to suffer much.' "They shall be all taught of God," John 6:45, must be changed to 'God shall teach them all.' Such changes are very easy if both the actor and the recipient of the action (the goal) are both stated in the sentence. If they are not explicitly indicated, it is not always the easiest thing to supply them. In John 7:39 the expression "Jesus was not yet glorified" requires the addition of the actor. The passive construction must be changed to an active one, but in every active verb expression in Eastern Aztec the subject must be explicitly stated. On the basis of such parallels as, John 17:5, "O Father, glorify thou me," the expression in John 7:39 may be changed to read 'God had not yet glorified Jesus.' There is no way to avoid indicating the subject, and on the basis of John's usage this would be the logical subject.

In Mark 2:5 the situation is somewhat confusing. "Thy sins be forgiven thee" must be shifted into the active form. One might assume that 'God' could be used as the subject. However, the Jews immediately accused Jesus of having assumed the prerogative of God in forgiving sins. Accordingly, one must translate, 'I forgive you your sins.'

"He that believeth on him is not condemned," John 3:18, must undergo two changes in being shifted into the active voice. First 'God' must be introduced as the subject. This is easily done on the basis of the context. However, the translation 'God does not condemn the one who believes on him' is incorrect. The final 'him' would refer to God. One must substitute 'the Son' from the context. Hence the translation into Eastern Aztec reads 'God does not condemn the one who believes on the Son.'

In some instances it is probably not satisfactory to shift every passive form to an active form of the same verb. For example, in "given among men," Acts 4:12, the verb may be shifted somewhat in meaning. Of course it could be rendered 'which God gave to men,' but this is hardly the implication of the passage. It is probably more satisfactory to translate "given" by 'exists,' e.g., 'which exists among men.'

In some languages it is necessary to indicate in all verbs the volitional source of the action; that is to say, one must indicate if the one who designed and desired the action is also the one who performs it. In Mark 4:12 the translation of "lest at any time they should be converted" must indicate in the Totonac language whether the situation was the result of the people's own volition or that of someone else. There is no way in the Totonac to be ambiguous in this verse.

In many instances the translator will find that transitive and intransitive verbs do not correspond in two different languages. Verbs which take objects in one language will not take objects in another, and vice versa. For example, in the Eastern Aztec one cannot translate literally, John 4:20, "Our fathers worshiped in this mountain." The Indian will always ask, "Worshiped whom?" The verb 'to worship' is always transitive; that is to say, it must have an object. One must insert, therefore, an object for the verb. Accordingly, the translation reads 'Our fathers worshiped God in this mountain.'

The type of so-called expletive construction, as in "it was noised that he was in the house," Mark 2:1, cannot be duplicated in most languages. Such constructions must generally be shifted into a direct actor-action type of sentence, e.g., 'people were hearing that he was in the house.'

14.2.2.6   MODE

The grammatical mode (or mood) defines the psychological atmosphere of an action. The more common modes have been given such names as indicative, imperative, subjunctive, potential, conditional, optative, interrogative, and dubitative. These are simply terms to describe the psychological atmosphere which the speaker gives to an action. For example, he may say *This man is going*. There is no doubt, hesitation, or condition indicated or implied. The statement *This man may be going immediately* indicates that the speaker is himself somewhat uncertain about the situation or that the event itself is contingent upon other matters, hence uncertain of fulfillment. This type of statement may be called in some languages a potential mode. An imperative mode is one which demands or commands an action, e.g., *Do it!* The subjunctive denotes a contingent mode, something that is dependent upon some other practical or linguistic feature. The conditional mode may be employed in conditions introduced by such words as 'if,' 'provided that' and 'although.' The optative mode expresses hope rather than definite possibility: e.g. *May he come*, an optative expression vs. *He may come*, a potential expression. An interrogative mode is a special set of forms which occur only in questions. A dubitative mode indicates that there is more or less doubt as to the action.

In some languages the modal features are quite complex. In the Kwakiutl language of the Northwest Pacific Coast every expression must indicate whether the report is based on self-experience, on inference, on hearsay, or on a dream. Such modal features might be a great help to the modern newspaper reader.

Problems of mode are very frequently combined with problems of aspect. The psychological conditioning of an action and the type of action are very closely associated factors. For example, "the Son of man sitting on the right hand of power," Mark 14:62, must be translated in Mixtec by the potential mode, for though the action of 'sitting' is continuous and would seem to call for the continuative form of the verb, the action is postulated for the future and so must take the potential mode.

14.2.2.7   POSSESSION

The indication of possession differs considerably with various languages. Many languages make a distinction between alienable and inalienable possessions, that is to say, possessions which are classed as dispensable and those which are classed as indispensable. Sometimes languages show interesting differences in the classification of various items. In one of the Indian languages of the Middle West, a 'horse' is classified as an inalienable possession, but a 'wife' is classed as alienable. Linguistically speaking a horse is a more indispensable feature than a wife.

In Aztec there are different forms of the nouns, depending upon whether they are alienable or inalienable. 'My bone,' if it is the bone I am chewing on or the one which I may use in soup, is one form, but 'my bone' in my body is a different form. Similarly, 'my breath' as part of respiration is one form, but 'my breath' after it has gone to fill a balloon becomes a different form.

In many languages there are certain words which must always be possessed. In the Aztec one can cut off a foot, so that this type of item may occur unpossessed, but a name can never occur without the statement of a possessor. Hence in Acts 4:12 "none other name" must be translated 'no other person's name.' A name cannot exist without some possessor. This is also true of "the spittle" in John 9:6. It must be possessed. Hence it is translated 'his spittle.'

The terms 'father' and 'son' give the most difficulty, for in many languages these words may not occur without an indication of the possessor. It is impossible to speak of a 'father' without indicating whose father it is; likewise with such words as 'son,' 'daughter,' and 'mother.' In John 5:20 "the Father loveth the Son" must be modified in Aztec to indicate the proper relationships. "The Father" in this sense of a Heavenly Father is generally indicated as 'our Father' in Aztec. "The Son" is related to 'our Father,' so the translation reads 'our Father loveth his Son.' The translation 'his Father loveth his Son' would not be intelligible, for "the Father" is more than just the Father of Jesus.

Similarly, "Lord" must be possessed in some languages. One cannot be a 'master' without being someone's master. Hence, "the Lord" becomes 'our Lord' in most contexts.

14.2.2.8   DEGREE

Degree is very rarely expressed in a manner similar to the forms of expression in English or Greek. We are so accustomed to such forms as *fine, finer, finest, as fine as, finer than,* and *finest of,* that we assume that all languages must have such types of expression. When we are rudely awakened to the fact that other languages do not express comparison and degree in this manner, we tend to complain that these languages are very deficient vehicles for expressing our thoughts. We are only being deceived by our own linguistic egotism. All languages may express degree, but few of them follow the forms which the Indo-European languages possess.

In stating the superlative degree in the Yipounou language, "Who is the greatest in the kingdom of heaven?" (Matthew 18:1) must be translated literally, 'Who surpasses the big ones in the kingdom of heaven?' One who surpasses those who are already big must surely be the biggest. The comparative degree is likewise stated by means of the verb 'to surpass.' For example, "It shall be more tolerable for Tyre and Sidon . . . than for you" is literally translated as 'It will surpass in being well for Tyre and Sidon . . . and not for you.' A double comparative corresponding to the English "the more he charged them, so much the more a great deal they published it," Mark 7:36, is literally in Yipounou 'When he surpassed in charging them, they surpassed very much in proclaiming it.'

The comparative expression is rendered in some languages by a positive plus a negative clause. In the Eastern Aztec, "My Father is greater than I," John 14:28, is literally 'My Father is really great; I am not great.' Note that this is an idiom, and that the second clause is only true in terms of the first clause. The only way of expressing a comparative in Aztec is by such a positive-negative construction.

14.2.2.9   RESPECT

Linguistic systems which indicate varying degrees of respect are exceedingly complex. Several languages of the Orient, e.g., Japanese, Korean, and Thai, make certain distinctions depending upon to whom or of whom one is speaking. The classification of these groups is determined usually by such factors as wealth, age, education, and familiarity to the speaker. Many of the usages are highly specialized, and some foreigners spend almost a lifetime learning to use these forms in a natural manner.

Many aboriginal languages also indicate various degrees of respect or familiarity. The Ponape language of the Southwest Pacific has a rather elaborate classification of nouns on the basis of whether the individual involved is a commoner or one to whom special dignity is normally given. For example, the word written *nä* designates the foot of an ordinary man, but *aluwilu* denotes the foot of a distinguished person. Any commoner's 'name' is *ad*, but the 'name' of a superior individual is *mar*. There are many corresponding words in the language which exhibit similar alternations.

In the Eastern Aztec, when one is addressing another person he must always indicate the degree of respect which must be accorded that individual. The so-called respectful form covers a rather wide area of meaning. It indicates that the person addressed is (1) probably older, (2) more respected in the community, and (3) more or less unfamiliar to the speaker. In translating the words of Jesus which were addressed to the Pharisees and Sadducees it might be assumed at first that Jesus would not use the form indicating respect. But this factor of respect is not one of actual respect so much as of social position, and surely the Pharisees and Sadducees as a class had a higher social position than Jesus, whose close associates included uneducated fishermen and a publican. Furthermore, Jesus was comparatively young. In addition to all this, the Pharisees and Sadducees were not very well known to Jesus personally, even though he was well acquainted with their practices. All these factors determine the choice of forms to be used in translating. The denunciations of the religious leaders, though occurring in forms which indicate formal respect, are all the more powerful. The contrast between the social forms and the personal qualities of men becomes a striking feature of the Aztec translation. Accordingly, the translator for the Eastern Aztec employs the forms of respect when Jesus is speaking to the Pharisees and Sadducees, but when they are speaking to Jesus the common or disrespectful forms are used. In all situations in which the cultural and linguistic factors are so closely combined, the translator must project the native cultural situation into the Biblical account and find the closest sets of equivalents.

14.3   Syntax

Syntax deals with the arrangements of words. No two languages correspond in the types of arrangements which occur. Any attempt to follow another language word for word is bound to result in absurd combinations. Every word may be correct in form, but the entire expression may be meaningless. Not only must the translator have the right words and the right forms of the words, but he must also combine the words into the proper idiomatic arrangements which the language uses. This is the syntax of the language.

The following analysis of problems of syntax is no attempt to cover the field in any comprehensive manner. It is only designed to introduce the reader to the more important syntactic problems which translators have encountered. These include (1) word order, (2) use of pronouns, (3) types of modification, (4) apposition, (5) prepositional phrases, (6) conjunctions, and (7) length of sentences.

14.3.1   Word Order

Most people are rather naïvely of the opinion that the word order in their language is so logical and superior to that which any other language may have, that they see nothing at all wrong in shifting the normal order of the native language in order to make it conform to what appears to the translator as a much better order. As in every other feature of translation, the best form is that which conforms most closely to the native usage.

It is difficult for the translator to develop a natural word order, even with the assistance of native translation helpers. There is a strong tendency in translating anything from one language to another to preserve more or less the order of the text language. We do it almost unconsciously when translating from some foreign language into English. The same thing is true when the native informant is translating from such languages as English, Spanish, Portuguese, and French into his own language. In many instances the native informant will not know just how to correct the order so that it may sound natural. The translator must be in a position to suggest alternate orders. To do this, the translator must analyze several hundred pages of native text material. He will want to make a chart of all possible word orders and check for frequency. For example, he may find that the order of the subject, verb, and object is not always the same. In some instances the order may be subject-object-verb and in other cases object-subject-verb. He should immediately attempt to find out the basis for this difference. It may be that if the object is a pronoun, it follows the subject, but if it is a noun, it precedes the subject. A similar check must be made of all types of constructions, involving such parts of speech as conjunctions, prepositions (in many languages these may always follow their so-called objects and are accordingly called 'post-positions'), adjective-like words, and adverb-like words. No language has ever been found in which there are not some preferred orders. The translator must find these orders and employ them.

A very common mistake in order occurs when people translate such a verse as Luke 9:10 from the AV, "And the apostles, when they were returned, told him . . ." This order is unnatural even in modern English. It is very likely to be so in an aboriginal language. It should be changed in very many instances to, 'And when the apostles were returned, they told him . . .'

In some languages a subordinate verb must always follow the principal verb of a sentence. If this is the case, then all clauses with dependent verbs must be made to follow. The above verse must then be changed to, 'And the apostles told him . . . when they had returned.'

In many languages it is very important that the relative pronoun immediately follow its antecedent (the word to which it refers). A close translation of many passages results in a completely erroneous translation. For example, in Romans 1:4–5 "and declared to be the Son of God with power, according to the spirit of holiness, by the resurrection from the dead: By whom we have received grace and apostleship." In some languages a literal translation of this passage would be entirely misleading or unintelligible. The 'whom' would be interpreted as referring to the 'dead.' There are relatively few languages which permit a relative pronoun to refer to something so far separated from it. In this instance, it is probably impossible to shift the order of the verses. What one must do is to repeat the words 'Son of God.' The first sentence will end with 'from the dead.' The second sentence will begin, 'The Son of God is the one by whom we received . . .' Such a change is necessitated by the syntactic structure, which makes certain orders of words obligatory. In a passage such as Ephesians 1:12 one may change the order from, "That we should be to the praise of his glory, who first trusted in Christ" to, 'That we who first trusted in Christ should be to the praise of his glory.' In this latter case it is not necessary to repeat words from the context.

The order of certain syntactic constituents is frequently important. In Greek the three personal pronouns usually occur in the relative order of first, second, and third. This order is generally preserved in translations into English, e.g. Mat. 17:27 "give unto them for me and thee," and John 10:30 "I and my Father are one." In normal usage, however, we reverse the relative order of Greek. This should be done in translating, for normal orders should be paralleled by normal orders, even though the actual orders are different. In English this lack of syntactic equivalence is not too serious, but in some languages the disregard for the relative order of pronominal elements may result in considerable misunderstanding or misinterpretation.

If the order of words in a language is very rigid, the translator will be able to conform to it more easily, for it will be obvious in almost all instances which order should be employed. In most languages, however, there is no complete rigidity. The various potential orders each have special subtle meanings and connotations. These may be very difficult for the translator to master thoroughly, but in so far as is humanly possible he should attempt to make the translation speak the language of the people. His translation should be designed to reveal the truth of the Word of God, not the peculiarities of Greek or English word order.

14.3.2   USE OF PRONOUNS

Languages exhibit many varieties of pronominal systems. Languages may differentiate between such features as (1) subjective and objective forms, (2) singular, dual, and plural number, (3) personal and impersonal reference, (4) shape and size of the antecedents, (5) distance of the antecedents from the speaker, and (6) sex of the antecedent. In fact, there is almost no category in the language which may not be paralleled by the pronouns, for these are words which substitute for other words.

Two things are important about pronouns: (1) the words for which they substitute and (2) the constructions in which they may substitute. The words for which a pronoun may substitute may be called the "class meaning" of the pronoun. The constructions in which such a pronoun may substitute for these words may be called the "substitution type."

Pronouns, like all other types of words, have areas of meaning. The word *she* in English is not restricted to substituting for feminine persons. We may use *she* to refer to a country, a school, an automobile, a ship, and such an abstract term as virtue. Such an area of meaning is quite arbitrary, but we must expect arbitrary classifications in all languages.

Pronouns usually have very restricted positions of occurrence. One cannot start a discourse in English by *She came to see us*. The hearer immediately asks, "Who is she?" This pronoun may only be used when the object for which it substitutes is already completely identified, either (1) by having a noun used first, as in *My aunt said she would come to see us*, or (2) by having this person so evident in a situation that no one can miss the identification. For example, someone might point to a person and say, "She is entirely too highbrow." The practical context of gesturing completely identifies the person.

This explanation of the meaning and the function of a pronoun in English may not seem exactly pertinent to the problems of translation. It is, however, very important. Translators tend to make as many mistakes in the handling of pronouns as in any syntactic feature in a language. Some translators are fully aware that in different languages pronouns have different meanings, that is to say, they substitute for different classes of words. Few translators are fully aware of the problems resulting from differences in the way in which pronouns are used. They assume that wherever a pronoun occurs in the English or the Greek or Hebrew, the native language can also employ a pronoun. Nothing could be further from the truth. In English and Greek, once the noun has been used, one may generally use a pronoun to refer to it. In fact, we must usually do this. For example, we say *My father will do it when he comes*. We do not repeat *my father*, e.g. **My father will do it when my father comes*. The latter statement is completely confusing.

In many aboriginal languages one does not use pronouns with the same frequency and in the same types of constructions as in

English. For example, in translating the first chapter of Ephesians into some languages it is absolutely necessary to change some of the pronouns to nouns. In Ephesians 1:4 one must often translate, 'according as God hath chosen us' in place of the AV "according as he hath chosen us," for in some languages the 'he' would refer to "Christ," verse 3, which occurs just before this phrase. There are innumerable instances in which the pronouns of the text must be changed to nouns in the translating, and vice versa, in order to make the syntactic constructions conform to the native usage.

Many languages in no way approximate the frequency of usage of pronouns which we have in English. For example, a literal translation of Acts 4:13 would be almost unintelligible in some languages. Note the frequency of the pronouns "they" and "them" in the following: "Now when they saw the boldness of Peter and John, and perceived that they were unlearned and ignorant men, they marvelled; and they took knowledge of them, that they had been with Jesus." In a language which does not employ a more or less elaborate type of reference system, as exists in English, such a verse must be considerably changed. The first 'they' is entirely too far away from its antecedents to be properly understood. One must substitute 'the rulers' or 'the headmen' from verse 5. Other identifications must also be made, so that the verse reads something like, 'Now when the headmen saw the boldness of Peter and John and perceived that Peter and John were not educated and were ignorant men, the headmen marvelled, and they realized that Peter and John had been with Jesus.' All these changes are dictated by the fact that the particular aboriginal language in question does not employ pronouns in the same way that English does. Such a translation seems clumsy in English, but a word-for-word translation into the aboriginal language is unintelligible.

14.3.3   TYPES OF MODIFICATION

There are five types of modification which cause most translators difficulty: (1) noun attributives, (2) adjective attributives, (3) participial attributives, (4) articles, and (5) classifiers.

14.3.3.1   NOUN ATTRIBUTIVES

Such expressions as "remission of sins," "love of God," "bread of life," and "gift of the Holy Spirit" are so common in English that it seems inconceivable that other languages cannot construct similar expressions including two nouns. In Greek, the second noun expression is in the genitive form. In English a prepositional phrase is employed. The basic problem is one of a noun modifying a noun, but the relationship between these nouns is often quite different. For example, in "the cares of this world" the second noun describes the type of cares. Such a relationship may be called a descriptive attribution. In "the deceitfulness of riches" the second noun is fundamentally the subject of the deceitfulness, for the riches are the items which deceive. This relationship may be called a subjective attribution. In "the lusts of other things" the second noun expression denotes the object of the lusting. Hence, this relationship may be called an objective attribution. In some aboriginal languages these expressions, which occur in Mark 4:19, must be considerably changed, for nouns may not be combined in these types of descriptive, subjective, and objective relationships. One must change the expressions to read 'the cares which are in this world, and the fact that riches deceive people, and the fact that people lust for other things.' The descriptive relationship is changed into a phrase which describes the manner in which the situation exists. The subjective relationship is changed so that the subjective element is the subject of the predicative element. The objective relationship is changed so that the object element is the object of the predicative element. In many languages one cannot avoid such changes of expression if the translation is to be understood by the native speakers. Such changes are the logical adaptations which must take place when any two languages are related in the translation procedure.

In many instances it is not possible to know precisely the relationship between the two nouns of a construction. For example, "the love of God," I John 2:5, may refer to 'man's love for God' or 'God's manner of loving.' In I John 2:15 there is a clue to the apparent ambiguity of the expression "the love of the Father" because the preceding parallel clause, "if any man love the world," gives basis for interpreting "the love of the Father" as a type of objective relationship. Hence, the verse may be translated as 'if any man loves the world, he does not love the Father.' This is the type of translation which must be employed in the Mazatec, for this language has no noun for 'love.' A subjective relationship, "They loved the praise of men more than the praise of God,"

John 12:43, may be changed to, 'they desired that men praise them more than they desired that God praise them.'

14.3.3.2   ADJECTIVE ATTRIBUTIVES

In some languages there are no such parts of speech as adjectives. A word meaning 'good' may occur as a verb, but not as an adjective. In such a language one must translate *the good man goes away* by making both *good* and *goes* verbs. It might be translated literally as 'the man goods [a single independent verb] and goes away,' or perhaps better, 'the man being-good goes away.' The necessity of substituting verbal forms for adjectival ones may greatly alter the form of the translation.

Some adjectives in the Greek or English do not correspond to any adjectives in the aboriginal language. "Faithless generation" must be changed in Eastern Aztec to 'people who do not believe.' "False Christs" must be changed to 'Christs who really are not.'

These problems will not give the translator much difficulty provided he follows the native language usage and does not attempt to force some unnatural forms.

14.3.3.3   PARTICIPIAL ATTRIBUTIVES

Greek is full of participial attributives. Instead of saying 'when the man came, he did it,' Greek says 'having come, the man did it.' Many pages of the Greek New Testament text contain a dozen or more attributive participles. This is a much greater frequency than occurs in English. In many instances the AV, as well as the ARV and ERV, follows the Greek with rigid consistency: e.g. Mark 10:21, "Then Jesus beholding him loved him"; Mark 10:27, "And Jesus looking upon them saith"; Mark 10:50, "And he, casting away his garment, rose."

Very seldom does another language even approximate the extensive use of participial attributives which occurs in the Greek or in the more literal translations into English. In no case should the translator attempt to conform the syntax artificially so as to represent this special feature of Greek. The translations in English are themselves frequently awkward and ambiguous. Such participial constructions should be broken up into separate independent verbs or clauses, e.g. Mark 10:21, 'Then Jesus beheld him and loved him' or 'Then when Jesus beheld him, he loved him.'

Note the changes which must frequently be made in the participial constructions in Romans 1:1, 'Paul, who is a servant of Jesus Christ, who has also been called to be an apostle, and who has been separated unto the gospel of God.' Note that in some instances it is impossible to string one relative clause after another in this manner. The verse must frequently be broken into three sentences, 'Paul is a servant of Jesus Christ. He has been called to be an apostle [Or, 'He has been called an apostle,' or 'He has been called and an apostle']. 'He has been separated unto the gospel of God.' The problem of apposition in "Paul, a servant of Jesus Christ" will concern us in the next principal section.

14.3.3.4   ARTICLES

Some languages do not possess articles, either definite or indefinite. New Testament Greek possesses only a definite article, and Latin possesses no articles. The articles which occur in the modern Romance languages are derived from pronouns.

Some translators have been very much concerned that they cannot render literally such an expression as "the Christ," Mark 8:29. If the language has no definite article, there is little point in trying to invent one. The language gets along perfectly well without one, even as classical Latin fared quite well without one. Sometimes a demonstrative adjective such as 'this' or 'that' may be used in place of the definite article *the*. 'Some' or 'any' may sometimes be employed for the indefinite article *a*. However, one should not attempt to force the construction. The distinction may appear quite unnecessary in the aboriginal language.

14.3.3.5   CLASSIFIERS

Some languages possess classifiers. These are words or particles which denote the class of the object that is being spoken of. In some instances they are used only with numerals. For example, if one is counting money, one does not say 'one, two, three,' etc., but 'one flat object, two flat objects, three flat objects,' etc. If sugar cane is being counted, then the count may be 'one long object, two long objects, three long objects,' etc. Some languages distinguish ten to fifteen different classes of objects, depending upon such factors as the size, shape, value, social position, supernatural power. and age.

In many languages, classifiers are not restricted to numbers but are extended to other classes of words and are used particularly with proper names. In such a language one cannot say 'Jordan' but rather 'river Jordan,' not 'Jerusalem' but 'city Jerusalem.' There may be many objects which always occur with such a generic classifying term, e.g. 'cloth silk,' 'animal camel,' 'man Pharisee,' and 'ruler Pilate.' Such a situation will demand the addition of many words to the text, but these classifiers are demanded by the syntactic structure. They must be added if the translation is to conform to the obligatory patterns of the language.

The use of classifiers is a great advantage in some instances. They are very convenient devices in giving some meaning to otherwise meaningless proper names.

14.3.4   Apposition

The grammatical construction in which a word or phrase is in apposition to another word or phrase is quite frequent in the Bible. Note four instances of apposition in the first seven verses of Romans: "Paul, a servant of Jesus Christ," Romans 1:1; "his Son Jesus Christ our Lord," Romans 1:3; "God our Father," Romans 1:7; and "the Lord Jesus Christ," Romans 1:7. Such grammatical constructions do not exist in some aboriginal languages. Accordingly, one should not attempt to make the native language conform artificially to the text language.

Generally, appositional expressions may be changed to relative clause constructions. For example, "Paul, a servant of Jesus Christ" may be changed to 'Paul, who is a servant of Jesus Christ.' "His Son Jesus Christ our Lord" must be modified in some languages to read 'his Son, who is Jesus Christ, who is our Lord.' Such a translation seems 'clumsy' to us, but the alternate literal translation into the aboriginal language would be almost unintelligible.

14.3.5   Prepositional Phrases

The problems connected with the translation of prepositional phrases have been considered briefly above, p. 249. The problems are essentially those of word classes. However, these constructions are so important, particularly for one who is attempting to translate from a text in a modern European language, that it is well to consider the principal difficulties to be encountered with the entire prepositional phrase construction. It should be noted that there are fewer prepositional phrases in the Greek text than in the English. Many of the case relationships in the Greek are translated by prepositional phrases in English. This very lack of correspondence should give us an excellent basis for judging the merits of even further modifications which are sometimes necessary in languages possessing very limited types of prepositional phrase constructions.

The principal problems which translators confront in handling the prepositional phrases of the text language are (1) the lack of correspondence in the areas of meaning between prepositions in the respective languages and (2) the necessity of employing verbal expressions of process in the native language to correspond to certain prepositions in the text language.

The lack of correspondence in areas of meaning is not particularly strange. We should expect it. However, the subtle distinctions in meaning of some relational words may be very perplexing. The native word for 'under' may correspond in almost all contexts to the meaning of English *under*, but in certain contexts the meaning may be strikingly different. Note the translation in one language in which "under the fig tree," John 1:48, actually denoted that Nathanael was beneath the surface of the earth, not that he was beneath the shade of the tree. One translator rendered "the angels of God ascending and descending upon the Son of man" in such a way that the native impression was that the Son of man constituted a ladder for the angels to climb up and down on in their journeys between heaven and earth.

The necessity of shifting from a prepositional usage to a verb expression indicating a process is much greater than may be suspected at first. Such situations may be conveniently illustrated by considering three different prepositional expressions: *by* (denoting 'means by which'), *for* (denoting 'on behalf of'), and *from*.

"John the Baptist was risen from the dead," Mark 6:14, must be changed in the Eastern Aztec to 'John the Baptist has left the dead and lives again.' There is no way of saying "to arise from" without indicating two processes: (1) the leaving and (2) the living again. This latter expression has been employed throughout for "resurrection" and related words. One does not say in Eastern Aztec to 'go from here to there' but rather to 'leave here and arrive there.' Similarly in Mazatec "have passed from death unto life" must be translated 'leave death and come to life.' It is very frequently the case that all indications of process must be made by means of verb expressions.

"Peace by Jesus Christ," Acts 10:36, cannot be translated literally word for word into Mazatec. The word which might be construed as meaning 'by' in certain contexts would mean 'with' or 'and' in this context. The English "by," Greek *dia*, also translated "through," is quite difficult to translate in many languages. In fact, almost all such expressions which indicate an agent or an instrumentality must in some languages be shifted into verb expressions. In the Mazatec the phrase "peace by Jesus Christ" is rendered literally as 'peace which Jesus Christ produced.' This may not be identically the same meaning which is intended in the Greek text, but it is the closest approximation which may be made in the Mazatec.

Expressions denoting benefaction are equally hard to translate. "My flesh, which I give for the life of the world," John 6:51, must be changed in Eastern Aztec to 'my flesh, which I give in order that the people of the world may live.' Several features of the language necessitate such a change. First, there is no preposition in Eastern Aztec such as English "for," Greek *huper*, which denotes benefaction. Similarly, there is no noun for "life" except one denoting an area of meaning similar to Greek *bios*, 'elementary existence' and 'the implements of existence,' namely, 'possessions.' Since a verb expression for "life" must be used in place of the noun of the English and Greek, the verbs 'give' and 'live' must be related. The closest equivalent in the Eastern Aztec is an expression of purpose. The use of 'people of the world' in place of 'world' is dictated by the fact that the word 'world' cannot stand for 'the inhabitants of the world' as it does in English. This figure of speech does not exist in Aztec. Someone may object that the translation in the Aztec is a rather extensive paraphrase of the Greek or English. Such paraphrases are not recommended when they can be avoided, but in some circumstances they cannot be avoided if the translation is to make sense. The literal rendition of the phrase in John 6:51 would mean 'my flesh, which I give to the existence of the ground.' As in many instances one must choose between (1) meaningful paraphrase which conforms to the meaning of the text and (2) literal renderings which give quite wrong meanings. The translator is constantly called upon to steer a careful course between unwarranted paraphrase on the one hand and literal absurdities on the other. Either extreme is to be avoided.

14.3.6   CONJUNCTIONS

Few languages are as plentifully supplied with subordinating and coordinating conjunctions as English and Greek. Translators usually find that certain conjunctions must do double or triple duty. That is to say, one conjunction in the native language is used to translate two or three different conjunctions in English. One relational expression in Maya covers an area of meaning including English 'concerning,' 'for,' 'because,' 'in order that,' and 'in behalf of.' In almost all instances the context makes the relationship clear. If it does not, another type of expression may be employed.

One should not be too concerned about potential ambiguity. Such ambiguity is very common in the Greek New Testament, where certain participial constructions may indicate purpose, time, concession, cause, and means. For example, the first seven words of the Greek text of John 8:30 may be translated as follows: (1) 'When he was saying these things, many believed on him,' (2) 'As he was saying these things, many believed on him,' (3) 'While he was saying these things, many believed on him,' (4) 'Although he was saying these things, many believed on him,' (5) 'Because he was saying these things, many believed on him,' (6) 'Since he was saying these things, many believed on him,' and (7) 'By means of his saying these things, many believed on him.' Actually of course there is no such ambiguity as has been suggested by these alternate translations. The context makes it evident that the introductory participial construction is essentially temporal. Hence, we may translate 'When (as, while) he was saying these things, many believed on him.'

The translator generally does not need to fear ambiguity half so much as artificial combinations of phrases and clauses. A Greek sentence may be strung out almost without end. Sentences which cover eight to ten verses in the New Testament text are not rare. Most languages will not, however, permit such long sentences. Two or three clauses put together with conjunctions are about the limit which such languages normally employ. Accordingly, one should make the translation conform in this matter of style.

14.3.7 LENGTH OF SENTENCES

Persons who have the opportunity to observe natives reading translations in their own language will quite frequently note that the people understand each word that they are reading and yet they fail to understand the entire passage because the sentences are abnormally long. The native language may possess a very simple sentence structure. Any attempt to modify or distort radically the native structure in order to make it fit the text language can result only in misunderstanding.

The essential problems involving sentence structure are not necessarily ones of length but of complexity of organization. Even a short sentence in the text language may be exceedingly complex and contain a series of constructions which cannot be combined into one sentence in the native language. For example, a verse such as Acts 13:23 is particularly confusing in Mazatec. "Of this man's seed hath God according to his promise raised unto Israel a Savior, Jesus." This sentence, even though it is comparatively short, must be broken up. The appositional construction "a Savior, Jesus" must be made into a clause, and the phrase "according to his promise" must be made into a clause. Not all these clauses can be included in one sentence and still conform to the syntactic structure of the Mazatec. Accordingly, the verse is changed to read 'God gave to Israel a Savior who is Jesus. Jesus belonged to the family of David. This was just as God promised.' Several factors may be noted about this translation. (1) The appositional construction has been broken into a dependent relative clause, namely, 'a Savior who is Jesus.' (2) The expression "seed" has been changed to 'family of,' for 'seed' cannot be used to denote progeny. In a passage where it may be necessary to introduce the specialized meaning of 'seed' the literal meaning of the Greek may be given in the margin, but it is probably not necessary here. (3) "This man" must be replaced by the proper name 'David.' If one were to translate 'family of this man' for the text "this man's seed," the words 'this man' would not refer to David, for they are too far removed from the reference to David in the preceding verse. The Mazatec habitually repeats proper names, e.g. the repetition of the name of Jesus and of the subject 'God' in the last clause.

One should not get the impression that this type of breaking up of sentences is an effort to conform to so-called "baby talk." Primitive languages are not "childish" languages. They are only different languages. Anything that is different is usually classified by us as awkward, illogical, or childish. There is as much innate beauty and elegance in an aboriginal language as in our own. It is only a different type of beauty and elegance. In the same way as some aboriginal peoples do not appreciate our singing several notes at once in various harmonic patterns, so we find it difficult to become accustomed to the rhythmic patterns of some aboriginal peoples in which as many as ten different rhythms may be integrated into one intricate form. When the translation in the Tarascan language changes "That he would grant unto us, that we being delivered out of the hand of our enemies might serve him without fear," Luke 1:74, to read, 'That he would permit us that we should be freed from the hands of our enemies and that we should be without fear and that we should serve him,' there is no appreciable destruction of the linguistic beauty or effectiveness of the passage. It is simply that in the Tarascan one cannot follow word for word the more or less complicated wording of the English or Greek texts.

Several long or intricate sentences in the New Testament have been broken up in various translations. Perhaps some of the most conspicuous of these sentences are Luke 1:1-4, Acts 1:1-4, 10:37-38, Romans 1:1-7, I Corinthians 1:1-3, Ephesians 1:3-14, Titus 1:1-4, Hebrews 1:1-4, and 7:1-3.

Sentences are not to be changed in accordance with the translator's own interpretation or because the adoption of some paraphrases constitutes the way of least resistance in the translation of some difficult passages. Sentences are to be changed only in accordance with the demands of the lexical, morphological, and syntactic structure of the native language. The necessity of making some adjustments to the grammatical features of the native language must not be interpreted as constituting a basis for translating only the 'gist' of a passage. The translator must make the closest possible translation in terms of the linguistic structures of the languages involved.

14.4   Lexicon

The lexicon, treated from the standpoint of descriptive linguistics, designates that part of linguistic analysis which treats the meanings of language forms: parts of words, words, and combinations of words. It may seem confusing to the student to introduce such a section as this so late in this treatment of Bible translating when it would seem that throughout this entire analysis of expressions we have been dealing with the meaning of forms which denote the various aspects of man, his natural environment, and his cultural environment. However, the meanings of the words which have been discussed in Chapters 8–13 have been dependent primarily upon the cultural and physical factors of the environment. The problems of meaning which this section treats concern the linguistic factors in the meaning of words.

In English we speak of the *foot of a mountain*. Perhaps we are oblivious of the fact that this type of expression is a very specialized form of speech. The mountain does not actually have a *foot* in the literal or primary sense of this word. Not all languages possess this figure of speech. In some languages one speaks of the 'belly of the mountain,' not the 'foot of the mountain.' Where, however, we have such commonplace expressions as *to mend nets*, the Totonac says 'to tie up the face of the nets.' In the Mazatec the compound 'embroidered-lion' is the designation of the mountain jaguar. In the Kiowa language white men are called 'big-eared men,' while Indians are called 'red-meated ones.' All such expressions are basically figures of speech. The forms and meanings of such expressions are part of the linguistic structure of the respective languages.

In the Bible there are many figures of speech, that is to say, words or combinations of words with very specialized meanings. These are very difficult to translate. Such expressions as "come to pass," Genesis 6:1 and Matthew 7:28, and "being fallen into a deep sleep," Acts 20:9, can only very rarely be translated literally into another language with any semblance of corresponding meaning. Translations such as 'to happen' and 'to become asleep' must usually be substituted. In the Eastern Aztec "He hath opened mine eyes," John 9:30, must be changed to 'He made me see.' The literal translation would mean nothing more than propping open the eyelids. "Shall not taste of death," Mark 9:1, must be changed to 'shall not die.' The figure of 'tasting death' is completely confusing.

The translator is usually confronted with three general types of figures of speech which produce difficulty. The first of these are expressions which include the words "son of," e.g. "sons of thunder," "son of peace," "Son of man," and "son of wickedness." The second class of figures of speech are hyperboles. The third class may be said to include the rest of those words (or combinations of words) with specialized meanings.

Expressions such as "son of peace" and "Son of man" give unlimited difficulty in some languages. The literal translation of "son of peace," Luke 10:6, may mean 'offspring of quietness.' This is potentially a figure of speech in English, but it may have absolutely no meaning in some languages. It may be nothing more than a confusing combination of words. If this is the case, one should translate such an expression by 'man who has peace' or 'man who is of a peaceful nature.' It may be valuable to place the literal translation in a footnote or margin if such a note would assist in any way in the understanding of the Semitic idiom. Parallel expressions such as "son of wickedness," "son of the morning," and "son of perdition" may be treated similarly. "Sons of thunder" has been discussed above, p. 134.

Such an expression as "Son of man" is equally troublesome, but the problem is more complicated. In many instances there is no word for mankind. Hence, one must say 'the Son of a man,' if the phrase is to be translated literally. This is not altogether satisfactory, but if there is no generic word for 'man,' it is often the best which can be done. Some translators have attempted to use an expression such as 'one having the character of a man.' Such translations have not been reported as successful. The parallelism of 'Son of God' and 'Son of man' is too great. In general, it is best to translate this expression "Son of man" in a literal manner, and then if necessary give the meaning of such an expression by means of a footnote.

There is a considerable tendency to reduce the hyperboles of Jesus' statements. In particular, translators have attempted to find some types of less exaggerated parallels for such expressions as "a camel to go through the eye of a needle," Matthew 19:24, and "the beam that is in thine own eye," Matthew 7:3. The translator is not justified in substituting 'Needle's-Eye Gate' for "eye of a needle" or 'small piece of wood' for "beam." The hyperboles of Jesus are intentional hyperboles. They are part of the Semitic linguistic culture and should be reproduced as literally as possible. The interpretation should be left to teaching.

There is no way of predicting which figures of speech can and which cannot be literally translated into the native language. Each figure of speech must be tested for itself. In so far as possible, one should attempt to reproduce all figures of speech as literally as is possible and still convey the meaning of the original text. However, such an expression as "fruit of his loins," Acts 2:30, may have to be changed in many languages. A literal translation is generally meaningless and in some instances vulgar. In the Mazatec this figure of speech has been translated 'the child he would have.'

In Eastern Aztec "innocent blood," Matthew 27:4, cannot designate a man. In order to give some meaning to the passage, one must translate 'I have betrayed an innocent man to die.' Note that in instances of such change of figures of speech it is often valuable to introduce the literal rendering into the margin or footnote.

The expression "verily, verily" is sometimes very artificial, if translated literally. In fact, in some instances such a phrase occurring at the beginning of a sentence only confuses the reader, for it is not in accordance with his own native idiom. The repetition of such adverbs is frequently quite unintelligible. Almost all languages have some idiomatic ways of rendering such an expression as "Verily, verily, I say unto you." In one language the closest equivalent is 'I am really telling you the truth.' If the literal translation is not meaningful, then such an alternate translation may be adopted.

"What have I to do with thee?" must very frequently be changed in translating. Note that this expression is not a literal translation of the Greek, which reads 'What to me and to you?' or 'What is it to you and to me?' A literal translation of the Greek is not, however, an accurate translation. This expression had a highly specialized meaning in Greek, and it is translatable by such an expression as 'What have I to do with you' or in some such fashion as Goodspeed has rendered it, "Do not try to direct me." As has been pointed out several times, the literal translation may not be the accurate translation. The translator must not be a blind hunter of words but the careful explorer into the realm of equivalence of meaning.

Chapter 15

PREPARATION OF THE MANUSCRIPT

THE preparation of the manuscript is a very essential process in producing a translation. It is true that this is to some extent only a mechanical type of work, and yet it demands great care if mistakes are to be avoided. Perfection may never be attained, but one should aim at it. Very slight mistakes may make a considerable difference in the meaning of a passage. The difference of only one letter made a passage read in Eskimo 'snowshoe shall rise up against snowshoe,' in place of 'kingdom shall rise up against kingdom.' In a more recent translation a mistake was discovered in which an r had been typed instead of an x. This made the passage mean 'I indulge in illicit practices with you' instead of 'I command you.'

The various factors in the preparation of the manuscript may be most easily understood by grouping them under the following headings: (1) form of the manuscript page, (2) number of copies, (3) corrections, (4) proofreading, (5) additional and inadmissible matter, (6) title page and imprints, and (7) formats.

15.1 FORM OF THE MANUSCRIPT PAGE

The form of the manuscript page is important if one wants to be assured of (1) a proper checking of the material by the Bible Society and (2) an accurate handling of the manuscript by the printers. One will save a great deal of time in the long run by careful preparation of the manuscript. A sample page of a manuscript occurs in the Appendix. The following rules will be found helpful in preparing the form of the manuscript:

1. Type the manuscript.

A manuscript in longhand is almost impossible to use. The countless errors that are made in checking and printing from a manuscript which is written by hand would more than justify the requirement that every manuscript be typed. The typist should be careful to observe the following rules:

    a. Use a dark ribbon.

    b. Do not strike over. Erase, or cross out and type again.

    c. If possible, use typewriter with pica-size type.

2. Special care should be employed in indicating diacritical marks.

Even typed diacritical marks are often difficult to distinguish. Accent and tone marks are frequently so short that they are easily confused. When they occur over an *i* they are often distorted in shape because of the dot of the *i*. It is valuable to extend such accent and tone marks with a pen, in order that there may be no mistaking the form.

3. Provide margins of at least one inch all the way around the page.

It is necessary to have some margin space to indicate corrections. Preserve a margin of $1\frac{1}{2}$ inches at the bottom if possible.

4. Triple-space material.

This may seem a waste of paper, but those who have made it a practice to triple-space all manuscript material have found that it is much easier to incorporate corrections and still make them legible. Triple spacing will often save writing over an entire page.

5. Use good, heavy, white paper, size $8\frac{1}{2}$ by 11 inches.

This is the standard typewriter size. The use of good paper is important, for cheap paper cannot be satisfactorily erased. White paper will be most easily read. Onion skin paper should not be employed. The slight saving in mailing costs does not compensate for its unsatisfactory features.

6. Employ four sets of numbers. (See sample page in Appendix.)

    a. The first number, that of the page, should occur at the middle of the top.

    b. The second set of numbers, indicating the contents of each page according to chapter and verses, should occur in the top right-hand corner, e.g. 12:24–13:4.

    c. The third set of numbers includes the numbering of the verses at the beginning of each verse.

    d. The fourth set includes the numbering of the chapters at the beginning of each chapter.

7. Place the chapter heading in the center of the page.

8. Do not permit verses to go over to the next page.

9. No hyphens should occur at the ends of lines, except ones which indicate types of compound junctures and which must occur whether the word is printed at the end of the line or in the middle.

10. Each chapter should be typed separately, beginning at the top of a new page. The chapters may then be typed in any sequence, and the pagination (numbering of the pages) may be inserted later.

11. All passages that are to be printed in poetic form should be clearly indicated in the manuscript. The material must be typed out line for line to correspond either with the diglot form or to represent the native poetic patterns.

12. The translator must supply with his manuscript a statement to the printers indicating where words may be divided. He must list the various types of sequences of consonants and vowels and indicate precisely where the syllabic divisions may be made. It is frequently not enough to say that words may be divided between consonants, for in some instances combinations such as *mb*, *nd*, and *ng* cannot be divided, whereas combinations of *rb*, *ld*, and *zg* can be divided. Such statements as to patterns of word divisions should be clear, comprehensive, and concise. If the text includes foreign words and the divisions of such words are different from native words, such differences must be noted.

13. The translator should supply with his manuscript a list of all special letters and diacritical marks.

15.2 NUMBER OF COPIES

It is extremely important that the copyist make at least three copies of any manuscript. The first copy should be sent to the Bible Society. One carbon should be kept by the translator. The other carbon copy should be stored in some safe place. There is considerable danger of manuscripts being lost in transit. A third copy will prevent great delay in getting out another copy of the manuscript, which must then be carefully proofread. One should not under any circumstance send away his only manuscript.

The two manuscripts kept on the field should not be stored together. One cannot afford to have the consecrated labor of many months or years destroyed by lack of proper precautionary measures.

Any changes that are made on any one manuscript must be transferred to the other manuscripts.

15.3　　　　Correcting the Manuscript

The following rules may be observed with profit:

1. All corrections should be typed or printed with pen and ink above the line in which the correction is made.
2. When printing with pen and ink employ the same form of letters as are used in the typed copy. For example, do not print e and ε interchangeably for the same phoneme. This is confusing to the typesetters.
3. Use a fine-point pen in printing.
4. Indicate by a wedge, i.e. $\wedge$, where any correction is to be inserted.
5. If the corrections are to be connected with the preceding or following words in the text of the copy, this should be indicated by the symbol $\subset$ to show the connection.
6. If there are extensive changes or insertions to be made, these should be made on a separate sheet, with a clear indication of where they are to be inserted, and what, if any, of the text of the manuscript is to be deleted.

15.4　　　　Proofreading

It is not the number of times that one goes over a text that assures one of the accuracy of the form, but the care that one takes in checking it. Those who have had some experience in proofreading are, however, continually amazed at the number of mistakes which escape their attention. The statement that people are fallible is nowhere better proven than in the proofreading of manuscripts and printers' proofs.

For printers' proofs it is advisable to employ the standard signs and symbols used by proofreaders. These are listed and illustrated in *The Guide for Translators*. See Appendix.

The translator normally has at least two proofreading tasks and possibly three, in the case of every translation. First, he must proofread the manuscript, second, the galley proof, and third, if he is available, it is wise for him to proofread the page proof. The proofreading is somewhat different in the three instances.

15.4.1   Proofreading of the Manuscript

Proofreading of the manuscript includes comparing the final manuscript with the rather marked-up manuscript which has been used for checking the translation for accuracy and meaning. There are four ways in which this may be done:

1. The translator may examine the two manuscripts carefully, looking from one to the other and comparing each word, phrase, and sentence. He will usually pick up some omissions and misspellings.
2. One person may read the prior manuscript, naming each mark of punctuation, while the translator compares the final manuscript. This is an excellent method of finding omissions, additions, and misspellings.
3. One person may spell out each word and name each mark of punctuation on the prior manuscript, while the translator checks the final manuscript. This is a very thorough means of insuring agreement.
4. One person may read the final manuscript while the translator reads the English, Spanish, Greek, or whatever other language has been used as a text language. This process is only designed to check for deletions, additions, and versification. This last process is more frequently employed with the pre-final manuscript than with the final manuscript.

It is not always necessary to employ all four of these methods. It is generally wise, however, to use at least two of them. It should be noted that while one is checking a manuscript for form, he should not at the same time attempt to check for meaning. These two processes must be separated. If one is thinking of the meaning, the forms of the words are frequently almost completely overlooked. One must concentrate on the form only.

In proofreading one must not overlook such items as the title, the running heads, the numbering of verses, and paragraphing.

15.4.2   Proofreading of the Galley Proofs

When a manuscript is first set up in type there is no division into pages. It is usually printed on long sheets of paper, one line after another, just as it occurs in the galley. There are often many mistakes in the galley proof, particularly when the translation is in a strange language with strange symbols. There are also many problems as to the division of words.

The proofreader of the Bible Society always proofreads the galley proof in order to discover any lack of conformity to the manuscript. He also checks for the division of words in accordance with the instructions sent him. The translator is always asked to read the galley proof if this is at all possible, for the translator generally will be able to find some mistakes which one unaccustomed to the language may not readily perceive. The translator may also find some last-minute errors in the text which may have escaped his notice before. If they are serious errors, they should be corrected, but very minor and inconsequential items should not be changed unless the translator is able to give adequate justification for the change or is willing to stand the extra cost, for changes which are not included in the original manuscript involve an added expense.

In reading the galley proof, one may employ any one of the three first methods suggested under proofreading of the manuscript. Special attention should be paid to numbering of verses, division of words, and spelling.

All corrections in the galley proof should be made with symbols regularly employed by proofreaders and editors.

Proofreading is at best a tedious job. But one cannot afford to spoil a good book by failing to see it through to the end.

15.4.3 PROOFREADING OF THE PAGE PROOFS

After the galley proofs have been corrected by the printer, the lines are divided according to pages, and the pagination and running heads are inserted. In checking the page proofs one should compare the galley proofs and the page proofs. If the material is set up in linotype, the entire line which contains any mistake will be recast. There are possibilities of other mistakes being made which were not made originally. If the material is set up by hand with individual letters or by a monotype machine, then presumably only the wrong symbols are changed. Nevertheless, in checking the page proofs one should examine every line. The proofreading of the page proofs may be done in any of the three methods employed for proofreading the manuscript or the galley proofs. Another method which may be used to very good advantage, since the material on each line is almost identical, is to superimpose the galley proofs upon the page proofs. This is done by folding under the top of the galley proof until the line of the galley proof can be placed immediately below the corresponding line in the page proof. As one goes down the page, one may continue to fold under successive lines of the galley proofs so that the corresponding lines of the two proof sheets may be placed next to each other and compared.

If the translation is to be published as a diglot, special attention must be given to seeing that the pages of the native text correspond verse for verse with the pages of the trade-language text. These problems of adjustment are often quite complicated.

15.5   ADDITIONAL AND INADMISSIBLE MATTER

The following paragraphs taken from the *Guide for Translators*, published by the Bible Society, explain clearly the types of additional and inadmissible matter:

"20. The Board desires that the chapter headings of the English AV, the subscriptions to the Epistles, and Ussher's system of chronology be not reproduced in the Society's editions.

"Page, chapter, and sectional headings (if introduced) must be simple summaries without doctrinal bias and as far as possible in the words of the text, and in any doubtful case should be submitted in English to the Secretary in charge. Sectional headings should be separated from the text by a space and, if possible, should be in different type.

"21. In accordance with the Society's Constitution, no Confession of faith, doctrinal notes, or table of lessons or festivals, may be printed in, or be bound up with, any of the Society's editions.

"22. It is not permissible to include descriptive indexes, glossaries, collections of historical, or of geographical or of other notes. Collections of the headings of pages, chapters, or sections are inadmissible."

15.6   TITLE PAGE AND IMPRINTS

All features of the title page and imprints are considered fully in the *Guide for Translators*, pp. 15–16.

It is important that the title be plain, concise, and in the native language.

15.7   FORMATS

The details of the format of the printed page are handled by the Bible Society in conference with the missionary. In order that the book may be as handy to use as possible, it has been considered valuable to keep down the size of the page. On the other hand, there is great need for the letters to be large in any book which is put out for those who are only becoming literate. Aboriginal people are not accustomed to reading and many of them suffer from eye trouble of one type or another. The conflicting factors of convenient size of the book and large size of the type are not easily resolved.

The translator is concerned principally with two problems in the format: (1) the indication of paragraphs and (2) printing the translation as a diglot.

15.7.1   PARAGRAPHING

For a discussion of the value and methods of indicating paragraphs in the translation, see pp. 15–16 of the *Guide for Translators*.

In general, translators are of the opinion that the indication of paragraphs are valuable, but the traditional form is so strongly intrenched in many cases that changes are frequently not too well received.

15.7.2   DIGLOTS

The value of publishing a translation as a diglot cannot be overemphasized for certain types of circumstances. In very many instances the native church tends to move toward the Christian community of the trade language. In Latin America those Indians who learn to read their native language are usually the progressive individuals who also want to learn and are learning to read the Spanish or Portuguese. Moreover, the assimilation of the Indian church groups into the national church community is an important goal of missionary work. The cultural and economic forces in the countries are almost all directed toward the ultimate assimilation of the Indians into the national life and into the dominant language group. For this reason the American Bible Society is publishing all such translations into aboriginal languages as diglots. This makes it possible to reach those bilingual members of the Indian communities with a text in both languages and also to assist in the general education of the Indian people toward the national languages. The result of such translations will no doubt be the disappearance of the Indian languages much more rapidly than would otherwise be the case. This does not mean that the Society is interested in the destruction of such native languages, nor is it interested necessarily in their preservation. The purpose is to reach men with the truth of the Word of God and to do it in a manner which will be most effective in preparing them to take their full responsibility of leadership in the Christian community of the countries of which they are citizens.

In several instances it has been found that government officials in Latin America who have been opposed to teaching Indians to read their own languages have reacted very favorably to diglot translations, for they see in them the possibilities for more rapid extension of the use of Spanish and Portuguese. It may very well be the case that colonial government officials in Africa, India, and the South Pacific may likewise be more favorably disposed to Bible translation if they see in the use of diglots the possibilities of more extensive knowledge of the trade languages. Translators should in all cases investigate such possibilities thoroughly.

If the translation is published as a diglot, the native text must correspond to the trade-language text. Any failure to do so will be looked upon immediately with suspicion by natives, who will not be able to understand the problems of textual criticism and alternate renderings and readings.

Whether or not one prints the translation as a diglot, the text in the native language should not have to lean on the trade language for its meaning. The translation should speak the language of the aboriginal people in such a simple, clear, and dignified manner that men will recognize its truth as being for them.

APPENDIX

A GUIDE FOR

TRANSLATORS, REVISERS, & EDITORS

WORKING IN CONNECTION WITH THE

AMERICAN BIBLE SOCIETY

By kind permission of the
BRITISH AND FOREIGN BIBLE SOCIETY
based upon and in harmony with
the Rules of that Society

———

AMERICAN BIBLE SOCIETY
New York
1932

TABLE OF CONTENTS

ON recommendation of the Society's Committee on Versions, the Board of Managers has approved the provisions of this Guide for Translators, Revisers, and Editors of versions prepared for publication by the Society. The Guide is based on, and is to a large degree verbatim, the "Rules for the Guidance of Translators, Revisers, and Editors working in connection with the British and Foreign Bible Society," which have been tested by wide use for many years. The Board acknowledges with gratitude the permission of the British Society's Committee for this use of its invaluable and comprehensive experience.

These rules express the main principles according to which translations of the Holy Scriptures should be undertaken. They have been considered and approved by translators and revisers in all parts of the world. They cannot, however, cover every difficulty that may arise. It is requested that all doubtful questions be referred to the Committee through the Secretary in charge, whose counsel is always available to translators and revisers. Procedure proposed on certain specified points should always be taken up with the Committee.

It is expected that the rules will be strictly followed and that any proposed departures therefrom will be referred to the Committee in New York.

ERIC M. NORTH
General Secretary

BIBLE HOUSE
ASTOR PLACE
NEW YORK
1932

A GUIDE for TRANSLATORS, REVISERS, and EDITORS working in connection with the AMERICAN BIBLE SOCIETY

The Spirit in which the Work is to be Done

1. Every translation or revision of a version of the Holy Scriptures should be undertaken in the Name of our Lord Jesus Christ, be touched with reverent and loving hands, and be carried on with the utmost fidelity and accuracy, in prayerful dependence on the Holy Spirit. Translators will doubtless remember that they are helping to fashion the religious language of many generations.

Translation and Revision Committees

2. All translation and revision work should, where practicable, be undertaken only after consultation with representatives of the leading Churches using the language. In selecting translators, next to spiritual fitness, scholarly and linguistic qualifications are of paramount importance. Wherever it is possible to form a small Committee of competent persons, representing different Christian communions, to translate or revise a version of the Scriptures, the work of a single translator or reviser is inadmissible for publication.

The actual revising executive should be a small Translation or Revision Committee, one member of it acting also as secretary for securing tentative proofs, conducting correspondence, etc. It is advisable to form also a Committee of Reference, embracing representatives, so far as practicable, of all the Churches and Missions which use the version. This Committee should be consulted by the working committee in cases of doubt or difficulty, and, in a revision, in every important change of words or phrases proposed. When these points cannot otherwise be settled, they should be referred to the Committee in New York.

Much caution should be exercised in adopting religious words or phrases suggested by non-Christian assistants.

Warning Against Needless Versions or Revisions

3. It is most important not to multiply versions needlessly in adjacent dialects; and careful inquiry should be made as to exist-

ing translations before a new one is undertaken. Intercommunication between neighboring Churches and Missions may lead to such modifications in a version as will make it available beyond the area for which it was originally intended.

Before any important Revision is taken up, the need for it should be clearly established, and arrangements framed for its execution with all practicable efficiency and speed.

Limitations of Revision

4. A Revision should, in most cases, be limited to the correction and improvement of a version which has already stood the test of practical use; but occasionally a retranslation is needful. To expedite such translations and revisions as they deem desirable, the Board of Managers of the Society is ready to consider any financial proposals which would secure for the work the whole time of the scholars essential for its prosecution. For many reasons—among which the great expense involved is not the least—the very prolonged revisions such as have sometimes taken place should be avoided.

List of Proposed Changes

5. Before a Revision is published, a statement of the principal changes contemplated should be circulated for criticism among all competent missionaries and other scholars on the field, and submitted to the Committee in New York.

Preference for Generally Accepted Interpretations

6. In passages where the original admits of more than one possible rendering, translators and revisers are expected, in view of the grave responsibility involved, to weigh the case fully before departing from a generally accepted interpretation which has been well established.

Text to be Followed

7. The Board desires that, wherever practicable, versions should be made and revised from the original Hebrew, Aramaic, and Greek, advantage being taken of any previous translations in the particular language, and of versions in cognate languages.

8. For the Old Testament, the use of Ginsberg's edition of the Old Testament (published by the British and Foreign Bible Society) or of Letteris' edition is strongly recommended both as regards consonants and vowels, but any other standard edition

may be used, liberty being given to translators and revisers to follow the *Kethib* or *Qeri* or renderings sanctioned by the English Authorized Version or the English Revised Version (1885) or the American Revised Version (1901) or by their marginal readings. In using the English versions preference, however, should be given to the readings given by the text rather than the marginal readings.

9. For the New Testament, translators and revisers are recommended to follow the text of the original Greek edited for the British and Foreign Bible Society by Dr. Eberhard Nestle, but are at liberty to follow that underlying the English Authorized Version (edited by Dr. F. H. A. Scrivener, for the Cambridge University Press), or that underlying the English Revised Version (edited by Archdeacon Edwin Palmer, for the Oxford University Press).

10. Translators who are unacquainted with the originals are desired to follow the text or margin of the English AV or ERV (1881, 1885), or the ARV (1901), or, in the case of translators unacquainted with English, some other version sanctioned by the Committee.

11. Words and sentences for which the English or American Revisers in their marginal notes declare that there exists ancient authority should find a place either in the text or in the margin. The Committee deprecates their entire omission.

Translations to be Faithful

12. Versions and revisions should be faithful translations, in a style easily understood by the people; on the one hand avoiding vulgarisms and colloquial expressions unworthy of the Book, and on the other hand avoiding forms of speech which are classical rather than intelligible to ordinary readers. It is not the object of the Society to produce versions in a language as it should be, but in a language as it is. The simplest and best-known words should be used in the idiomatic forms of the living tongue, and paraphrase should be avoided as far as practicable. Every version should be as literal as the idiom of the language will permit.

Alternative Renderings and Translational Helps

13. While restricting the translational work of the Society to the rendering of the text of Holy Scripture, the Board does not

regard the Constitutional provision, prohibiting note and comment, as excluding marginal helps, which may be needed to overcome certain classes of difficulties in a translation. It does not approve of any helps which are not included under the following heads:—

(a) *Alternative readings.* These would include those instances in which there may be various readings of the original text which are of generally accepted authority. It is permissible for translators to put in the margin a translation of an alternative reading in cases which seem to them to be of sufficient importance.

(b) *Alternative renderings.* In important passages where the original admits of more than one meaning, or where the meaning cannot be expressed adequately in one word or phrase, translators may put preferred renderings in the text and alternatives in the margin.

(c) *Difficulties in the original language.* Words in the original which cannot be rendered literally without obscurity (e. g., technical terms, or words peculiar to the time and circumstances when the books were written) are usually rendered in the text either by (1) a very brief explanatory phrase, or (2) transliteration from the original, or other suitable language, or (3) the adoption of some generally known term which fairly represents the original idea. In such cases, in order to give as faithful a rendering of the *text* as possible, it is helpful and permissible to add in the margin some local equivalent or expansion of the term adopted; but every such marginal addition must be limited to an honest attempt to provide *an intelligible translation of the words and idioms of the original text.*

(d) *Difficulties in the language into which the translation is made.* Special difficulties are often due to the ideas and customs peculiar to the people into whose language the Bible is being translated. Occasionally there are words and phrases the literal translation of which, because of ideas peculiar to the country, would not convey to the reader the sense of the original. In such cases, with a view to the attainment of the ultimate end of translation, it is permissible to add in the margin a phrase which, *without attempting to interpret the meaning of the passage,* is calculated to prevent misunderstanding.

> Translational helps of this class should be rare and be introduced only when absolutely necessary. They should be discontinued in any version as soon as the necessity for them ceases.

(e) *Proper names.* Where the name of a place or a person

merely transliterated into a foreign tongue would not convey the idea of place or personality, it is permissible to add the generic title; e. g., Jordan (river), Jeremiah (prophet), when such addition is necessary to give the sense. At the first occurrence of a proper name which conveys no meaning to the reader, a few words may be placed in the margin to make the historical or geographical reference intelligible.

When the sense of a passage turns on the meaning of a name in the original tongue, a translation of the name may be given in the margin.

(f) *References*, as explained in paragraph 19.

(g) *Added words*. In the English Bible, words implied but not expressed in the original text are printed in italics, *when it is desirable to call attention to the addition* of the words. If a similar printing-device (such as ⌊. . . .⌋) cannot be adopted in other versions, a marginal indication of the addition should be made.

Every marginal addition must be limited to an honest attempt to provide an adequate rendering of the original text, and must not be of the nature of interpretation. Cases of doubt should be referred to the Secretary in charge.

Before versions containing translational helps are published by the Society, a list of marginal additions proposed must be submitted (in the text of the version and in English) to the Committee on Versions, and the approval of the Board of Managers must be obtained.

Uniformity in Rendering

14. The Board recommends that care should be taken to translate, or transliterate, *uniformly*, as far as possible, where the meaning is the same, the most important Scripture names and terms, such as—

(a) The Divine names and attributes.

(b) Psychological terms; e. g., soul, spirit, heart, will, desire, pleasure, and conscience; also, such words as body and flesh.

(c) Moral and spiritual attributes; e. g., faith, hope, love, truth, grace, mercy, peace, joy, patience, meekness, humility, righteousness, holiness, and their opposites.

(d) Words that have to do with temptation and sin.

(e) Words for repentance, pardon, conversion, etc.

(f) Ceremonial words for washing, sprinkling, etc.

(g) Sacrificial terms.

(h) Words connected with worship; e. g., prayer, praise, temple, synagogue, church.

(i) Official terms for prophet, priest, king, judge, minister, apostle, disciple, presbyter, bishop, deacon, etc.

(j) Words relating to death, the grave, the place of the departed, eternity, the destiny of the saved and the lost, etc.

The treatment of proper names and the designation of the books of the Bible should, as far as possible, be uniform over wide areas, and especially in neighboring and cognate versions.

To accomplish the provisions of this paragraph a member of the Translation or Revision Committee should be definitely assigned to make the necessary collations of passages, especially where a group of subcommittees or individual translators have each primary responsibility for different books.

New Words

15. Words that must be transliterated rather than translated should be carefully adapted to the grammatical and phonetic principles of a language.

16. When any material object mentioned in Scripture, such as a plant or an animal, is unknown to the people for whom the translation is intended, the Board prefers the introduction of an explanatory phrase, or of a loan word, the precise meaning of which can be explained by a teacher, rather than the use of a word meaning a different object.

The Sacred Names

In the Old Testament

17. (a) אֱלֹהִים (Elohim), Θεός, God.—The name used in Hebrew for "God" in its most general sense is *Elohim*. The Septuagint accepted the Greek Θεός as its equivalent. Every care should be taken to select the highest native term for God that a language affords. The teaching of the Bible will by degrees purify and raise the ideas associated with the word used.

(b) אֲדֹנִי (Adonai).—The Hebrew word *Adonai* is translated Κύριος by the Septuagint, and is generally rendered "Lord" in English. In most languages a word conveying the idea of "lordship" is to be found.

(c) יְהֹוָה (YHWH, called the Tetragrammaton as having four letters in the Hebrew).—This is a proper name, the exact pronunciation of which is unknown. In reading the Hebrew Scriptures, *Adonai*—less frequently *Elohim*—was substituted for it at a time considerably before the Christian era. The translators of the Septuagint (the earliest Greek version of the Old Testament) followed this substitution by the use of Κύριος (Lord). The Septuagint version was quoted and its example followed by the writers of the New Testament. The same course was adopted in all translations, so far as is known, from the Syriac of the second century down to the close of the 15th century.

The pronunciation "Jehovah" arose in the 16th century through confusion of the word *Adonai* with the Tetragrammaton. This pronunciation is incorrect. In the English AV and ERV the name *Jah* or *Jehovah* is introduced in only a few places where the translators wished to indicate that the force of the passage turned upon the name. In other passages "Lord" in small caps was substituted for it. Several translators, for example, the American Revisers in the ARV, have preferred to retain some approximate transliteration of the Hebrew Tetragrammaton in all cases.

Translators in other European languages followed one or other of three courses; e. g.:

1. Substitution: Luther (1530), de Sacy (1668) and many others followed the precedent of the Septuagint and New Testament; using, e.g., "Herr" (Lord); "Seigneur" (Lord).

2. Transliteration: The Spanish translators, de Reyna (1569) and Valera (1602), preferred to approximate transliteration and used the word *Jehová*.

3. Translation: Ostervald (1724) sought an equivalent for Jehovah and used the expression *L'Eternel*.

In view of this divergence in practice, the Board does not desire to lay down any fixed rule. But it considers that when the force of a passage clearly turns upon the name, the word should be transliterated; and it desires (1) that in other cases, where one usage has become established, no change should be made unless it is supported by the general wish of the Christian community using the version; and (2) that wherever there are languages belonging to the same family, and in use side by side, there should be, as far as possible, uniformity of practice.

(d) Where the transliteration is not adopted, the difference between "Lord" (for the Tetragrammaton) and "Lord" (for *Adonai*) should be shown, if not by capitals, by different type, spacing, or other device, and the significance of the variation may be explained by a note at the back of the title-page.

IN THE NEW TESTAMENT

(e) Where quotations from, or references to, the Old Testament in the New involve the presence of the Tetragrammaton, it is permissible to mark the word answering to it in capitals or otherwise.

(f) In adjacent districts and cognate versions, care should be taken to secure corresponding renderings of the sacred name 'Jesus.'

Similarity of treatment should also prevail in adjoining districts in reproducing the designation 'Christ' or 'Messiah.' Forms like 'Masiya' from the Hebrew are free from objection, but to retain the link with 'Christian,' 'Christianity,' etc., an adaptation of the Greek 'Christos' may be preferable.

It may sometimes be found necessary to explain in a prefatory note that Jesu, Jesus and Isa, are different forms of the name of the same person, and that Christos and Masiya are two forms of a title meaning Anointed.

(g) In translating 'Holy Spirit' or 'Spirit,' care must be taken to indicate His Personality *beyond all question*. Though the Greek word πνεῦμα is neuter, its treatment as masculine (e. g., by the use of ἐκεῖνος in apposition to it in John 14: 26) usually leaves no doubt as to the intent of speaker, or writer. A *Person*, and not a mere *influence*, was meant. The double sense of the Greek word (breath or wind, and spirit) sometimes makes it difficult to decide whether the Divine Person Himself is intended. In such cases the Committee recommends that the guidance afforded by the use of capitals by the American and English Revisers or by Nestle should be followed. In alphabets devoid of capitals, recourse can be had to different type or spacing.

All cases of doubt or difficulty as to the use of any of the sacred names should be referred in English to the Committee in New York.

The Word "Baptize"

18. Without expressing any preference, the Board desires the term transliterated *baptize* in English, and its cognates, to be

either translated in the text, provided all Missions using, or likely to use, the version are agreed upon a rendering embracing both interpretations;

or transliterated—without any translation in either text or note;

or transliterated—with the two alternative renderings in the margin to express both interpretations.

References and Quotations

19. When old and established versions belonging to recognized Protestant communities are reproduced by the Society, their marginal references, their chapter and page headings and other accepted forms of printing have usually been retained. When marginal references are to be specially prepared for the Society's versions, the Board requests consultation or correspondence with the Committee on Versions before proceeding.

Where possible, it is desirable that references for quotations by one Biblical writer from another should be given in all editions of the complete Bible issued by the Society.

Where considered essential, it is permissible for translators and editors to use quotation marks to indicate a quotation from one part of the Bible in another, or to show a speech within a speech; but in the case of most languages it is possible as in English to indicate quotations without special marks; and this is preferable.

Additional and Inadmissible Matter

20. The Board desires that the chapter headings of the English AV, the subscriptions to the Epistles, and Ussher's system of chronology be not reproduced in the Society's editions.

Page, chapter, and sectional headings (if introduced) must be simple summaries without doctrinal bias and as far as possible in the words of the text, and in any doubtful case should be submitted in English to the Secretary in charge. Sectional headings should be separated from the text by a space and, if possible, should be in different type.

21. In accordance with the Society's Constitution, no Confession of faith, doctrinal notes, or table of lessons or festivals, may be printed in, or be bound up with, any of the Society's editions.

22. It is not permissible to include descriptive indexes, glossaries, collections of historical, or of geographical or of other notes. Collections of the headings of pages, chapters, or sections are inadmissible.

Arrangement of the Text

23. Inasmuch as the ordinary chapter and verse divisions (which are comparatively modern) are liable to interrupt and

obscure the meaning and connection of Holy Scripture, many translators ask that new translations, and revisions of existing translations, be published in paragraph form, with or without sectional divisions or headings.

The Board does not object to this course where it will not create difficulties by introducing a change of form to which readers are unaccustomed and the value of which they cannot appreciate. Where paragraphs are adopted, the old chapter numbers should for convenience of reference be placed in the margin, and the verse numbers there or in the body of the text. Arabic figures are generally preferable to Roman. The Board leaves each body of translators or revisers to arrange the sections, if adopted, as they think fit, suggesting, however, consultation of the arrangement of Nestle's Greek Testament or of the ERV or ARV.

On the other hand, when the text is arranged in verses, the grouping which would be exhibited by paragraphs may be shown by blank spaces dividing the successive topics, or preferably, by ¶ as in the AV.

It is recommended that the numeration of chapters and verses should follow that in the AV and RV, though it occasionally differs from that in Hebrew and Greek editions. Editors should carefully examine, correct and collate pages, chapters, and verses in the copy and in the proofs.

Characters and Spelling

24. Where a version is to be published in a language not yet reduced to writing, or in which the orthography is varied or incomplete, it is often difficult to decide the question of the characters to be used. In this situation individual ingenuity and provincial views greatly need to be supplemented by the counsels of national and international linguistic authorities. A considerable body of tested experience is available in many areas, the principles of which hold good generally. To ignore them may retard the educational and religious development of the people. The Secretary in charge will be glad to put translators and committees in touch with competent assistance.

In general, the use and, certainly, the multiplication of accents and diacritical marks should be avoided if at all possible; the same phonetic sound should be rendered by the same symbol and only one sound by one symbol. If a choice of symbol is possible, the relation of the language to neighboring or dominant languages should be carefully considered.

Title-Page and Imprints

25. The title-page should contain:

(a) The name of the book stated as concisely and plainly as possible, in the language of the version.

(b) The imprint of the Bible Society in the language of the version or, if that is impossible or undesirable, in English or some other European language. This imprint should include (1) the place of publication, (2) ordinarily, the name "American Bible Society," (3) and usually the year of publication.

Words and phrases appearing on the title-page should all be in the same language as the version, unless otherwise required by government regulation.

The title and imprint are usually given without any punctuation marks.

26. In the case of foreign versions, except those in the chief European languages, there should be an inconspicuous indication of the language and part in English, French, German, Spanish, Latin or other widely known European language, on the verso or back of the title-page (or on the last page), not on the title-page itself, and preferably in small type, as follows:

(N. T., Tentative Ed., Pampangan) *indicating*		A New Testament in preliminary tentative version.
(N. T., Cakchiquel)	"	A New Testament, original version.
(N. T., Cakchiquel & Spanish)	"	A diglot.
(Rv. N. T., Tswa)	"	A Revised N. T.
(Rv. Gos. John, Tswa)	"	A Gospel of John in the revised version.
(1926 Rv. Psa., Quechua)	"	The 1926 Revision of the Psalms in Quechua.

Following this, or below on the next line (or possibly on the last page) is desirable an indication of the date of the edition and the quantity; e. g.:

3M-1928	—*meaning*—	1928 edition of which 3,000 were printed.
5C-1930	—*meaning*—	1930 edition of which 500 were printed.
5M-6, 1931	—*meaning*—	edition of June, 1931, of which 5,000 were printed.
8C-2 Ed. 1929	—*meaning*—	2d Edition, printed in 1929, 800 copies.

Combined notations would read thus:

(Rv. N. T., Siamese, 5C-1931)—*meaning* the Revised Version of the New Testament in Siamese, 1931 edition, of which 500 were printed.

Occasionally it will be necessary to print in small type on the verso of the title-page a description of the book in the language of the government of the country; e. g.:

Novo Testamento na Lingua Tswa do Districto de Inhambane

27. In some countries, the law requires the name of the printer and of the place of printing to be put on each book. This should be inserted in small type at the end of the book, often on a single line on the last page; e. g.:

Impresso em Gran-Bretanha, na tipographia de
Richard Clay & Sons, Limited, Bungay, Suffolk.

28. Binding title, to be stamped or printed on the cover, should be in the language of the version and should consist solely of the vernacular words for "The Bible" or "The Holy Bible," "The New Testament," "The Four Gospels," "The Gospel according to St. John" or "St. John," etc., as the case may be, in as short a form as possible.

29. Before printing, all title-pages and binding titles should be submitted to the Secretary in charge in New York or, when the printing is done in a Foreign Agency, to the Agency Secretary. With the text should be sent a line for line translation and, if the characters of the version are not roman, a line for line transliteration.

30. In cases where the text is to be reproduced by photographic process (as unsuited for type composition) application for instructions should be made to the Secretary in charge or to the Secretary of the Agency in which the printing is to be done.

Accuracy of Transcription and Preparation for Printing

31. The manuscript from which the type is to be set should preferably be typewritten and double-spaced. If not typewritten, great care should be taken to insure legibility. The manuscript should be written on one side of the paper only, with good margins. The edge should not be bound.

Pages should be numbered consecutively. It will be found helpful to have at least the chapter number (and preferably the number of the first verse) indicated in the upper right hand corner of each page of the manuscript.

32. Every possible care should be taken to insure accuracy. In the recopying and correcting, letters, words, whole lines may drop out unobserved and the most careful comparison should be made. Care should also be taken that standards of capitalization,

punctuation, and spelling are adhered to throughout the text. Revision in proof form may add very seriously to the cost of the book and delay publication and should be avoided by the accuracy of the manuscript. The correction of MS by pasting on correction slips should be avoided, unless the adhesive is exceptionally strong and nonstaining.

33. In sending forward a complete manuscript, it is desirable to send at the same time copy for binding title, title-page, back of title-page, and text of contents page (i. e., names and page location of books in the volume). It is also desired that a list be submitted of the characters used bearing diacritical marks or otherwise differing from those in a standard font of type.

34. Proofs will be sent to the translator for correction. Standard symbols in use in correcting proof are given on pages 18–20. In returning proof, the corrector is asked to indicate whether he wishes to see further proof or not.

Original Manuscript

35. The MS of the first translation of any portion of Scripture into a new language or dialect should always be permanently preserved in the Bible House, New York.

In the case of a subsequent translation or a revision, the preservation of the MS is desirable, unless in any particular case or cases the Committee directs otherwise.

Information Through the Agency Secretary

36. Where a translation or revision is carried on in a field for which the Society has an accredited Agency Secretary, in order to expedite the work, he should be kept informed of its progress and be the channel through which official correspondence with New York is conducted.

Copies for the Bible House Library

37. As early as possible, on its publication, five sample copies of every new translation or version should reach the Secretary in charge. In the case of books printed abroad, the copies should be sent to him by the Agent of the Society or by the Editor responsible for their production; in the case of those printed in the United States, they must be supplied by the Publication Department.

GENERAL DIRECTIONS FOR PROOFREADING

1. Read all proof slowly, letter by letter, in order to detect every error.

2. Read through the proof several times with a definite point in view. Consider carefully punctuation, correct usage, typographical errors, general alignment, spacing, general effect.

3. Make all corrections in ink of a color contrasting with that used by the professional proofreader.

4. Put all corrections in the margin near the word marked. If several are made, place them in the order of their appearance with a slanting line between them; as, *wf/tr/sc/*.

5. Do not erase a correction made which you have found unnecessary. Draw a line through the correction and write ***stet,*** which means ***Let it stand.*** If necessary, rewrite a correction.

6. Underline three times a word or words to be written in large capitals and write "caps" in the margin; underline twice to indicate small capitals and write "s. c." in margin.

7. When a word is incorrectly capitalized, draw a line through the letter and write "l. c." in the margin to indicate "lower case."

Pages 18–20 are from **Taintor and Monro, "The Secretary's Handbook."** By permission of The Macmillan Company, publishers.

8. Underline a word once to indicate that it is to be italicized, and write "ital" in the margin.

9. Place a circle in the margin around a period **or** colon to be inserted. To indicate a comma write ,/or ^,; to indicate an apostrophe write ˇ'; to indicate quotation marks write ˇ" ˇ".

10. To indicate that a word or expression should be removed draw a line through the word or expression and write in the margin the sign ℘ (dele), which means *Take out.*

11. Write in the margin all new material to be inserted and indicate by caret (∧) where it is to be placed.

12. Write in the margin a double (=) to show that a hyphen is to be placed where indicated by a caret sign.

13. Use the space sign # to indicate that more space is needed where indicated by the caret.

14. Use the sign ⁀‿ to indicate that space between letters or words is to be eliminated.

15. Be careful to answer all queries made by the publisher's proofreader. To indicate your approval, cross out the question mark and allow the correction to stand. To show disapproval of the correction suggested, cross out the question or answer it in full.

SIGNS USED IN CORRECTING PROOFS

⌐⌐	Push down the lead which is showing with the type.
ꝺ	Delete; take out.
↻	Turn inverted letter right side up.
stet ·····	Let it remain; change made was wrong.
□	Indent one *em*.
⊙	A period.
=	The type line is uneven at the side of the page; straighten it.
×	A broken letter.
"	A hyphen.
ital.	Use italics.
( )	Join together; take out the space.
ℭ	Take out letter and close up.
center	Put in middle of page, or line.
≡	Straighten lines.
⌄	Insert an apostrophe.
⌃	Insert a comma.
[	Raise the word or letter.
]	Lower the word or letter.
⌐	Bring matter to the left.
⌐	Bring matter to the right

#	Make a space.
lead	A thin metal strip used to widen the space between the lines.
space out	Spread words farther apart.
¶	Make a paragraph.
no ¶	Run on without a paragraph.
cap.	Use a capital.
l.c.	Use the lower case (small type), *i.e.* not capitals.
s.c.	Small capitals.
w.f.	Wrong font — size or style.
font.	Kind of type.
tr.	Transpose.
rom.	Use roman letter.
overrun	Carry over to next line.
<	Indicates where an insertion is to be made.
Qy. or (?)	Doubt as to spelling, etc.
≡	Indicates CAPITAL letters.
≡	Indicates SMALL CAPITAL letters.
—	Indicates *italic* letters.
～	Indicates black type letters.
≋	Indicates **BLACK CAPITALS.**
≋	Indicates **BLACK SMALL CAPITALS**
≈	Indicates ***black italic.***

PROOF SHOWING CORRECTIONS

ADDRESS AT GETTYSBURG

Fourscore and seven years ago our fathers brought forth on this continent a new nation, conceived in liberty, and dedicated to the proposition that all men are created equal. Now we are engaged in a great civil war, testing whether that nation, or any nation so conceived and so dedicated, can long endure. We are met on a great battlefield of that war. We have come to dedicate a portion of that field as a final resting-place for those who here gave their lives that that Nation might live. It is altogether fitting and proper that we should do this.

But, in a larger sense, we cannot dedicate — we cannot consecrate — we cannot hallow — this ground. The brave men, living and dead, who struggled here, have consecrated it far above our poor power to add or detract. The world will little note nor long remember what we here say. but it can never forget what they did here.

It is for us, the living, rather, to be dedicated here to the unfinished work which they who fought

(Address at the dedication of the Gettysburg National Cemetery, Nov. 19, 1863. Reprinted, by permission of The Macmillan Company, from Abraham Lincoln, the Man of the People, by Norman Hapgood.)

CORRECTED PROOF

ADDRESS AT GETTYSBURG

Fourscore and seven years ago our fathers brought forth on this continent a new nation, conceived in liberty, and dedicated to the proposition that all men are created equal.

Now we are engaged in a great civil war, testing whether that nation, or any nation so conceived and so dedicated, can long endure. We are met on a great battlefield of that war. We have come to dedicate a portion of that field as a final resting-place for those who here gave their lives that that nation might live. It is altogether fitting and proper that we should do this.

But, in a larger sense, we cannot dedicate — we cannot consecrate — we cannot hallow — this ground. The brave men, living and dead, who struggled here, have consecrated it far above our poor power to add or detract. The world will little note nor long remember what we say here, but it can never forget what they did here. It is for us, the living, rather, to be dedicated here to the unfinished work which they who fought here

(Address at the dedication of the Gettysburg National Cemetery, Nos. 19, 1863. Reprinted, by permission of THE MACMILLAN COMPANY, from "Abraham Lincoln, the Man of the People," by Norman Hapgood.)

INDEX

(The numbers refer to sections unless pages are indicated)

The Rendering of Biblical Terms

of

Weights and Measures

AMERICAN BIBLE SOCIETY

GUIDE FOR TRANSLATORS AND REVISERS

Supplement No. 1

1943

The Translation of Biblical Terms for Weights, Measures, Distances, Money, etc.

THE summary and suggestions which follow are intended to simplify the task of the translator in dealing with these terms. No attempt to lay down a rigid rule is made, in view of the varied resources of different languages.

I. Underlying Principles

1. The object of the translation is to convey to the reader the sense of the passage, not a mathematical formula.

E.g.: Ezekiel 45:10 — "Ye shall have just balances, and a just ephah, and a just bath"; *not* "Ye shall have just balances, and a just sixty-five pints, and a just eight gallons."

2. Relative value or size may be more important than the precise equivalence.

E.g.: 2 Kings 7:1 — The point lies in the cheapness of the price, not in the number of grains of silver in the shekel, nor the cubic content of the seah or measure.

3. It must be recognized that even an approximate mathematical equivalent may not meet the problem in a given instance, because the current local value now may be very different.

E.g.: Luke 10:35 — The AV has the Good Samaritan give the innkeeper "two pence," the ARV "two shillings," for the care of the sufferer. Even if the English penny is associated with the Roman denarius by the abbreviation "d," it by no means represents now the same purchasing power.

4. It must be recognized also that, while translation is intended to make the original text understandable and in a certain sense indigenous, it is by no means desirable to translate so as to give the reader the impression that the events described happened yesterday and just across the street. The historical nature of the Scriptures, their witness that certain events occurred at particular places and times in the world's life, and under conditions then existing, warrants the retention of such terms as preserve that historical atmosphere. For this reason, transliteration of a term, when it appears necessary, may be an advantage.

(2)

5. It is not always possible for the text, or the text combined with a minimum translational help in the margin, to give a fully satisfactory rendering. Yet it is often more important *not* to interrupt the flow of the reader's thought by the interjection of a marginal reference, than to set forth with exactness the significance of a single word or phrase in the passage.

6. As a general principle, where there is a native measure or weight substantially equivalent in size, then use it; i.e., translate the term. If there is no such equivalent, then one may either transliterate from the Hebrew or Greek original, or use an equivalent term from some other language current in the neighborhood. But some words probably must be transliterated because of context, or because used for more than one precise value: e.g., gerah, beka, shekel, maneh, talent.

7. In some instances a useful solution might be to alter the number of units, in order to make the equivalents appropriate; e.g., if there is no word in the native language for *fathom*, but a word for *yard*, in Acts 27:28 "twenty fathoms" might be translated "forty yards." (*Note:* in a seafaring country, measures of sea depth may be different words from "dry" length). But care must be taken to avoid unnatural ways of expression; e.g., in John 2:6 it would probably be better to translate "containing two or three metretes apiece" as "two or three measures apiece," than to say "containing eighteen to twenty-seven gallons apiece."

8. The use of marginal notes or an appended table to indicate values and relationships is a question of importance. In the Society's editions their use is justified only as translational helps (see Rule 13 in the *Guide for Translators*). The following points may be useful in applying the rule:

(*a*) Avoid marginal notations in all introductory editions of the New Testament books, and preferably in the first edition of the New Testament.

(*b*) Exceptions to this may be where a transliteration is obscure in meaning, and the point of the passage depends on understanding the relative value. This may be illustrated by Matthew 18:24, 28, where the *talent* is in contrast to the *shilling;* but even here a note is hardly needed, as the contrast is exhibited by the difference between 10,000 and 100!

(*c*) In full editions of the Bible, it is probably desirable in the case of *transliterated* terms to use a marginal note, such as those in column 5. Such a note need not appear at every occurrence of the word. It may be given at the first occurrence in each Biblical book. Or, if a relatively lengthy note is needed, it may be given at the first occurrence in the Bible, and at other points a reference be made back to this. When a word appears more than once in a chapter, the marginal notation should be indicated only at the first occurrence.

Where it seems clearly desirable in the case of a *translated* term, a marginal notation may be used to give the original form in Hebrew or Greek and its value.

9. Where such words as "shekel" are not in the original, the provisions of the Guide for Translators, par. 13g, should be followed.

10. With these provisions the Committee would regard the introduction of tables of weights, measures, and other values as unnecessary.

II. Explanation of the Tables

11. Old Testament terms and New Testament terms are treated separately. The names and values are usually different. Also, the problems involved in translation are limited, for the great majority of Bible translators, to the New Testament terms. Yet, the persistence of such terms as "bath," "cor," "seah" (in "saton") from Old Testament times into those of the New Testament makes it desirable, even for translators of New Testament books only, to have this entire table before them. Renderings in the New Testament books ought always to be chosen with an eye to the future, when possibly some or all of the Old Testament may be translated into the same language.

The definite mathematical terms of each Testament are divided into the following categories:

Old Testament:	*New Testament:*
1 Weights, Money, Coins	1 Weights, Money, Coins
2 Length and Distance	2 Length and Distance
3 Area	3 Cubic Contents
4 Cubic Contents	4 Time
5 Time	

12. Indefinite terms involving measurement, such as "money," "age," "length," "bowshot," are omitted from these tables. Under

each heading the terms are for the most part arranged in order from smaller to greater. Some terms, admitted to the tables because they can be definite, are also used indefinitely, such as "hour," "day," "measure," "reed," etc.; in such cases of course what is given in the tables has no application to their meaning when used indefinitely. Care should be taken to observe this distinction.

13. Instead of giving references to authorities for each separate term in these tables, the following more or less exhaustive articles are suggested for translators interested in the history and relations of the various items: (a) in the *Dictionary of the Bible* (ed. Hastings), art. "Money," vol. iii. pp. 417–432, and art. "Weights and Measures," vol. iv. pp. 901–913, both articles by Prof. A. R. S. Kennedy; (b) in the *International Standard Bible Encyclopaedia* (ed. Orr), art. "Money," vol. iii. pp. 2076–2080, and art. "Weights and Measures," vol. v. pp. 3079–3081, both articles by Prof. H. Porter; (c) appropriate articles in *Dictionary of the Bible* by Davis, and similar works of reference, with the literature listed there.

• •

Summary of Old Testament Dry and Liquid Measures

Dry			*Liquid*		
			12 logs	=	1 hin
10 omers, or					
10 tenth parts, or		= 1 ephah	6 hins, or		= 1 bath
3 seahs, or			3 third parts		
3 third parts					
10 ephahs	= 1 homer		10 baths	=	1 cor

N.B.—The ephah (about a bushel) and the bath (about 8 gallons) were equivalent measures.

Translators' Tables of Biblical Weights,

Column 1 gives the words used in the ARV to render the original terms standing opposite them. When the AV differs, its rendering is added in parentheses. The letters in parentheses appended to some items in this column distinguish identical renderings of different originals. Column 2 gives the number of times the original word occurs in the Hebrew or Greek text. Most of such occurrences are listed either in column 1 or on page 22. Columns 3 and 5 contain the renderings, or kind of renderings, suggested by the "principles" formulated in the Introduction to these tables. The blank column 4 is reserved for the choice made by the translator for his own text and marginal note, if any. Column 6 is intended to help in two ways: by showing relationship of the term to

In considering column 3, attention must be given

A.   In the Old

1. Weights, Money, Coins

1 Term ARV	2 No. of occurrences	3 Suggested Renderings Text	4 Renderings Adopted by Translator
gerah גֵּרָה (gērāh) Ex. 30:13; Lev. 27:25; Num. 3:47; 18:16; Ezek. 45:12	5	tlt: gera	
beka (AV bekah) בֶּקַע (beqa') Gen. 24:22 marg.; Ex. 38:26	2	Gen. 24:22: tr: half; tlt: shekel Ex. 38:26 tlt: beka	
shekel שֶׁקֶל (šeqel) for refs. see p. 22	88	tlt: shekel	
piece of silver (A) כֶּסֶף (keseph) (ARV, 3 times: piece of silver) for refs. see p. 22	18	tlt: shekel tr: of silver	
shekel of silver (ditto) for refs. see p. 22		tlt: shekel; tr: of silver	
silverling (ditto)		tlt: shekel; tr: of silver	
piece of money קְשִׂיטָה (q·sīṭāh) (AV once: piece of silver) Gen. 33:19; Jos. 24:32; Job 42:11	3	tr: piece of money	
piece אֲגוֹרָה ('ᵃghōrāh) 1 Sam. 2:36	1	tr: bit	
pieces רַצֵּי (raṣṣē) Ps. 68:30	1	tr: pieces (of)	
maneh מָנֶה (māneh) Ezek. 45:12	1	tlt: maneh	

(6)

Measures, Distances, Money, Etc.

other terms, and by giving the actual dimension as measured in standards familiar to the translator. Column 7 gives suggestions as to translation or transliteration recommended in columns 3 and 5, specifies passages calling for the notes in column 5, and warns against possible neglect of the "underlying principles" laid down in Sec. I.

The abbreviation "tr" stands for "translate by nearest equivalent to"; "tlt" stands for "transliterate from the original Hebrew or Greek"; "borrow," like "tlt," refers to taking over a term by suitable transliteration, but is here applied to the taking over of foreign terms from other languages than the original.

to the statement of principles and to column 7

Testament

5 Suggested Marginal Notes (if any)	6 Equations with Other Terms, and with Current Standards	7 Remarks
	1/20 part of a shekel	Mentioned only to specify size of shekel.
Heb. *beka.* See Ex. 38:26	½ shekel	
On Gen. 23:15: The silver shekel weighed about 14½ grams, or ½ ounce troy. *Elsewhere:* See note on Gen. 23:15	20 gerahs, or 2 bekas 14.55 grams, or 224 grains of silver	
See note on Gen. 23:15	*See shekel*	The words *shekel* and *piece* are not in the text. See Intr., par. 9.
Heb. *kesitah,* value unknown		Gen. 33:19; Josh. 24:32; Job 42:11 should all have the footnote.
Heb. *agorah,* value unknown		The context calls for a word meaning a trifling wage.
Heb. *ratse,* value unknown		The word is in the plural, governing *silver*.
Nearly a kilogram, or over 2½ troy pounds	60 shekels, Babylonian standard	The context requires transliteration of *maneh*. The interpretation of Ezek. 45:12 is difficult. See commentaries.

(7)

1 Term ARV	2 No. of occurrences	3 Suggested Renderings Text	4 Renderings Adopted by Translator
pound (A) מָנֶה (māneh) 1 Kin. 10:17; Ezr. 2:69; Neh. 7:71, 72	4	tr: pound, or tlt: maneh	
darics אֲדַרְכֹּנִים ('ᵃdharkōnīm) (AV drams) 1 Chr. 29:7; Ezr. 8:27 דַּרְכְּמֹנִים (dark·mōnīm) Ezr. 2:69; Neh. 7:70–72	2 4	tr: gold pieces	
talent כִּכָּר (kikkār) Ex. 25:39 etc.; see p. 22	46	tlt: talent	

2. Lengths and Distances

finger אֶצְבַּע ('etsba') Jer. 52:21	1	tr: finger	
handbreadth טֶפַח (ṭephaḥ) 1 Kin. 7:26; 2 Chr. 4:5; Ps. 39:5 טֹפַח (ṭōphaḥ) Ex. 25:25; 37:12; Ezek. 40:5, 43; 43:13	3 5	tr: handbreadth	
span זֶרֶת (zereth) Ex. 28:16(2); 39:9(2); 1 Sam.17:4; Isa. 40:12; Ezek. 43:13	7	tr: span, or half a cubit	
cubit (A) אַמָּה ('ammāh) Gen. 6:15 etc.; see p. 23	247	tr: cubit	
cubit (B) גֹּמֶד (gōmedh) Judg. 3:16	1	tr: cubit	

5 Suggested Marginal Notes (if any)	6 Equations with Other Terms, and with Current Standards	7 Remarks
On 1 Kin. 10:17: See note on Ezek. 45:12, Heb. maneh	The heavy gold maneh equalled 50 heavy, or 100 light, gold shekels. (Comp. 1 Kin. 10:17 with 2 Chr. 9:16)	If the native currency is based on some other monetary system, the equivalent (if any) of the English pound may be used. Otherwise tlt. Heb. maneh.
On Ezr. 2:69; Neh. 7:71, 72: Heb. maneh, equal to 50 shekels; see Gen. 23:15	The silver maneh equalled 50 silver shekels (Ex. 38:25f), or 727.5 grams, or 11,200 grains	
On 1 Chr. 29:7; Ezr. 8:27: Heb. adarkon, perhaps the light gold shekel. See 2 Chr. 9:16	1 light gold shekel	
On Ezr. 2:69; Neh. 7:70, 71, 72: Heb. darkemon. See note on Ezr. 8:27	8.425 grams, or 130 grains, of gold, or about a guinea	
On Ex. 38:24: Heb. kikkar, nearly 59 kilograms, or 158 troy pounds, of gold	The gold talent (kikkar) equalled 60 heavy gold manehs, and weighed 58,941 grams, or 909,600 grains, of gold	Kikkar has other meanings besides a weight of metal. Such occurrences are not reckoned in col. 2. See Intr., par. 12.
On Ex. 38:25: Heb. kikkar, nearly 44 kilograms, or 116⅔ troy pounds, of silver Elsewhere: See notes on Ex. 38:24, 25	The silver talent (kikkar) equalled 60 heavy silver manehs, and weighed 43,650 grams, or 672,000 grains, of silver	

	¼ handbreadth	The thickness of a finger, not its length.
	⅙ cubit 7.44 cm., or 2.93 in.	
On Isa. 40:12: That is, a builder's rule	3 handbreadths (i.e., reach of outspread hand), or ½ cubit	If the language has no word for this unit, render by half cubit, or its equivalent. But in Is. 40:12 use a word for the instrument in common use for measuring.
On Gen. 6:15: Heb. ammah, about 45 cm., or 17½ in.	6 handbreadths 44.64 cm., or 17.58 in.	The distance from elbow to tip of the middle finger. If the language lacks a name for this primitive measure, cubit may be borrowed, or ammah may be tlt. Reference to note on Gen. 6:15 may be added wherever desired.
On Judg. 3:16: Heb. gomed, length uncertain	Probably a short cubit of 5 handbreadths About 37 cm., or 15 in.	Perhaps distance from elbow to knuckles of the clenched fist.

1 Term ARV	2 No. of Occurrences	3 Suggested Renderings Text	4 Renderings Adopted by Translator
reed קָנֶה (qāneh) Ezek. 40:5 (2), 6 (2), 7 (3), 8; 41:8; 42:16, 17, 18, 19	13	tr: reed or rod	

3. Area

acre (A) צֶמֶד (ṣemedh) 1 Sam. 14:14 (AV: yoke) Is. 5:10	2	tr: acre	
furrow's length מַעֲנָה (ma'anāh) (AV: acre (B)) 1 Sam. 14:14	1	tr: length of a furrow	

4. Cubic Contents

kab קַב (qabh) (AV: cab) 2 Kin. 6:25	1	tr: pint, or half a liter, or tlt: kab	
omer עֹמֶר ('ōmer) Ex. 16:16, 18, 22, 32 (ARV: omerful), 33 (ARV: omerful), 36	6	tlt: omer	
tenth part עִשָּׂרוֹן ('issārōn) (AV: tenth deal) Ex. 29:40 etc.; see p. 22	31	tr: a tenth	
measure (A) סְאָה (s'āh) Gen. 18:6; 1 Sam. 25:18; 1 Kin. 18:32; 2 Kin. 7:1, 16, 18 (twice each here)	9	tr: measure, or tlt: seah or saton	
measure (B) שָׁלִישׁ (šālīš) Is. 40:12	1	tr: measure, or tlt. or tr: seah	
measure (C) אֵיפָה ('ēphāh) Deut. 25:14(2),15; Prov. 20:10(2); Mic. 6:10	6	tr: measure	
measure (D) כֹּר (kōr) 1 Kin. 4:22 (2); 5:11 (2); 2 Chr. 2:10 (2); 27:5	7	tr: measure	

5 Suggested Marginal Notes (if any)	6 Equations with Other Terms, and with Current Standards	7 Remarks
On Ezek. 40:3: Heb. kaneh, equal to six cubits of seven handbreadths each	6 long cubits, each cubit 7 handbreadths About 3 meters, or 10 ft.	If natural reeds are locally known and used to measure with, use word for reed. If not, then use a word for a rod or stick of about 10 ft. length.

On Is. 5:10: Heb. tsemed, a yoke. See 1 Sam. 14:14 On 1 Sam. 14:14: Heb. tsemed, a yoke		Compare Roman area jugerum, from Lat. jugum, a yoke. In 1 Sam. 14:14 it is a different word that is rendered in AV "acre"; see below.
On 1 Sam. 14:14: Comp. Ps. 129:3		If the ARV text is followed, this word is not a measure of area but of distance. If the margin (and AV) is followed, then the above word tsemed follows and explains it. (Consult commentaries.)

On 2 Kin. 6:25: The Heb. kab was equal to about 2 quarts, or 2 liters	⅙ seah; 1/18 ephah About 2 lit., or 2 qts.	Of course, if pint is used, the preceding words the fourth part of must be omitted; also the marginal note.
On Ex. 16:16: The Heb. omer was equal to nearly four liters, or half a peck	1/10 ephah (Ex. 16:36) About 3.7 lit., or 7 pts.	If there should be a local measure approximating this size, better use its name than tlt. omer.
On Ex. 29:40: That is, of an ephah. See note on ch. 16:16	1 omer; 1/10 ephah C. 3.7 lit., or 7 pts.	The phrase of an ephah may be introduced into the text (see Intr., par. 9), or a ref. in the margin to note on Ex. 29:40, at any of the remaining occurrences where it seems needed.
On Gen. 18:6: The Heb. seah was about 13 liters, or a peck and a half	⅓ ephah About 13 lit., or 1½ pecks	If no local measure approximates, then seah, or its N.T. equivalent saton, may be tlt.
On Is. 40:12: That is, a container for measuring meal holding a "third" (of an ephah), i.e., a seah	⅓ ephah About 13 lit., or 1½ pecks	If there is such local measure of cubic contents as suits seah, use it for this also. If not, seah must be tlt. The passage calls for an insignificant measure; comp. on span.

1 Term ARV	2 No. of Occurrences	3 Suggested Renderings Text	4 Renderings Adopted by Translators
measure (E) מְשׂוּרָה (mᵉsūrāh) Ezek. 4:11, 16	2	tr: by the cupful	
large measure שָׁלִישׁ (šālīš) (AV: great measure) Ps. 80:5	1	tr: by the gallon	
ephah אֵיפָה ('ēphāh) See measure (C) Ex. 16:36; for all refs. see p. 23	34	Deut. 25:14, 15; Prov. 20:10; Mic. 6:10: tr: measure Elsewhere tlt: ephah	
homer חֹמֶר (ḥōmer) Lev. 27:16; Num. 11:32; Is. 5:10; Ezek. 45:11 (3), 13 (2), 14 (2); Hos. 3:2	11	tlt: homer	
half-homer לֶתֶךְ (lethekh) (AV: half homer) Hos. 3:2	1	tr: half; tlt: homer	
log לֹג (lōgh) Lev. 14:10–24	5	tlt: log	
hin הִין (hīn) Ex. 29:40; for other refs. see p. 23	22	tlt: hin	
bath בַּת (bath) 1 Kin. 7:26, 38; 2 Chr. 2:10 (2); 4:5; Ezr. 7:22 (2); Is. 5:10; Ezek. 45:10, 11 (2), 14 (4)	15	tlt: bath	
cor כֹּר (kōr) See measure (D) Ezek. 45:14	1	tlt: kor	
hour שָׁעָה (šā'āh) The same hour: Dan. 3:6, 15; 4:33; 5:5 for a while: Dan. 4:19 (AV, the same hour)	5	tr. as in ARV	

5 Suggested Marginal Notes (if any)	6 Equations with Other Terms, and with Current Standards	7 Remarks
		Any measure expressing a pitiful dole.
Literally a "third" (of a bath)	⅓ bath	Here the figure is hyperbole. Render by a familiar liquid measure too large to be taken literally.
On Deut. 25:15, Mic. 6:10: Heb. ephah On Deut. 25:14; Prov. 20:10: Heb. an ephah and an ephah On Ex. 16:36: About 37 liters, or a bushel	3 seahs; 1/10 homer; 1 bath (liquid) About 37 lit., or 1 bu.	On Amos 8:5; Zech. 5:6, and elsewhere as desired, a footnote may refer to the note on Ex. 16:36.
On Lev. 27:16: About 370 liters, or over 10 bushels	10 ephahs; 1 cor (sometimes liquid) About 370 lit., or 10 bu. 5 qts.	On Num. 11:32; Is. 5:10; Hos. 3:2, and elsewhere as desired, a footnote may refer to the note on Lev. 27:16. The homer, like the cor, was also used for liquids (Ezek. 45:11, 14).
On Hos. 3:2: Heb. lethek	½ homer; ½ kor About 185 lit., or 5 bu. 5 pts.	
On Lev. 14:10: About half a liter, or nearly one pint	1/12 hin About ½ lit., or nearly 1 pt.	
On Ex. 29:40: A little more than six liters, or nearly a gallon and a half	⅙ bath A little over 6 lit., or nearly 1½ gals.	On Lev. 19:36; Num. 15:4; Ezek. 4:11; 45:24, and elsewhere as desired, a footnote may refer to the note on Ex. 29:40.
On 1 Kin. 7:26: About 37 liters, or a little over 8 gallons. See Ezek. 45:11	6 hins; 1 ephah (dry); 1/10 kor (sometimes dry) or 1/10 homer (dry) About 37 lit., or a little over 8 gals.	On Is. 5:10, and elsewhere as desired, a footnote may refer to the note on 1 Kin. 7:26.
On 1 Kin. 5:11: 370 liters, or over 80 gallons (liquid measure), or 10 bushels (dry measure)	10 baths; 10 ephahs; 1 homer (dry) 370 lit., or over 80 gals. (liquid) or 10 bu. 5 qts. (dry)	On any of the remaining occurrences, if desired a footnote may refer to the note on 1 Kin. 5:11.
	An indefinite but short space of time	This word occurs only in the Aramaic parts of Daniel; it is not Hebrew.

5. Time

1 Term ARV	2 No. of Occurrences	3 Suggested Renderings Text	4 Renderings Adopted by Translator
watch אַשְׁמֹרֶת ('ašmōreth) Ex. 14:24, Judg. 7:19 1 Sam. 11:11	3	In Ps. 63:6; 119:148: tr: watch of the night; elsewhere tr: watch	
אַשְׁמוּרָה ('ašmūrāh) Ps. 63:6; 90:4; 119:148; Lam. 2:19 (night-watch: Ps. 63:6; 119:148; AV: *night* watch)	4		
day יוֹם (yōm) Gen. 1:5, etc.	very often	tr: day	
week שָׁבוּעַ (šābhūa')	25	tr: week	
month יָרֵחַ (yārēaḥ) Ex. 2:2; Deut. 21:13; 1 Kin. 6:37, 38; 8:2; 2 Kin. 15:13; Ezr. 6:15; Job 3:6; 7:3; 29:2; 39:2; Dan. 4:29; Zech. 11:8	13	tr: month	
חֹדֶשׁ (ḥōdheš)	very often		
year שָׁנָה (šānāh)	very often	tr: year	

6. General

Lev. 19:35. Literally "Ye shall not do unrighteousness in judgment, in length (מִדָּה, middāh), in weight (מִשְׁקָל, mišqāl), and in measure (מְשׂוּרָה, mᵉsūrāh)"; ARV: . . "in measures of length, of weight or of quantity." So render or use verb forms, such as "in measuring and weighing."

See also 1 Chr. 23:29: "for all manner of measure (mᵉsūrāh) and size."

5 Suggested Marginal Notes (If any)	6 Equations with Other Terms, and with Current Standards	7 Remarks
	First, middle and last third of the night, the length varying with the time of year	The Hebrews had three night watches (see Lam. 2:19; Judg. 7:19; and Ex. 14:24). If the language has no word for such periods, it may be necessary to paraphrase.
	24-hr. day Also, period of daylight	Discriminate, if the language has a different word for these two meanings. The Hebrew *day* was reckoned from evening to evening, e.g., Gen. 1:5; Dan. 8:14. See note below.
	7-day period	If the language lacks a word for this, borrow *week*, or the equivalent in some other language giving cultural background, or tlt. Heb. word in some such form as *shabu*. Avoid making it resemble the totally different root *shabbath*.
	One lunar cycle, from new moon to new moon	If the language has but one word for *moon* and *month*, be careful of the phrase chosen for *new moon day*.
	One solar cycle, consisting of 12 lunar months to which a 13th was added at intervals to make the lunar year agree with the solar	New year reckoned from the autumnal equinox, was celebrated at the first new moon thereafter (Tishri). The religious year began with Nisan (Ex. 12:2).

Note: Words and phrases denoting times of the day, as translated in the ARV, are as follows:

the eyelids of the morning (Job 3:9)   the rising of the morning   the dawning of the day
the dawning of the morning   when the morning arose   the spring of the day   dayspring
at break of day

Various phrases referring to the rising of the sun. (N.B. *from the rising of the sun to the going down thereof* is not a reference to time, but to space or direction, as, *from east to west.* So also *toward the sun rising.*)

morning
by the time the sun is hot   until the heat of the day
noon   noontide   noonday   midday
until the day declineth (AV afternoon; Judg. 19:8)
twilight   when the gates . . . began to be dark   when it was dark
evening   at even (eventide, AV)   evening time

Various phrases referring to the *setting* or *going down of the sun*
night   midnight   the dark

(15)

B. In the New

1. Weights, Money, Coins

1 Term ARV	2 No. of Occurrences	3 Suggested Renderings Text	4 Renderings Adopted by Translator
mite λεπτόν (lepton) Mark 12:42; Luke 12:59; 21:2	3	tr: mite	
farthing κοδράντης (kodrantēs) Matt. 5:26; Mark 12:42	2	tr: farthing	
penny ἀσσάριον (assarion) (AV: farthing) Matt. 10:29; Luke 12:6	2	tr: penny	
piece of silver (B) δραχμή (drachmē) (twice piece only); Luke 15:8 (2), 9	3	tr: silver coin	
shilling δηνάριον (dēnarion) (Matt. 22:19; Mark 12:15; Luke 20:24—ARV: denarius) Matt. 18:28; 20:2, 9, 10, 13; Mark 6:37; 14:5; Luke 7:41; 10:35; John 6:7; 12:5; Rev. 6:6 (2). (AV: always penny, pence)	16	tr: shilling, or use local equivalent, or tlt: denarion	
half-shekel δίδραχμον (didrachmon) (AV:tribute money, tribute); Matt 17:24 (2)	2	tr: half, tlt: shekel	
shekel, στατήρ (statēr) (AV: piece of money) Matt. 17:27	1	tlt: shekel	
piece of silver (A) ἀργύριον (argurion) (AV: Matt. 27:6, silver piece, Acts 19:19, piece of silver) Matt. 26:15; 27:3, 5, 6, 9; Acts 19:19	6	tlt: shekel, or tr: piece of silver	
pound (A) μνᾶ (mna) Luke 19:13–25	9	tr: pound, or use local equivalent, or tlt: mna	

Testament

5 Suggested Marginal Notes (if any)	6 Equations with Other Terms, and with Current Standards	7 Remarks
Gr. *lepton*, the smallest copper coin	½ farthing About 1½ grams, or 23 grains, of copper, coined	The rendering of *lepton* and *kodrantes* hinges on the translation of Mark 12:42, where 2 *lepta* make one *kodrantes*. *Lepton* should be the smallest copper coin in use and *kodrantes* double that value.
Gr. *kodrantes*, a Roman copper coin	¼ assarion About 3 grams, or 40–50 grains, of copper, coined	
Gr. *assarion*, a Roman copper coin of various values	1 as; 1/16 denarius. Also 1/24 drachma; 1/32 denarius	*Assarion* should be still larger. If such a relationship cannot be substantially preserved, transliteration of one or more of the terms may be required.
Gr. *drachme*, a local silver coin worth one quarter of a shekel. See note on Matt. 26:15	¼ shekel About 3.64 grams, or 56 grains, of silver, coined	If a small silver coin is known locally, esp. if used by women as an ornament, its name may be used. Otherwise tr. *silver coin* but drop the word *silver* in second and third occurrences.
Gr. *denarion*, a Roman silver coin, worth a little more than a drachma	4 Roman assaria 1 drachma (roughly). Up to nearly 4 grams, or 60 grains, of silver, coined	In order to keep this distinct from the drachma and shekel, the use of *shilling* or its equivalent is recommended, as a coin more or less foreign. Footnote on the first 3 passages given in col. 1, and any others desired.
Gr. *didrachmon*, a coin worth half a shekel, the amount of the temple poll-tax. See Ex. 38:26	2 drachmas; ½ shekel (O.T. *beka*) About 7.27 grams, or 112 grains, of silver, coined	
Gr. *stater*, a silver coin worth four drachmas. See note on 26:15	4 drachmas About 14.55 grams, or 224 grains, of silver, coined	Same as O.T. shekel.
Gr. *argurion*, a silver coin worth four drachmas, of about 14½ grams, or half an ounce weight	4 drachmas About 14.55 grams, or 224 grains, of silver, coined Heavy shekel of O.T., or Greek stater	Put footnote, if anywhere, at Matt. 26:15 and Acts 19:19. These *pieces of silver* were worth four times as much as the *piece of silver* in Luke 15:8.
Gr. *mna*, worth a hundred drachmas, or 25 shekels. See note on Matt. 26:15	25 shekels; 100 drachmas. (O.T. silver maneh) 363.7 grams, or 5,615 grains, of silver	If pound sterling or no approximately equivalent value is available, tlt: *maneh* or *mina*.

(17)

1 Term ARV	2 No. of Occurrences	3 Suggested Renderings Text	4 Renderings Adopted by Translator
pound (B) λίτρα (litra) John 12:3, 19:39	2	tr: pound (as a weight), or use a local equivalent, or tlt: litra or libra	
talent πάλαντον (talanton) Matt. 18:24; 25:15-28	15	tlt: talent	

2. Lengths and Distances

cubit (A) πῆχυς (pēchus) Matt. 6:27; Luke 12:25; John 21:8; Rev. 21:17	4	tr: cubit	
fathom ὀργυιά (orguia) Acts 27:28 (2)	2	tr: fathom	
reed κάλαμος (kalamos) Rev. 11:1; 21:15, 16	3	tr: reed	
furlong στάδιον (stadion) Luke 24:13; John 6:19; 11:18; Rev. 14:20; 21:16	5	tr: or tlt: stadia (plur.)	
mile μίλιον (milion) Matt. 5:41	1	tr: or tlt: milion	
sabbath day's journey σαββάτου ὁδός (sabbatou hodos) Acts 1:12	1	tr. as a phrase	

3. Cubic Contents

measure (F) χοῖνιξ (choinix) Rev. 6:6 (2)	2	tr: or tlt: quart or liter	
measure (A) σάτον (saton) Matt. 13:33; Luke 13:21	2	tr: measure, or tlt: seah or saton	

(18)

5 Suggested Marginal Notes (if any)	6 Equations with Other Terms, and with Current Standards	7 Remarks
Gr. *litra*, a Roman weight for merchandise, over three quarters of a (Br.-Amer.) pound	1/25 of heavy talent About 349 grams, or, 5,376 grains, weight of merchandise	If the pound weight ar its equivalent is not locally available, then tlt: *litra* or *libra*. Avoid confusion with metric "liter."
The silver talent was of the value of sixty pounds or minas	3,000 light shekels 60 minas 21,820 grams, or 336,000 grains of silver	The footnote may appear at Matt. 18:24. Elsewhere, as desired, a note may refer back to the note on Matt. 18:24.

On John 21:8; Rev. 21:17: Gr. *pechus*, about 46 cm., or 17½ in. On Matt. 6:27; Luke 12:25: no footnote	See on O.T. *cubit* 44.64 cm., or 17.58 in.	
Gr. *orguia*, a measure of depth of about 6 ft. or nearly two meters	4 cubits About 1.78 m. or 5 ft., 10 in.	If the language has no equivalent, either tr. or borrow *meter* or *yard* giving *double* the figures used in Acts 27:28, or borrow *fathom*.
Gr. *kalamos*, a measure of about 3 meters, or ten ft.	See on O.T. *reed* About 3 m., or 10 ft. 3 in.	See on O.T. *reed*. But note Rev. 11:1 requires both *reed* and *rod*.
On Luke 24:13: a Greek measure equalling about 178 meters, or 194 yards	400 cubits 600 Greek ft. About 178 m. or 194 yds.	In the other occurrences a footnote may, if desired, refer to the note on Luke 24:13. If the language has an equivalent term, use it.
	5,000 Roman ft., or 1,000 double paces About 1,480 m., or 1,618 yds.	If the mile is unknown, any approximately similar distance may be used.
That is, the distance of nearly one kilometer, or a thousand yards	2,000 cubits About 890 m., or 970 yds.	

Gr. *choinix*, a little less than a liter, or quart, implying great scarcity	About 1 lit., or 1 qt.	
Gr. *saton*, the Heb. *seah*, a measure containing about 13 liters, or a peck and a half	⅛ of an ephah About 13 lit., or 1½ pks.	If no local measure approximates, then *seah* or *saton* may be tlt.

1 Term ARV	2 No. of Occurrences	3 Suggested Renderings Text	4 Renderings Adopted by Translator
measure (G) μόδιος (modios) Matt. 5:15; Mark 4:21; Luke 11:33	3	tr: measure	
measure (C) βάτος (batos) Luke 16:6	1	tlt: bath	
measure (D) κόρος (koros) Luke 16:7	1	tlt: kor	
firkin μετρητής (metrētēs) John 2:6	1	tr: measure	

4. Time

hour ὥρα (hōra) Matt. 8:13, etc.	very often	tr: hour or tlt: hora	
the space of half an hour ἡμίωρον (hēmiōron) Rev. 8:1	1	tr: for half an hour	
watch φυλακή (phulakē) Matt. 14:25; 24:43; Mark 6:48; Luke 2:8; 12:38	5	Matt. 24:43; Luke 12:38: tr: watch of the night Elsewhere: tr: watch	
day ἡμέρα (hēmera)	very often	tr: day	
week σάββατον (sabbaton), or σάββατα (sabbata) Matt. 28:1; Mark 16:2, 9; Luke 18:12; 24:1; John 20:1, 19; Acts 20:7; 1 Cor. 16:2	9	tr: week	
month μήν (mēn) Luke 1:24, etc.	18	tr: month	
year ἔτος (etos) or Matt. 9:20, etc. ἐνιαυτός (eniautos) Luke 9:14, etc.	47 14	tr: year	

5 Suggested Marginal Notes (if any)	6 Equations with Other Terms, and with Current Standards	7 Remarks
Gr. *modios*, a measure containing a *seah*, or *saton*. See note on Matt. 13:33	⅛ of an ephah About 13 lit., or 1½ pks.	As the reference in every occurrence is to the container as such, and not to the contents, a word meaning such container should be used.
A Heb. measure of about 37 liters, or over 8 gallons	1 ephah (dry) About 37 lit., or 1 bu.	See note on 1 Kin. 7:26.
A Heb. measure of about 370 liters, or over 10 bushels	10 ephahs (dry)	See note on 1 Kin. 5:11.
Gr. *metretes*, a liquid measure of about 40 liters, or 9 gallons	"Working equivalent of the ephah-bath" About 40 lit., or 9 gals.	A slightly larger quantity than the Heb. *bath*.

		See supplement page 30.
	Four quarters of the night, their length varying with the seasons	The Romans had four night watches. If the language has no name for approximately the same, then paraphrase.
	24-hour day Also, period of daylight	In New Testament times the day from sunrise to sunset was divided into twelve hours (John 11:9); the night likewise from sunset to sunrise (Acts 23:23). See note on page 22.
	week	See col. 7 on O.T. *week*.
	The lunar cycle, from new moon to new moon	
	The solar cycle	

Note: See note on next page.

Note: Words or phrases denoting times of the day are translated in the ARV
      as follows:

    until the day dawn   at early dawn   as it began to dawn
    when the morning was come   at the cock-crowing
    when it was day   dayspring   till break of day
    at the rising of the sun   when the sun was up
    morning   early in the morning
    midday   noon
    when the day was far spent   the day began to wear away
    toward evening
    even   evening   eventide   when (the) even was come
    at even, when the sun did set (was setting)
    night   it was now dark
    midnight   early, when it was yet dark

References Not Specified in the Preceding Table

Numbers in ( ) are the number of occurrences within the chapter or verse.

shekel

The 88 occurrences in the original are:

Gen. 23 (2)	2 Kin. 7 (6); 15:20
Ex. 21:32; 30 (6); 38 (7)	1 Chr. 21:25
Lev. 5:15 (2), 27 (12)	2 Chr. 3:9
Num. 3 (4); 7 (26); 18 (2); 31:52	Neh. 5:15; 10:32
Josh. 7 (2)	Jer. 32:9
1 Sam. 9:8; 17:5, 7	Ezek. 4:10; 45 (4)
2 Sam. 14:26; 24:24	Amos. 8:5

In addition the word occurs, in italics, in both ARV and AV 12 times,
viz. Ex. 30:23; 38:28; Num. 3:50; Deut. 22:19, 29; Judg. 8:26; 2 Sam.
21:16; 1 Kin. 10:16, 29; 2 Chr. 1:17; 9:15, 16. In the AV there are 8
additional occurrences, viz. Ex. 30:23 (two); Judg. 17:2, 3, 4, 10;
2 Sam. 18:11, 12.

silver (keseph)

The 22 occurrences in the original are:

Gen. 20:16; 37:28; 45:22	2 Chr. 1:17
Deut. 22:19, 29	S. of S. 8:11
Judg. 9:4; 16:5, 17 (4)	Is. 7:23
2 Sam. 18 (2)	Hos. 3:2
1 Kin. 10:29	Zech. 11 (2).
2 Kin. 6 (2)	

Except for Is. 7:23, rendered by *silverling*, everywhere either *piece of silver*
or *shekel of silver* occurs (with *piece* and *shekel* in italics, except in
Gen. 20:16; 37:28; 45:22 in ARV, where by error *piece* is in roman),
as follows: *shekel of silver* in Deut. 22:19, 29; 1 Kin. 10:29; 2 Chr. 1:17
in both ARV and AV, and in Judg. 17 (4) and 2 Sam. 18 (2) in the AV
besides; and *pieces of silver* everywhere else.

talent (kikkar)

Ex. 25:39; 37:24; 38 (6)	1 Chr. 19:6; 20:2; 22:14 (2),
2 Sam. 12:30	29 (4)
1 Kin. 9 (2); 10 (2); 16:24; 20:39	2 Chr. 3:8; 8:18; 9:9, 13; 25 (2);
2 Kin. 5 (4); 15:19; 18:14 (2);	27:5; 36 (2)
23:33 (2)	Ezr. 7:22 (Aram.); 8:26 (3)
	Est. 3:9

cubit (ammah)

Gen. 6 (4); 7:20
Ex. 25 (8); 26 (8); 27 (11); 30 (3); 36 (6); 37 (11); 38 (11)
Num. 11:31; 35 (5)
Deut. 3 (3)
Josh. 3:4
1 Sam. 17:4
1 Kin. 6 (20); 7 (23)
2 Kin. 14:13; 25:17 (2)
1 Chr. 11:23

2 Chr. 3 (14); 4 (7); 6:13 (2); 25:23
Ezr. 6:3 (2)
Neh. 3:13
Est. 5:14; 7:9
Jer. 52:21 (2), 22
Ezek. 40 (40); 41 (26); 42 (8); 43 (13); 45:2; 46:22; 47:3
Dan. 3:1 (2)
Zech. 5:2 (2)

tenth part (issaron)

Ex. 29:40
Lev. 14 (2); 23 (2); 24:5

Num. 15 (3); 28 (11); 29 (11)

In the first 11 occurrences ARV adds in italics *of an ephah*. AV never adds. In the four passages where AV reads *a several tenth deal* (Num. 28:13, 21; 29:10, 15), the original repeats *issaron*; this is ignored by ARV.

ephah

Ex. 16:36
Lev. 5:11; 6:20; 19:36
Num. 5:15; 28:5
Deut. 25:14 (2), 15
Judg. 6:19
Ruth 2:17
1 Sam. 1:24; 17:17

Prov. 20:10 (2)
Isa. 5:10
Ezek. 45 (8); 46 (9)
Amos 8:5
Mic. 6:10
Zech. 5 (5)

From "*measure* (C)," p. 10, it will be seen that ARV and AV render *ephah* as measure or *diverse* (AV *divers*) measures in Deut. 25:14, 15; Prov. 20:10 and Micah 6:10.

hin

Ex. 29:40 (2); 30:24
Lev. 19:36; 23:13

Num. 15 (6); 28 (5)
Ezek. 4:11; 45:24; 46 (4)

Illustrations of Translators' Practices

A S illustrations of translators' practices the table which follows shows the general procedure in the case of a number of translations. On page 28 are some specific instances giving the actual transliterations or meanings of translations that have been adopted by recent translators.

It should be understood that these illustrations do not necessarily carry the recommendation of the Society, but are entered here solely as information.

The languages and versions examined are as follows, the date given being either that of the translator or of the edition used. The practices of translators are indicated only in the case of the reference given.

1 Latin Vulgate, Bagster, 1933
2 French, Segond, 1928
3 French, Synodale, 1929
4 Italian, Revised, 1927
5 Spanish, Valera Revised, 1928
6 Spanish, Hispano-Americana, 1923
7 Portuguese, Brasiliera, 1924
8 Arabic, Van Dyck, 1931
9 Modern Greek, 1925
10 German, Luther, 1939
11 German, Menge, 1931

12 Dutch, States General, NBS, 1918
13 Dutch, NBS, N.T., 1940
14 Danish, DBS, 1931 (N.T., 1907)
15 Norwegian, 1930 Rev.
16 Swedish, 1917 Rev.
17 Ganda, 1899 (N.T., 1925)
18 Kongo: Buende, 1933
19 Hausa, 1932
20 Swahili (Zanzibar), 1937
21 Venda, 1936
22 Malinké, N.T., 1942
23 Luba-Lulua, 1941 (Rev. N.T.)

24 Mongo-Nkundu, 1930
25 Fiji, 1902 (1906; N.T., 1931)
26 Hawaiian, 1929
27 Tagalog, 1933
28 Panayan, Rev. N.T., 1941 MS
29 Japanese (Rom.), N.T., 1923
30 Javanese, N.T. parts
31 Siamese, N.T., Rev. 1930
32 Mam, N.T., 1939
33 Quechua, N.T., 1943 MS

A. In the Old Testament

1. Weights, Money, Coins

gerah	Ex. 30:13	Transliterated from the Hebrew (tlt.) by all except 1, 5, 7, 21, which translate (tr.).
beka	Ex. 38:26	Tlt. by all except 1, 2, 5, 8, 10, which tr.
shekel	Gen. 23:15	Tlt. by all except 10, 20 and 21, which tr. 11 and 27 add notes.
piece of silver	Gen. 20:16	Tr. by all except 18 and 25, which tlt. *keseph.*
piece of money	Gen. 33:19	Tr. by most. Tlt. by 2, 8, 14, 15, 16, and 19, e.g. French *kesita.* 2, 5 and 15 add notes.
piece	1 Sam. 2:36	Tr. by all except 11, which paraphrases.
pieces	Psa. 68:30	Tr. by all except 1, 10, 11, which paraphrase, 11 adding a note.
maneh	Ezek. 45:12	Tlt. by all except 12, 14, which tr.
pound	1 Ki. 10:17	Tlt. by all from *maneh* except 5, 7, 10, 12, 14, 17, 19, 21, 25, 26, which tr 17 borrows from French. 11 adds a note.
darics	Ezr. 2:69	Tlt. from Greek *drachma* by 5, 9, 12, 14, 18. From *daric* by 2, 3, 4, 7, 11, 15, 16, 17, 19, 20, 27. From *dram* by 25, 26. Tr. by 1, 8, 10, 21.
talent	Ex. 25:39	Tlt. from the Greek *talanton* by all except 8, 10, 20, which tr.

2. Lengths and Distances

finger	Jer. 52:21	Tr. by all.
handbreadth	1 Ki. 7:26	Tr. by all.
span	Ezek. 43:13	Tr. by all except 25, which borrows from English, and 15 and 16 which paraphrase. 11 adds a note.
cubit (A)	Gen. 6:15	Tr. by all except 25, 26, which borrow from English. 11 adds a note.
cubit (B)	Judg. 3:16	Tr. by all except 14, which tlt. as *gomed* with a note, and 25 and 26, which borrow from English *cubit*.
reed	Ezek. 40:3	Tr. by all.

3. Area

acre	1 Sam. 14:14	Paraphrased by 1, 2, 3, 4, 5, 7, 9, 11, 15, and 16. Tr. by 8, 10, 12, 14, 17, 18, 20, 25, 27. 19 and 26 borrow from English *acre*, and 21 borrows from Dutch.
furrow's length	1 Sam. 14:14	As above except that 14 paraphrases, 19 and 21 tr., and 27 borrows *acre*.

4. Cubic contents

kab	2 Ki. 6:25	Tlt. by all except 11, 20, 21, 25 and 27. 14 adds a note.
omer	Ex. 16:16	Tlt. by all except 20 and 21. 3 adds a note.
tenth part	Ex. 29:40	Tr. by all except 25, which paraphrases. 15 adds a note.
measure (A)	Gen. 18:6	Tr. by all except 1, 16, 19, 26. 1, 19 and 26 tlt. from Greek *saton*. 16 renders as "seah-measure" and 11 adds a note.
measure (B)	Is. 40:12	Tr. by all except 1, 5, 14, which paraphrase.
measure (C)	Dt. 25:14	Tr. by 1, 4, 8, 9, 10, 11, 17, 19, 20, 21, 25, 26, 27. Tlt. from *ephah* by 2, 3, 5, 7, 12, 14, 15, 16, 18. 3 adds a note.
measure (D)	1 Ki. 5:11	Tlt. from *kor* by all except 17, 21, 25 and 27, which tr. 11 and 20 add a note.
measure (E)	Lev. 19:35	Tr. by all.
large measure	Psa. 80:5	Tr. by all except 3, 9, 11, which paraphrase.
ephah	Ex. 16:36	Tlt. by all except 20 and 21, which tr.
homer	Hos. 3:2	Tlt. by all except 1, 10, 11 and 20, which tr.
half-homer	Hos. 3:2	Tlt. from *lethekh* by 2, 4, 7, 8, 14, 15 and 16. Tr. by all others.
log	Lev. 14:10	Tlt. by all except 1, 17, 20, 21, 25, which tr. 3, 4, 11, 15, 27 add a note.
hin	Ex. 29:40	Tlt. by all except 20, 21, 25, which tr. 11 adds a note.
bath	1 Ki. 7:26	Tlt. by all except 17, 21, 25, which tr. 3, 11, 20 add a note.
cor	Ezek. 45:14	Tlt. by all except 20 and 25, which tr. 3 and 15 add a note.

5. Time

hour	Dan. 4:33	Tr. by all except 26 and 27, which borrow from Spanish or English.
watch	Ex. 14:24	Tr. by all.
	Psa. 63:6	Tr. by all but 1, 10, 11, which paraphrase, and 26, which seems to borrow from English.
day	Gen. 1:5	Tr. by all.
week	Jer. 5:24	Tr. by all except 1, 10, 17, 26, which tlt. from Greek *sabbaton*.
month	Ex. 2:2	Tr. by all.
	Gen. 7:11	Tr. by all.
year	Gen. 5:3	Tr. by all.

B. In the New Testament

1. Weights, Money, Coins

mite	Mk. 12:42	Tr. by all except 26, 27, 28, 29, which tlt. *lepton* from Greek. 2 adds a note.
farthing	Mk. 12:42	Tr. by all except 1, 6, 7, 17, 32 and 33, which tlt. *kodrantes*; and 22, which borrows from French. 2, 4, 6 add a note.
penny	Mt. 10:29	Tr. by all but 1, 7, 26 which tlt. *as* or *assarion*, and 17 and 22, which borrow from French; 19 and 21 from English; 11 paraphrases. 4, 7 and 16 add notes.
piece of silver	Lk. 15:8	1-7, 14 and 28 tlt. *drachma*; 20 and 21 borrow *shilling*; 24 borrows from French; 33 combines tr. and tlt.; all others tr.
shilling *(denarius)*	Mt. 20:9	Tlt. from *denarion* by all except the following: 8, 10, 12, 13, 15, 16, 19 and 31, which tr.; 20, 21, 24, 25, which borrow from French or English. 7 and 23 add a note. 33 combines.
half shekel	Mt. 17:24	Tr. by all except 1-7, 12, 17, 28, 30, which tlt. from Greek *didrachmon*; 11, 14, 15, 16 paraphrase; 32 and 33 combine tr. and tlt.
shekel	Mt. 17:27	Tlt. from *stater* by all except 11, 13, 16, 20, 21, 22, 24, 25, 26, 27, 29, 31 and 33, which tr.; and 18, 19 and 23, which borrow *shekel*. 2, 3, 4, 6, 7, 11, 16 and 29 add a note.
piece of silver(A)	Mt. 26:15	Tr. by all except 25, 26, and 30, which borrow *shekel*. 3, 4 and 29 add a note.
pound (A)	Lk. 19:13	Tlt. from *mna* (e.g., *mina*) by all except 10, 12, 17, 19, 20, 21, 23, 25, 26, 31 and 32. 19, 21, 25, 26 borrow *pound*; 20 borrows *shilling*; others tr. 2, 4, 6, 11, 14, 16, 22, 23, 29 add a note.
pound (B)	Jn. 12:3	Tr. by all except 17, 22-27, 32, which borrow from English, Spanish, or French. 18 adds a note.
talent	Mt. 18:24	Tlt. by all except 8, 10, 16, 20, 31, which tr. 2, 3, 4, 6, 7, 11, 14, 16, 23 and 28 add a note.

(26)

2. Lengths and Distances

cubit	Mt. 6:27	Tr. by all except 23, which borrows *cubit*, and 24, *metres*. 6 and 29 add a note.
fathom	Acts 27:28	Tr. by all.
reed	Rev. 11:1	Tr. by all except 1, which tlt. *calamus*.
furlong	Lk. 24:13	Tlt. from *stadion* by all except 8, 10, 19, 20, 22-25, 29, 31 and 33. Tr. by 8, 10, 20, 29, 31 and 33. 19 and 25 borrow from English and 22, 23, 24 from French. 2, 4, 7, 11 and 14 add a note.
mile	Mt. 5:41	Tlt. by all but 17, 20, 22, 28, 29, 30 and 31, which tr.; 19, 25 and 26, which borrow from English; 18, 23 and 24 from French. 1 and 7 combine tlt. and tr. 2 and 3 add a note.
sabbath day's journey	Acts 1:12	Tr. by 1, 2, 3, 10, 11, 18, 20, 23, 25, 28, 29, and 31 All the rest combine tlt. and tr. 2, 3, 4, 6 and 29 add a note.

3. Cubic Contents

measure (F)	Rev. 6:6	Tr. by all except 4, 7 and 32; 4 and 7 tlt. *choinix*, 32 borrows from Spanish. 2, 4, 6, and 7 add a note.
measure (A)	Mt. 13:33	Tr. by all except 1, 4, 17 and 26, which tlt. *saton*, and 24, which borrows from French. 7 and 16 add a note.
measure (G)	Mt. 5:15	Tr. by all. 7 adds a note.
measure (C)	Lk. 16:6	Tr. by all except 4, 6, 8, 18 and 26, which tlt. *batos*, and 32, which borrows from Spanish. 2, 4, 6, 16 add a note.
measure (D)	Lk. 16:7	Tr. by all except 1, 4, 5, 6, 7, 8 and 32, which tlt. *koros*, and 26, which renders *homer*.
firkin	Jn. 2:6	Tr. by all except 1, 7, 8, 12, 18, 28 and 30, which tlt. *metretes*; and 23 and 24, which use a French measure. 4, 7, 11 add a note.

4. Time

hour	Mt. 8:13	Tr. by all except 24, 26, 27 and 32, which borrow from English, Spanish or French.
the space of half an hour	Rev. 8:1	Tr. by all except 24, 25, 26, 27 and 32, which borrow *hour* as above. 25 (Fiji) "afanaua"(!)
watch	Mt. 14:25	Tr. by all except 25 and 26, which borrow from English. 2, 3, 4 add a note.
week	Mt. 28:1	Tr. by all except 1, 11, 19, 21, 24, 26, which tlt. *sabbaton*; and 32, which borrows from Spanish. 11 paraphrases.
month	Lk. 1:24	Tr. by all.
year	Mt. 9:2	Tr. by all.
	Jn. 11:49	Tr. by all.

Illustrations of Solutions
Other than Normal Translation or Transliteration

The translations below are literal; in the case of some European languages the
meaning is given as of the time the translation was made.

I. In the Old Testament

gerah	Ex. 30:13	Spanish Valera, Portuguese Brasiliera, and the Vulgate transliterate *obolos* (an ancient Greek coin).
piece of silver	Gen. 20:16	Spanish Valera, Portuguese Brasiliera, Danish and Norwegian translate as *shekel of silver*.
piece of money	Gen. 33:19	The Vulgafe uses *agnis*, and Spanish Valera uses *corderas*, both words related to *amnon (lamb)*, the LXX reading. Most others translate as in English, while Luther uses *groschen* (a common German small coin).
darics	Ezr. 2:69	The Vulgate and Luther translate *gold pieces*.
talent	Ex. 25:39	Luther translates as *hundredweight*.
span	Ezek. 43:13	Fiji uses *afa kiupiti*, a sort of pidgin English transliteration of *half a cubit*.
cubit (A)	Gen. 6:15	Most borrow some form of *cubit*, which comes from a Latin word meaning *elbow*. The Germanic translations use a form of *elle*.
reed	Ezek. 40:5	Luther and Menge (German), Danish and Norwegian translate as *rod;* almost all the others as some form of reed.
acre furrow's length	1 Sam. 14:14	AV—a half acre of land, which a yoke of oxen might plow. ARV—half a furrow's length in an acre of land. Most of the European versions paraphrase, paralleling the AV. Luther and the Dutch States General version parallel the ARV. Some others transliterate *acre* from English.
watch		Most European languages have a suitable word; others paraphrase it.

	Ex. 14:24 1 Sam. 11:11	morning watch	Luba-Lulua—	about sunrise
	Ju. 7:19	beginning of the middle watch	" "	midnight
	Psa. 63:6 119:48	night watches	" "	night
			" "	—time-for-watchers part of night
	Psa. 90:4 Lam. 2:19	watches [night]	" "	—when watchers begin their work

II. In the New Testament

mite	Mk. 12:42	English usage contemporary with AV meant a small coin or sum of money. Many translate as *little monies*. Quechua uses *blanca qolqe*, *blanca* being an old Spanish small copper coin, (used in the Spanish texts), to which is added the general Quechua word for *money*. It renders similarly all the money terms below.
farthing	Mt. 5:26	English contemporary meaning: one fourth of a penny. Transliterated from *kodrantes* by Vulgate, Hispano-Americana Spanish Version, Brasiliera Portuguese and Modern Greek. Many translate by some equivalent to a quarter of a coin. The Siamese simply says *all that is owing*. Some use current French money.
penny	Mt. 10:29	English contemporary meaning: a common Anglo-Saxon coin equivalent to the European denarius. Now a twelfth of an English shilling. Translated often as some local small coin or transliterated from some current small coin.
half shekel	Mt. 17:24	Menge (German), Danish, Norwegian, Swedish, Malinké, Mongo-Nkundu and Siamese paraphrase as *Temple tax or tax*.
piece of silver	Mt. 26:15	Variously translated as *pieces of silver* or *silver money* or *money*.
cubit	Mt. 6:27	See Old Testament *cubit*. Malinké and Panayan translate as *measure of forearm* with the use of a local term; the Quechua uses a term equivalent to the measure of 2 hands; and Mongo-Nkundu transliterates a French equivalent. Conob, at Jn. 21:8, 200 cubits, uses *four cords*, a common local measure, here equalling 92 yards.
fathom	Acts 27:28	English contemporary meaning—space to which a man can extend his arms. Malinké, Luba-Lulua, Mongo-Nkundu and Panayan use a local measure equivalent to the span of two arms extended. Others use some local equivalent length. Quechua translates *twenty fathoms* as *120 measures of foot*.
sabbath day's journey	Acts 1:12	Most versions simply transliterate *sabbath* and translate *journey*. Siamese has *distance allowed to be travelled on the sabbath day*. Panayan has *as far as may be walked on the sabbath day*. Luba-Lulua follows the note in the Segond (French) Version: *journey of Jewish Sunday*.
measure (F)	Rev. 6:6	Siamese, Mongo, and Luba-Lulua use a general word for measure. Malinké uses a word meaning locally a measuring rod.

(29)

measure (A)	Mt. 13:33	Siamese and Luba-Lulua use a general word for measure; Mongo uses *kilos*, and Malinké a flour measure.
measure (G)	Mt. 5:15	Siamese uses a word meaning *bucket*; Mongo and Malinké, one meaning *basket*; Luba-Lulua, one meaning *chest* or *box*.
measure (C)	Lk. 16:6	Siamese uses *bucket*; Mongo a term meaning *pots*; Malinké a *gourd measure* and Luba-Lulua a general term.
measure (D)	Lk. 16:7	Siamese uses a word meaning *bag* or *sack*, Mongo and Malinké one meaning *basket*, and Luba-Lulua a general term for measure used for A, D and F above.
firkin	Jn. 2:6	Luba-Lulua and Mongo-Nkundu express the measure in litres. Panayan transliterates the Greek, because water-jar, already mentioned, holds about 12 to 15 gallons. Siamese uses the same *bucket* as was used in measure C and G above. Conob translates *two or three firkins* as *five or six jugs* (each holding about four gallons).

watch

See Old Testament section.

	Mt. 14:25	*in the fourth watch of the night*	
		Luba-Lulua	*about the fourth time when it was dawning*
		Quechua	*dawn period*
		Malinké	*cock-crowing time*
	Mt. 24:43	*watch*	Luba-Lulua *in the night*
	Lk. 2:8	*keeping watch*	Luba-Lulua *tending . . . in the night*
	12:38	*second watch*	Luba-Lulua *midnight, . . .*
		third "	*second cock-crow*

Divisions of the Day Illustrated

third hour (of the day)
Aymará: *about three hours after sunrise*
Conob: *when high now the sun*
Malinké: *morning hour nine*
Moré: lit. *sun ripen*
Ec. Quechua: *mid-morning*
Peruvian Quechua: *from sunrise three hours*

third hour (night)
Aymará: *at the third night hour*
Conob: *when warms itself the night*
Malinké: *night hour ninth*
Moré: *night early*

sixth hour
Aymará: *the sixth hour*
Ecuadorean and Peruvian Quechua, Moré and Conob: *at about midday*
Malinké: *sun-reach-me-above hour*

seventh hour
Aymará: *one hour after midday*
Moré: *when the sun breaks* (after its zenith)
Ec. Quechua: *shortly after midday*
Peru. Quechua: *round about midday*

(30)

ninth hour
  Conob: *when little inclined sun*
  Malinké: *evening hour third*
  Ec. Quechua: *mid-afternoon*
  Peru. Quechua: *second rest time after midday*

tenth hour
  Conob: *when beneath middle day*
  Malinké: *day hour tenth*
  Moré: *place cooling*
  Ec. Quechua: *shortly past midday*
  Peru. Quechua: *time when sun casts shadows*

eleventh hour
  Aymará: *about the hour of the setting of the sun*
  Conob: *when about to leave workers*
  Malinké: *evening hour fifth*
  Moré: *sun which wants to enter time*
  Ec. Quechua: *toward end of afternoon*
  Peru. Quechua: *when evening begins*

when the evening was come   Aymará: *at the entering in of the sun*
very early in the morning   Aymará: *at the very first light*

Native Aymará division of the day and night: *light, sunrise, midday, sunset, night*

Day begins in Conob when: *comes color to the base of heaven* (the east)

The Malinké native always says: *night and day,* never *day and night*

APPENDIX

THE ACTS

WORD CHECK LIST

This list of words has been prepared as an aid in checking consistency in the use of terms. It does not mean that necessarily the same Greek word must everywhere be translated by the same native word and no other, nor that an English word expressing a particular meaning of the Greek word must necessarily be translated everywhere by the same native word. Idioms are not the same in any two languages, and terms assumed to be equivalent sometimes have different meanings in different languages though the context may be the same. The list, however, will serve to assist in securing consistency in the use of terms when there is no reason for inconsistency, will check any inadvertent or unnecessary differences and will aid in attaining the standard of faithful translation, using idiomatic forms but avoiding paraphrase and endeavoring to be as literal as the idiom of the language will permit.

The list makes no pretence at completeness except for the words which it includes. Not every occurrence of a Greek term is stated under every head but all of those uses are given where a Greek word is translated by the English term under which it is classified.

AV	— Authorized Version (King James)
RV	— English and American Revised Versions (1885, 1901)
ERV	— English Revision, 1885
ARV	— American Standard Revised Version, 1901
W & H	— Westcott & Hort
TR	— Textus Receptus
N	— Nominative case

The occurrences of the Greek or English word standing at the head of a section are indicated by the repetition of the first and second letters of the words, e. g. under the head GOOD, " κα. g. fruit," indicates that the Greek word used is "καλός " and the English word used is "good." If no abbreviation is indicated the Greek word used is the first one given at the beginning of the item. The addition of "s" to the English letter indicates the plural, e. g. "ds" for "disciples," "t" is used for "the," "N" indicates the nominative case.

(Sample Copy from American Bible Society Check Lists)

WORD CHECK LIST OF ACTS

HEAVEN οὐρανός

1:10
11
11
11
2:2
5
19
34 hs.
3:21
4:12
24
7:42
49
55
56 hs.
9:3
10:11
12 (AV. air)
16
11:5
6 (AV. air)
9
10
14:15
17 οὐρανόθεν
17:24
19:35 RV margin
22:6
26:19 οὐράνιος heavenly
26:13 οὐρανόθεν
(see also 22:23   air.)

HOPE, -ED

A. ἐλπίς
2:26
16:19
23:6
24:15
26:6
7
27:20
28:20

B. ἐλπίζω
24:26 -ed
26:7

HOLY -INESS

A. Holy Spirit (see Spirit A.)

B. Other Uses
2:27 ὅσιος H. one
3:12 εὐσέβεια   (holiness, AV)
         godliness

14 ἅγιος H. one
21   "   h. prophets
4:27   "   h. Servant (AV. h. child)

30   "   h. Servant (AV. h. child)

6:13   "   h. place
7:33   "   h. ground
9:13   "   saints
32   "   "
41   "   "
10:22   "   h. angel
13:34 ὅσιος h. (TR & AV omit)

35 ἅγιος H. one
21:28   "   h. place
26:10   "   saints

HUMILITY ταπεινοφροσύνη

20:19 AV (RV. lowliness)

INIQUITY ἀδικία

1:18
3:26 πονηρία -ies
8:23

JOY χαρά
(See also Gladness)

8:8
12:14 (AV gladness)
13:52
15:3
20:24 (TR & AV only)

MARK

LIST OF PARALLEL PASSAGES

This series of parallel phrases, clauses, and sentences has been prepared as an aid in checking the consistency of translation. The list is so prepared that the translation of the several parallels can be written in, in parallel form, and compared word by word. It differs from the "Word Check List" in that it deals with passages rather than with individual words.

As in the case of the "Word Check List," this is not intended to be an indication that passages that are parallel must necessarily be translated in exactly the same way, but simply to require that deviations from consistency in translation be avoided unless there is real reason for them. The standard of faithful translation of the Scriptures calls for the use of idiomatic forms, but also the avoidance of paraphrase and an endeavor to be as literal as the idiom of the language will permit.

It is believed that this document includes about as many parallel phrases as such a list justifies. There are, of course, other briefer phrases that occur and recur which could be checked up by the careful use of a Concordance but which seem too slight in significance to be included here.

Whenever a particular verse is under consideration an examination of the Index will show whether it contains a parallel phrase recorded in this list. Passages can therefore be checked, reference by reference, or by taking each group of passages and checking over the successive items in the main list.

A separate Index for the four Gospels will be available covering parallel phrases included in these lists appearing in more than one Gospel, and also parallels between the several Gospels that may not occur more than once in a given Gospel.

The references to the Gospel of Matthew are to items in the similar List of Parallel Passages and Phrases for that Gospel.

(Sample Copy from American Bible Society Check Lists)

Mark

Items 11 - 17

#11
1:23 ..he cried out, saying (with ἀνακράζω)
3:11 ..(they) "   "   "   ("   κράζω)
5:7 and crying out..he saith("   "   )
9:24 ..cried out, and said ("   "   )
10:47 he began to cry out and say(with "   )

#12
1:24 What have we to do with thee?
5:7 "   "   I "   "   "   " ?

#13
1:26 crying with a loud voice (φωνέω)
5:7 "   out "   "   "   "   (κράζω)
15:34 cried "   "   "   "   (βοάω)
37 uttered "   "   "   "   (ἀφίημι)

#14
1:27 they were all amazed   (θαμβέομαι)
2:12 "   "   "   "   (ἐξίστημι)
5:42 "   "   "   ...with a great amazement
6:51 "   "   sore   "   (ἐξ...ἐχστάσει)
(ἐξ.)
9:15 " .. " greatly "   (ἐκθαμβέομαι)
10:24 the ds." "   "   (θα.)
32 they "   "   (")
14:33 began to be greatly amazed(ἐκ.)

#15
1:31 he ..took her by the hand and raised her up
5:41 taking the child by the hand, ...Arise
9:27 But Jesus took him by the hand, and raised him up; and
he arose.

#16
1:32 And at even
4:35 when even was come
6:47 "   "   "   "
14:17 "   it was evening
15:42 "   even was (now) come
(in each case - ὀψίας γενομένης)
Cf. Mat. #55

#17
1:34 he...cast out many demons
39   casting out   "
3:15 to cast   "   "
22   casteth he out the demons
6:13 they cast out many demons
7:26 he would cast forth the demons out of ..
9:38   casting out demons
16:9 he had cast " seven demons
17 shall they cast out demons

CHECK LIST OF PROPER NAMES IN THE GOSPELS

	Mt.	Mk.	Lu.	Jn.
Calvary (See Skull)				
Cana				-
Canaan	-			
Canaanite (See Cananaean)				
Cananaean (AV. Canaanite)	-	-		
Capernaum	-	-	-	-
Caesar	-	-	-	-
Caesarea	-	-		
Cedron (See Kidron)				
Cephas				-
Chorazin	-		-	
Christ	-	-	-	-
Chuzas (ERV. and AV. Chuza)			-	
Cleopas			-	
Cleophas (See Clopas)				
Clopas (AV. Cleophas)				-
Corban		-		
Cosam			-	
Cyrene (AV. Mark, Luke Cyrenian)	-	-	-	
Cyrenian (See Cyrene)				
Cyrenius			-	
Dalmanutha		-		
Daniel (AV. in Mark only)	-	-		
David	-	-	-	-

	Mt.	Mk.	Lu.	Jn.
Decapolis	-	-		
Didymus				-
Eber (AV. Heber)			-	
Egypt	-			
Eleazer	-			
Eliakim	-		-	
Elias (See Elijah)				
Eliezer			-	
Elijah (AV. Elias)	-	-	-	-
Elisabeth			-	
Eliseus (See Elisha)				
Elisha (AV. Eliseus)			-	
Eliud	-			
Elmodam			-	
Emmanuel (See Immanuel)				
Emmaus			-	
Enoch			-	
Enos			-	
Ephraim				-
Er			-	
Esaias (See Isaiah)				
Esli			-	
Esrom (See Hezron)				
Ezekias	-			
Gabbatha				-
Gabriel			-	

(Sample Page of Maya Manuscript)

1 1:1-10

LE KILIICH MA'ALOB PEKTSIL JEE BIX MARKOS

Kapiitulo 1

1. U yaxchum u ma'alob pektsil Jesukristo, u Paal Yumbil.

2. Jee bix ts'iiba'an tumen Isaias le profeetae': Jee kin tuuxtik in j-bisaj-t'aan tu taan a wich u ti'al u yutskint a beel ta taan.

3. U t'aan un tuul maak tun k'a'am t'aan tej x-tokoy lu'umo': Utskinte'ex u bel Yumbil, tojkinse'ex u t'uut'ulbeiloob.

4. Juan tan u ts'ik ok-ja' ka'ach tej x-tokoy lu'umo', tan u tse'ektik u ok-ja'il k'ex-tuukul u ti'al sa'atsaj-siipiloob.

5. Kaj jook'oob tiknal tulaakal u ba'pachil Judea yetel le Jerusalemiloobe', ka tu ts'aaj ok-ja' ti'oob ichil u yaalkab-ja'il Jordan, tan u kaantikoob u k'eebanoob.

6. Juane' u buukintmaj u tso'otsel kaameyo yetel u k'ax-nak'tma k'eewel; u janle', saak' yetel u kabil k'aax.

7. Tu tse'ektaj, ka tu ya'alaj: Tun taal tin paach un tuul maak mas nojoch ket ten, ma'a tan in najmatik in xoltal tu taan u ti'al ka in wach' u taabil u xaanab.

8. Ten tu jaajile', tin ts'aj te'ex ok-ja' yetel ja'; ba'ale' leti'e' bin u ts'a te'ex ok-ja' yetel Kiliich Espiritu.

9. Kaj uch ti le k'iinoobo', taal Jesus tu Nasaretil Galilea, kaj ts'aab ok-ja' ti' tumen Juan, ichil u ja'il Jordan.

10. Le kaj jok' ichil le ja'e', tu yilaj u je'epajal ka'ano'ob yetel u yeemel le Espiritu bey un tuul tsutsuy yook'ol leti'.

GENERAL INDEX

351

BIBLICAL INDEX